Contents

ENGAGING ORGANIZATIONAL COMMUNICATION THEORY & RESEARCH

■ MULTIPLE PERSPECTIVES ■

EDITORS

STEVE MAY
University of North Carolina at Chapel Hill

DENNIS K. MUMBY
University of North Carolina at Chapel Hill

SAGE Publications
Thousand Oaks ■ London ■ New Delhi

For information:

Sage Publications, Inc.
2455 Teller Road
Thousand Oaks, California 91320
E-mail: order@sagepub.com

Sage Publications Ltd.
1 Oliver's Yard
55 City Road
London EC1Y 1SP
United Kingdom

Sage Publications India Pvt. Ltd.
B-42, Panchsheel Enclave
Post Box 4109
New Delhi 110 017 India

Printed in the United States of America

Library of Congress Cataloging-in-Publication Data

Engaging organizational communication theory and research : multiple perspectives / edited by Steve May, Dennis K. Mumby.
    p. cm.
Includes bibliographical references and index.
ISBN 0-7619-2848-0 (cloth) — ISBN 0-7619-2849-9 (pbk.)
  1. Communication in organizations. I. May, Steve. II. Mumby, Dennis K.
HD30.3.E54 2005
302.3'5—dc22

                         2004013890

This book is printed on acid-free paper.

04   05   06   07   08   10 9 8 7 6 5 4 3 2 1

Acquisitions Editor:	Todd Armstrong
Editorial Assistant:	Deya Saoud
Production Editor:	Julia Parnell
Copy Editor:	A. J. Sobczak
Typesetter:	C&M Digitals (P) Ltd.
Indexer:	Rachel Rice
Cover Designer:	Janet Foulger

ENGAGING ORGANIZATIONAL COMMUNICATION THEORY & RESEARCH

This book is dedicated to
Richard and Marilyn, who taught me to
appreciate and value learning, and to
Grace and Dennis, who deserve a second dedication

Acknowledgments

A book of this kind inevitably involves the support and cooperation of a number of people. It is an accomplishment shared among the authors, the publisher, and the editors. First, we'd like to thank the authors of the various chapters for agreeing to participate in this project and for producing such interesting and "engaged" work. Any success that this volume has will be due to their erudition and expertise. Todd Armstrong, our editor at Sage, encouraged us to pursue a project that explored scholars' engagement with theory and research. He shepherded the project through its various phases with his usual mixture of insight and good humor. Thanks also to Deya Saoud, editorial assistant at Sage, for seeing the book through to completion. Our three reviewers—Jim Barker at the U.S. Air Force Academy, Patrice Buzzanell at Purdue University, and Gail Fairhurst at the University of Cincinnati—provided extremely valuable feedback that greatly improved the quality of the final manuscript. Any limitations that remain are due to the incompetence of the editors.

1

Introduction

Thinking About Engagement

Dennis K. Mumby

Steve May

When we first discussed this project, one of the things we both agreed upon was that we didn't want to end up with a typical, "run-of-the-mill" reader. Many volumes out there do an admirable job of covering the various perspectives that exist in a given discipline. We wanted to produce a volume that presented the different perspectives that are current in the field of organizational communication, but we had a somewhat different agenda. Rather than provide a set of "overview" chapters, each of which surveyed a particular body of research, we wanted to bring together a group of prominent scholars, each of whom can write in interesting ways about how they "engage" with the research tradition out of which their scholarship is generated. The result is this volume.

In adopting this approach, we are pursuing a number of different objectives. First, we want to give students in the field of organizational communication a sense of the array of scholarly traditions that characterize the field. Clearly, it was not possible for us to be exhaustive in this objective; we necessarily had to pick and choose from among a large number of perspectives. However, we feel that our choices identify those perspectives that, at least in the last 10 years or so, have come to constitute much of the organizational communication "canon." We believe that each chapter represents a research tradition that all students of organizational communication must be familiar with in order to be considered educated in our field. Indeed, this is the first sense in which we intended the title of our book to be read; that is, these are the perspectives that students should be familiar with in order to feel "engaged" with the field.

Second, although we wanted to provide students with a view of the field that encompassed various perspectives, we also did not want to produce another "handbook" of organizational communication. There are several of those already out there (e.g., Clegg, Hardy, & Nord, 1996; Grant, Hardy, Oswick, Phillips, & Putnam, 2004: Jablin & Putnam, 2001; Jablin, Putnam, Roberts, & Porter, 1987), and we didn't want to reinvent the wheel. Given that, we asked each contributor to write a chapter that not only examined a particular perspective but also addressed the ways in which each scholar himself or herself "engaged" with that perspective. Thus, each chapter is written from a very personal—rather than a "god's eye"—point of view. The second meaning of the title of the book, then, gets at the idea that a particular theoretical perspective is not simply "adopted" by a researcher (rather like one might wear an article of clothing); rather, it becomes foundational to the way that he or she sees the world. "Engaging" a particular perspective, then, means entering into dialogue with it (and with the community of scholars that constitutes that perspective) and exploring how it challenges one's assumptions and prejudices about the world. It's interesting to note how, in a number of the chapters, the writers address the ways in which they are very much transformed as people by virtue of their encounter with a particular intellectual tradition. In this sense, we can say that good scholarship upsets our commonsense views of how things work, undermining the apparent naturalness of "the way things are."

Third, the notion of "engaging" organizational communication theory and research gets at the idea that, particularly in the last 10 to 15 years, the field has evolved in ways that could hardly have been imagined when organizational communication first emerged as a coherent subdiscipline in the late 1950s/early 1960s (Redding, 1985). Indeed, it is instructive to note that the National Communication Association did not even have a division devoted to organizational communication until the early 1980s (there had been a "commission" for some years, but full divisional status was not attained until around 1982). It is our sense that, given the forms of scholarship that are being produced, the field of organizational communication has become a pretty exciting place to be in the last 15 to 20 years. Certainly, in the wake of the "discursive turn" that took place in the early 1980s, the emergence of interpretive, critical, postmodern, and feminist research has radically altered the landscape of the field. At the same time, the more "traditional" areas of research have developed in exciting and innovative ways that bear little resemblance to the kind of variable-analytic research that was being done in the 1960s and 1970s. Thus, one of the goals of this volume is to convey to the reader the sense of excitement and "engagement" that researchers feel about the state of our field.

Finally, "engaging" organizational communication theory and research intends to convey the intimate connection between theory and practice. Scholarship does not emerge out of a vacuum, but instead generally is produced as the result of a confluence of factors—social, political, epistemological, and even economic. The emergence of a body of scholarship is generally a response to such confluences. It is probably no accident, for example, that the study of organizational culture emerged at a time when people were starting to ask questions about the quality and meaning of their work lives; efforts to understand how employees "made sense" out of their organizational lives certainly fits with this shift. Similarly, the growth of feminist scholarship—though a little late in our field—runs parallel to the increasing prominence of women in organizations and the growing awareness regarding the gender dynamics that have emerged out of this shift. In different ways, the authors of each of the chapters explore how they themselves have engaged the theory-practice dynamic.

The remainder of this chapter attempts to situate the chapters in this volume in the context of the transformation of the field of organizational communication that has occurred in the course of the last 15 to 20 years. As the chapter develops, we will be addressing questions such as: What are the central themes and problematics that have emerged out of the transformation of the field? In what ways are the perspectives developed in this chapter both convergent and divergent?

Framing the Chapters

As a way of orienting readers to the chapters in this book, we want to briefly address a set of issues and problematics that have helped to shape the terrain of organizational communication studies in the last 20 years or so. In many ways, the essays in this volume can be seen as various efforts to engage with these problematics, utilizing a number of different theoretical perspectives.

First, we want to unpack our thinking behind the choices that we made regarding what chapters and topics to include in this book. In other words, in what sense does this volume provide a coherent account of the current state of the field of organizational communication? Clearly, choice implies both presence and absence; in including certain perspectives we have necessarily excluded others. However, we feel that the choices we made cover most of the major perspectives currently influential in our field, and with which students of organizational communication must be familiar in order to be *au courant*. One caveat is in order, however. Rather than choose to focus on particular bodies of research (e.g., leadership, organizational identification, conflict and negotiation, etc.), we have instead chosen for the most part to highlight what we see as the major theoretical frameworks of our field. Our thinking here is that although it is important to be familiar with various areas of research, it is more important to come to grips with larger questions of epistemology, ontology, and so forth that drive those various research agendas. Of course, the phenomena that scholars study can never be fully separated—nor should they be—from the perspectives brought to bear on those phenomena (and indeed, each chapter addresses the intimate relationship between theory and research); however, understanding the ways in which our field exhibits both tensions and points of coherence is an essential step in appreciating the broader debates and conversations that underlie the scholarship that is published in our books and journals.

In what sense, then, does this volume articulate a coherent view of the field of organizational communication? The order of the chapters reflects both historical and theoretical developments in the field, although the trajectories of these two dimensions do not always coincide. Thus, Chapters 2 through 7 represent what are arguably the six most "dominant" perspectives in our field—dominant in the sense that they currently have a significant organizing effect on debates about the state of the field. The final three chapters before our conclusion address three more narrowly circumscribed problematics—structuration, "organization," and globalization. Although clearly there are numerous choices we could have made here, we feel that these problematics have had and continue to have considerable influence over how we choose to research the complex phenomenon of organizing.

Given postpositivism's historical position as the dominant theoretical frame for studying organizations, Steve Corman's chapter on that topic kicks off the book. Social science research in the variable-analytic tradition was, for a long time, the benchmark against which judgments about the validity of various forms of research were made. In the last 20 years, the proliferation of other research traditions has undermined its hegemonic status, but it still occupies a significant and important place in the field. Corman's chapter is particularly interesting because he undermines many of the current, knee-jerk responses to postpositivism, articulating its current form as very much convergent with many of the current developments in organizational communication, particularly those associated with the "discursive turn" and the rejection of "correspondence" theories of truth.

Brenda Allen's chapter on social constructionism represents a parallel tradition that was, for a long time, the poor relation to postpositivism. Although the social constructionist tradition has a long and storied history in the humanities and social sciences going back to the 19th century, it first only rose to prominence in organizational communication in the late 1970s/ early 1980s. In this sense, it represented the first significant challenge to the hegemony of postpositivism. The "interpretive turn" (Putnam & Pacanowsky, 1983) in our field was viewed as a sea change in assumptions about the relationship between communication and organization—many researchers moved from studying "communication in organizations" to examining how communicative processes constitute organizing (Pacanowsky & O'Donnell-Trujillo, 1982; Putnam, 1983). Allen explores the underpinnings of this tradition, situating its development principally in the work of Berger and Luckmann (1971) and assessing its impact on organizational communication theory and research.

In Chapter 4, George Cheney, assisted by Dan Lair, charts the development of the rhetorical tradition in organizational communication. Of particular interest here is the tracing of the multiple origins of rhetorical theory and criticism as those origins cohere in the study of organizational rhetoric. Indeed, the chapter is exemplary in its efforts to show the connections between what is traditionally thought of as the origins of organization studies in sociology, and the emergence of a rhetorical sensibility among organizational communication scholars in the early 1980s. In the context of this book, it is important to recognize rhetorical theory and criticism as a perspective that, in many ways, is social constructionist in orientation, but that at the same time has emerged out of a very different tradition, and with an analytic focus that is different from most social constructionist research.

Stan Deetz's chapter on critical theory similarly explores the various intellectual origins of this perspective, showing how a relatively coherent approach to organizations has emerged out of traditions as divergent as Nietzschean perspectivism, Marxism, phenomenology and hermeneutics, and Freudian theory. Of all the chapters in this volume, Deetz's is probably the most explicit in terms of the way in which he engages with critical theory to demonstrate how it is not simply a way of *looking at* the world, but rather lays out a blueprint for *living in* (and transforming) the world. His argument that being a critical scholar involves being simultaneously filled with care, thought, and good humor is, we think, a particularly insightful and provocative way of characterizing the critical enterprise.

In Chapter 6, Bryan Taylor takes on the almost impossible task of explaining postmodernism in a coherent and accessible manner. He does not ignore the fact that postmodernism creates discomfort, ambiguity, and (deliberate) incoherence in how it engages with the world. Taylor's task, then, is on one hand to explore, for example, the relationship between postmodernity as an ontological condition, and postmodernism as an intellectual resource to better analyze contemporary organizations, and on the other hand to show how postmodernism destabilizes comfortable ideas about what organizing really is. In this sense, his chapter provides insight into how postmodernism explores many of the same issues as critical theory (e.g., the relationships among power, discourse, and knowledge) but explores those issues in ways that both converge with and diverge from the latter.

Karen Ashcraft's chapter on feminism is one that—as she acknowledges up front—could not have been written as recently as 10 years ago. However, since the early 1990s organizational communication studies has joined fields such as critical management studies and organizational sociology in the systematic exploration of the "gendered organization" (Acker, 1990). Ashcraft's chapter is particularly useful in terms of (a) the way that it subtly characterizes the complex debates within feminist studies itself; (b) how it demonstrates that feminist studies as a theoretical, critical, and praxis-oriented enterprise has its own trajectory that is not simply derivative of other intellectual traditions such as critical theory or postmodernism; (c) its articulation of the potential for feminist organizational communication studies to make unique contributions to our understanding of gendered identities and organizing processes; and (d) its demonstration of the dialectical relationship between personal experience and engagement with a particular research agenda.

The final three chapters in the book before our conclusion are somewhat different in that they do not represent the kind of macrolevel perspectives characteristic of the preceding chapters. Rather, each in different ways can be characterized as explicating meso-level, or mid-range, theories that address a particular phenomenon or organization-related problematic. Each is included because we feel that these theories have had, and/or continue to have, a particularly formative influence on current research trends in our field.

In Chapter 8, Scott Poole and Bob McPhee draw on their considerable expertise to explore the impact of Anthony Giddens's structuration theory on organization studies. As they point out, structuration theory has been extremely influential across a range of disciplines, including organizational communication. The specific problematic that structuration addresses concerns the relationship between agency and structure. Which is primary in understanding human behavior—the possibilities for individual agency or the constraints of larger social structures? Poole and McPhee explore how Giddens's answer is to transcend this dichotomy altogether, theorizing the mutually constitutive character of agency and structure. As they show, structuration theory has profound consequences for our understanding of the dialectic of communicating and organizing.

Jim Taylor's chapter examines perhaps the most profound and basic problematic of all: What is organization? His answer to this question is to challenge the very idea of organizations as stable, objective, reified structures, and to put in its place a conception of organizations as simultaneously chaotic and co-orientational, concerned with discursive closure and yet involved in a never-ending search for meaning. In Taylor's view, then, organizations both embody and are sustained through the (never-ending) attempt to resolve contradiction.

Finally, Cynthia Stohl's chapter takes on the problematic of globalization. We would guess that this chapter was the most difficult to write because of (a) the exponential growth of research in this area in the last 5 years and (b) the remarkable eclecticism of the theoretical approaches adopted in this research. In this area of research, it is particularly futile to talk about "globalization theory" in the singular. Stohl provides an extremely engaged and engaging account of this vast array of literature, but more significantly she convincingly shows how well-positioned are scholars in the field of organizational communication to address the complexities and contradictions of the ongoing globalization process.

In the next section of this chapter, we look more closely at the issue of how each author addresses his or her particular perspective, and how this translates into "engagement"—a process that varies considerably across the chapters (and a variation that is itself worthy of attention).

Engaging Theory

In the last 20 years or so, scholars have become more sensitized to and self-reflective about the role of theory in the knowledge production process. While the 1960s and 1970s in organizational communication were characterized by a very narrow definition of theory circumscribed by strict social science parameters (in which theories were judged according to their ability to reflect, explain, and predict an objective world), current scholarship recognizes that theory is not just a conduit for truth but rather plays a constitutive role in the creation of truth claims. Indeed, a great deal of organizational scholarship in the last 25 years has been devoted to metatheory; that is, to exploring the assumptions and implications embedded in different forms of theorizing, and the consequences of these forms of theorizing for understanding organizational life (e.g., Burrell & Morgan, 1979; Deetz, 1996; DiMaggio, 1995; Sutton & Staw, 1995; Weick, 1995). One thing that has become particularly clear about such reflection is that there is no grand theory that will adequately explain or encapsulate the organizing process. Instead, all theories are partial, perspectival, political, and contested. All "truths" about organizational life therefore have to be situated within the set of epistemological, ontological, axiological, and political assumptions upon which such claims are built.

Does this mean, therefore, that a completely relativist position is the only one possible regarding scholarship? We do not believe so. In fact, no one would deny that despite (indeed, because of) the "paradigm proliferation" of the last few years (and the apparent incommensurability among these paradigms) the body of knowledge that organizational communication research has produced has greatly increased in its richness and profundity. Developments in postpositivist, critical, postmodern, and feminist research, among other developments, have greatly enhanced our insight into the communicative dimensions of organizing. For example, recent feminist research has moved us beyond treating gender as a variable, toward recognizing the fundamentally gendered character of the organizing process. Such a shift does not signal the discovery of a more objective truth about the relationship between gender and organizational communication. Rather, it sensitizes us to issues that lie outside the purview of research that views gender simply as one organizational variable among many; for example, that men have gender too, and that gender is a process that is accomplished through the everydayness of organizing.

As you read through these chapters in this book, then, we would like you to think about the relationship of each author to theory development. What are the various ways in which they engage with theory? What are the implicit definitions of theory with which each scholar is operating? To what extent does each author conform to the view of theory suggested here (i.e., as partial, contested, etc.)? Furthermore, what kinds of knowledge claims does each author make about his or her particular perspective?

A second and related issue that we would like to address concerns what might be called—in postmodern terms—the "discourse of vulnerability" (Mumby, 1997). This notion acknowledges that our understanding of the relationship between the researcher and knowledge production has shifted in the last two decades. No longer do we see the author of knowledge claims as a disinterested, objective bystander who adopts an all-seeing, "god's eye view" toward truth. Instead, scholars have come to recognize the extent to which the researcher is implicated in the construction of truth claims. This shift is perhaps most visible in ethnographic studies, where researchers from a number of perspectives have addressed their active roles in creating knowledge (e.g., Kauffman, 1991; Martin, 1992; Nelson, 1998; Van Maanen,

1988). Martin (1992), for example, is particularly explicit about the need for organizational researchers to "give up the authority game" and acknowledge that they can lay little claim to impartiality and objectivity. Indeed, many scholars would argue that attempts to maintain such neutrality result in research that is dessicated and often disconnected from everyday, real-world issues.

In the context of this book, the issue of the discourse of vulnerability speaks directly to the question of engagement and provides a way for us to think about how each author characterizes himself or herself as "engaging" with a particular body of scholarship. As editors, one of the things that we found most interesting about these essays was the various ways in which the authors made sense out of what it means to engage with theory. Some authors framed engagement in extremely personal ways, arguing for an intimate connection between their own biographies and the form of scholarship that they practiced. For Stan Deetz, for example, there would at first glance seem to be little connection between his upbringing in a rural Indiana community and his later development as a critical scholar. However, it is precisely his experience with issues of difference, community, and otherness that profoundly shaped this later evolution, as he came to recognize how marginality was constructed through the politics of experience underlying sameness and difference. On the other hand, Steve Corman's form of engagement—while just as compelling as Deetz's—is framed much more in terms of his own sense of his place in the larger disciplinary matrix of communication studies. Rightly recognizing that "positivism" has often been set up as a "straw man" by critical and other scholars in our field, he spends a good part of his chapter undermining the caricatures of positivism that have frequently substituted for genuine engagement with a theoretical perspective. Steve Corman's form of engagement, then, involves reframing postpositivism by reading against the grain of such caricatures, thus resituating it within the larger canon of organization studies. In this way, Corman resists being "assimilated to the naive positivist stereotype" (p. 17).

As you read these chapters, then, you may want to think about the ways in which the various authors engage with the "discourse of vulnerability." How does each author position herself or himself in relationship to the specific theory with which she or he engages? How, indeed, does each author make sense of the very notion of engagement? What does that concept mean to the various authors? To what extent does each author blur or break down the separation between knowledge claims, on one hand, and personal experience and biography, on the other? Certainly, the idea that there is a connection between personal experience and knowledge production is still a fairly controversial and much-debated issue in the social sciences, and we want to sensitize readers to the different ways in which this relationship is taken on. Do the authors in this book view their own personal biographies as peripheral to, or constitutive of, the ways that they produce knowledge?

A third framing issue that we would like you to think about as you read through these chapters concerns points of convergence and divergence among the theories represented in this book. As we indicated above, the field of organizational communication has gone through a period of ferment and paradigm proliferation, resulting in a "great blooming, buzzing confusion" of theories and models available to researchers. If you are a graduate student reading this volume, you probably have, at some point, experienced being overwhelmed by the effort required to make sense out of this confusion. Learning the specific constructs and concepts associated with a particular theory is one thing; understanding the relationships between and among those theories is quite another. In addition, given the fact that at some point you are expected to adopt a particular theory and call it your own, the need to make sense out of these points of convergence and divergence becomes particularly acute. A further complication here is that it is clearly erroneous to talk about perspectives such as "critical theory, "feminist theory," "globalization theory," and "postmodern theory" in the singular. Each perspective is made up of numerous theories and approaches that may ostensibly draw on the same tradition, but that appropriate that tradition in very different ways.

Of course, some of the chapters in this book are more easily identified as having points of convergence than others. For example, feminist theory and critical theory have much in common, and to some extent they draw on a shared intellectual heritage. For example, both focus on issues of power, resistance, marginality, and possibilities for emancipation from conditions of oppression. Furthermore, both draw quite heavily from the continental philosophical tradition. On the other hand, critical theory has been largely blind and deaf to the connection between gender and power, and the feminist and critical bodies of scholarship in our field often have developed in parallel rather than in an integrated fashion. Another apparently easy point of convergence is the relationship between critical and postmodern scholarship. In the last few years, the two perspectives often have been uttered in the same breath. Certainly, they have a number of issues in common, particularly in their shared view of the constitutive role of language in the construction of systems of meaning and identity. However, the two perspectives also have a number of points of divergence, particularly regarding how power works in modern society and in their respective conceptions of truth (Alvesson & Deetz, 1996). For example, Foucault's disciplinary conception of power is quite distinct from Marxist "top-down" conceptions; furthermore, postmodernists tend to operate with localized notions of truth, eschewing critical theorists' tendency to hang on to some kind moral foundation in which to ground truth claims (the debate between Foucault and Habermas comes to mind here—see Mumby (1992) for a discussion of their respective positions).

However, it is also interesting and illustrative to seek out points of convergence among the various chapters where none apparently exist. For example, Steve Corman's chapter on postpositivism may, at first blush, seem to have little in common with chapters by Brenda Allen on social constructionism, Karen Ashcraft on feminism, Stan Deetz on critical theory, or Bryan Taylor on postmodernism. Closer inspection, though, suggests that although there are certainly profound differences, there are enough points of connection to suggest that "incommensurability" is not an appropriate way to describe their relationship. For example, Corman points out that postpositivism recognizes the interpretive character of knowledge production, arguing that "subjective understandings have a key impact on the scientific process" (p. 31). Certainly, this is a claim that would resonate with Allen, Ashcraft, Deetz, and Taylor, although how they conceptualize the role of interpretation in research might well vary considerably. Furthermore, Corman situates postpositivism as a nonfoundationalist perspective in the sense that there is no completely objective, independently existing world to appeal to in making judgments about knowledge claims. Rather, such claims gain their validity from an appeal to the standards for knowledge set up by a particular community of scholars. Again, this is a position with which most scholars schooled in interpretive, critical, feminist, or postmodern theory would be comfortable, although again some debate undoubtedly would ensue over the features of nonfoundationalism and the standards appropriate for a particular community of scholars.

A final point of convergence across all the chapters is that each in its own way adopts a critical perspective toward the phenomenon of organizational communication. By this, we want to suggest that each author is engaging with organizational communication in a way that undermines our commonsense assumptions regarding the character of organizing processes. In this sense, each chapter "makes strange" both organizational life and the ways in which scholars theorize about the processes that constitute it. For example, Cynthia Stohl draws our attention to how globalization scholars have struggled (and often failed) to articulate a coherent set of constructs around which organizations can be studied as global phenomena. At the same time, she alerts us to the fact that the apparent morass that is the field of globalization speaks precisely to the incredible turbulence, uncertainty, and complexity associated with globalization processes. Similarly, Jim Taylor takes us through an argument that suggests that, far from being stable entities, organizations as communication phenomena are best understood as characterized by chaos and complexity. His chapter is exemplary in its efforts to undermine our commonsense understanding of organizations as stable, predictable, physical entities. Like all the essayists in the volume, Taylor demonstrates how important it is for us to develop *communication-based* theories that provide insight into the human (organizational) condition.

Conclusion

Our goal in this introduction has been to set up a number of framing issues that will aid in your reading of the chapters. Initially, we laid out a number of ways to makes sense of the notion of engagement, which is the central organizing principle in the volume. Second, we provided a brief overview of each chapter, providing a rationale for the choices we made. Third, we problematized the notion of "theory" itself in an effort to sensitize you to the different ways that the various authors engage with and produce theory. Fourth, we introduced the idea of the "discourse of vulnerability" as a way to frame the authors' myriad understandings of the very idea of engagement. One of our main goals in editing this book was to provide rich and vivid exemplars of the ways that the personal and the scholarly are inextricably entwined. In a number of ways, the scholars in this volume have made themselves vulnerable in writing about the relationship between their own lives and their connection to a larger body of scholarship. In this context, the theories that they each write about truly come alive. Finally, we suggested some ways in which the various perspectives in this volume both converge and diverge. Here, we wanted to draw your attention to both the complexity and the coherence of the field of organizational communication. Although there are significant amounts of divergence across perspectives, it is clear that all the scholars in this volume are dedicated to writing critically about the intersection of communication and organizing.

Ultimately, our goal is not to provide a set of definitive answers regarding the nature of theory and research in our field. Instead, we hope that this book does precisely the opposite, evoking in you a whole set of questions about where our field has been and where it is headed. Perhaps such questioning will help to produce the next major developments in the field of organizational communication.

References

Acker, J. (1990). Hierarchies, jobs, bodies: A theory of gendered organizations. *Gender and Society, 4*, 139–158.

Alvesson, M., & Deetz, S. (1996). Critical theory and postmodernism approaches to organizational studies. In S. Clegg, C. Hardy, & W. Nord (Eds.), *Handbook of organization studies* (pp. 191–217). Thousand Oaks, CA: Sage.

Berger, P., & Luckmann, T. (1971). *The social construction of reality.* London: Penguin.

Burrell, G., & Morgan, G. (1979). *Sociological paradigms and organisational analysis.* London: Heinemann.

Clegg, S., Hardy, C., & Nord, W. (Eds.). (1996). *Handbook of organization studies.* Thousand Oaks, CA: Sage.

Deetz, S. (1996). Describing differences in approaches to organization science: Rethinking Burrell and Morgan and their legacy. *Organization Science, 7,* 191–207.

DiMaggio, P. J. (1995). Comments on "what theory is not." *Administrative Science Quarterly, 40,* 391–397.

Grant, D., Hardy, C., Oswick, C., Phillips, N., & Putnam, L. L. (Eds.). (2004). *Handbook of organizational discourse.* London: Sage.

Jablin, F. M., & Putnam, L. L. (Eds.). (2001). *The new handbook of organizational communication: Advances in theory, research, and methods.* Thousand Oaks, CA: Sage.

Jablin, F. M., Putnam, L. L., Roberts, K. H., & Porter, L. W. (Eds.). (1987). *Handbook of organizational communication: An interdisciplinary perspective.* Newbury Park, CA: Sage.

Kauffman, B. J. (1991). Feminist facts: Interview strategies and political subjects in ethnography. *Communication Theory, 2,* 187–206.

Martin, J. (1992). *Culture in organizations: Three perspectives.* New York: Oxford University Press.

Mumby, D. K. (1992). Two discourses on communication, power, and the subject: Jürgen Habermas and Michel Foucault. In G. Levine (Ed.), *Constructions of the self* (pp. 81–104). New Brunswick, NJ: Rutgers University Press.

Mumby, D. K. (1997). Modernism, postmodernism, and communication studies: A rereading of an ongoing debate. *Communication Theory, 7,* 1–28.

Nelson, S. (1998). Intersections of eros and ethnography. *Text and Performance Quarterly, 18,* 1–21.

Pacanowsky, M., & O'Donnell-Trujillo, N. (1982). Communication and organizational cultures. *The Western Journal of Speech Communication, 46,* 115–130.

Putnam, L. L. (1983). The interpretive perspective: An alternative to functionalism. In L. L. Putnam & M. Pacanowsky (Eds.), *Communication and organizations: An interpretive approach* (pp. 31–54). Beverly Hills, CA: Sage.

Putnam, L. L., & Pacanowsky, M. (Eds.). (1983). *Communication and organizations: An interpretive approach.* Beverly Hills, CA: Sage.

Redding, W. C. (1985). Stumbling toward identity: The emergence of organizational communication as a field of study. In R. D. McPhee & P. K. Tompkins (Eds.), *Organizational communication: Traditional themes and new directions* (pp. 15–54). Beverly Hills, CA: Sage.

Sutton, R. I., & Staw, B. M. (1995). What theory is not. *Administrative Science Quarterly, 40,* 371–384.

Van Maanen, J. (1988). *Tales of the field: On writing ethnography.* Chicago: University of Chicago Press.

Weick, K. (1995). What theory is not, theorizing is. *Administrative Science Quarterly, 40,* 385–390.

2

Postpositivism

Steven R. Corman

S hortly after receiving the invitation to write this chapter, I attended a meeting at the University of Tübingen in Germany. This university (founded in 1477) is almost 200 years older than the oldest in the United States (Harvard). Accordingly, many of its buildings have an impressive, historic feel. The conference I attended was held in the Auditorium Maximum, so named, I was told, because it is (or was) the largest auditorium on campus. To the American professor who has taught in a few 500-seat auditoriums, it seemed surprisingly small, holding perhaps 200 people. Even more striking was how *antique* this auditorium looked. Each row was one continuous desk, its top made of a long plank that spanned the width of the auditorium. The seats were flat boards that hinged down from the desk of the row behind. The wood bore a dark patina of decades of lectures. It was your archetypal well-seasoned hall of learning.

Serendipity struck when, on the train going back from the conference, I read in Gellner (1985) that Tübingen was the location of a famous encounter between Karl Popper and Theodor Adorno in 1961. Their encounter must have taken place, though I have been unable to verify this, in the auditorium where I just spoke. After all, the conference was sponsored by the German

AUTHOR'S NOTE: I would like to thank John Jackson, Michele Jackson, Bob Krizek, Bob McPhee, Mike Monsour, and anonymous reviewers for helpful comments on earlier drafts of this chapter. I also thank Dorothea Wagner for making the visit to Tübingen possible.

Sociological Association, and those attending the conference were "spoiling for a fight" (Bryant, 1985, p. 126).

In one corner was Popper, a contemporary (but not a member) of the Vienna Circle, a group of philosophers that formulated and promoted the *logical positivist* philosophy of science. He was highly critical of logical positivism, and he promoted *critical rationalism* as the best alternative. In the other corner was Adorno, a member of the Frankfurt School of social theory, which can be credited with popularizing and legitimizing critical theory in the social sciences and humanities. He argued that *critical dialectics* should replace the logical positivist enterprise in social science.

It was not the battle that the audience had hoped for. Popper and Adorno basically agreed on the "central role of theoretical criticism" (Frisby, 1976, p. ix) in sociology. Their argument was over the details: What *kind* of critical enterprise was best suited to displace positivism? Dahrendorf (1976) recounts disappointment among the conferees in the lack of clash between Popper and Adorno, and he attributes it to a common foe:

> In terms of time and subject matter, however, the discussion was dominated neither by Popper nor Adorno, but instead by a "third man," conjured up by almost all participants in the discussion, but yet against whom the two symposiasts unreservedly adopted a common stance. This "third man" was given several names by his friends and enemies alike—"positive method," "unmetaphysical positivism," "empiricism," "empirical research," and so on. (p. 125)

This Third Man was also a straw man: In Adorno's introduction to a volume that grew out of the Tübingen discussions (Adorno et al., 1969/1976), he "holds up for criticism a naïve positivism which is hardly at issue amongst any of the disputants [at Tübingen] even though it may remain in operation in much of social scientific practice" (Frisby, 1976, p. xxix).

This story details my encounter with an important place in the history of postpositivism, but it also serves as touchstone for several points about my engagement with this perspective as a scholar. First, I want to make it clear that I am not writing this chapter as the Third Man in this volume. There is reason to worry about being slotted in that role because of a tendency (that I will detail below) for critics to caricature positivism, magnetizing it so as to collect all nearby persons and positions. Phillips (2000) does not mince words on this point:

> The general fantasy is that anyone who is impressed by the sciences as a pinnacle of achievement of human knowledge, anyone who uses statistics or numerical data, anyone who believes hypotheses need to be substantially

warranted, anyone who is a realist (another unanalyzed but clearly derogatory word) is thereby a positivist. (p. 157)

Because those statements describe me, I am a prime candidate for being assimilated to the naive positivist stereotype. So let me be clear that the postpositivism I will advocate in this chapter is not some half-hearted tweaking of old ideas. It is a fundamental reform of positivist principles that results in a perspective no more (or less) problematic than other popular alternatives.

A related danger is that this chapter will be read as documenting arcane beliefs that we must study only to know where we are coming from, on our way to going somewhere better in the other chapters. I have seen this pattern more than once in other books and texts. Thus, I argue that postpositivism is not some philosophical carcass but a *necessary* component of progressive research practices that is different from, yet compatible with, other parts of that mix. In the next section, I review the history of different kinds of positivism before outlining five principles of postpositivism. After that, I round out the chapter by commenting on the relationship of postpositivism to antipositivist positions.

A Brief History of Positivisms

Another point embedded in the opening story is this: Positivism is a very old and influential tradition with a longer history than most people understand. The core ideas of positivism were first formalized much more than a century ago, and many different versions followed. Support for the most infamous version had mostly collapsed by the end of World War II, when my parents were still children. The Tübingen conference was not even about positivism, but about alternatives to it that already had become institutionalized in the 15 years following the war. This decidedly post-positivist gathering took place more than 40 years ago, 2 years after I was born, when the patina in the Auditorium Maximum may have been a shade or two lighter.

These facts impress me now because antipositivist arguments never seemed so old when I began hearing them. In part this is because they were new ideas *to me*. Until graduate school, I had never encountered any serious criticism of the scientific method (the realization of positivist ideals). The Space Age yielded a steady stream of results demonstrating its basic soundness and effectiveness. It was the ideal in all my social science classes, and the studies we learned about seemed successful in that they made progress toward answering important questions. Thus, it was genuinely novel to hear arguments that, for example, observation is essentially theory laden and that observed facts could never confirm a theory.

Another reason the arguments against positivism may have seemed new is that they were relatively new *to my discipline*. Perhaps they were new to many disciplines in the United States, as the volume that resulted from the Tübingen conference was not published in English until 1976. In the communication discipline, it is fair to say the Alta Conference in 1981 marks the beginning of organized opposition to the Third Man (Miller, 2000). So just as I was entering graduate school, antipositivism was becoming trendy. Yet this movement that seemed "cutting edge" to me at the time was actually reproducing arguments at least 20 years old! This illustrates the importance of having a grasp of the history of positivism.

The word "positivism" has a *lot* of different forms and meanings. By breaking out commitments in different philosophical domains, Halfpenny (1982) identified a dozen different kinds. A somewhat more holistic perspective distinguishes three general kinds of positivism that will suit our purposes here: classical, logical, and instrumental. In the mid-1800s, *classical positivism* sprang from Comte's (1830/1970) efforts to develop a "positive" method for the study of society. The historical context for his proposals is important. Comte believed that the sciences progress from a primitive theological state where phenomena are explained as acts of God(s), to a metaphysical state where phenomena are attributed to mysterious invisible forces, to a positive state where phenomena are explained on the basis of natural laws. Science at Comte's time was decidedly oriented toward the first two approaches, and he sought to outline a philosophical alternative that would pave the way for a movement toward the latter. In its time, classical positivism was quite a radical idea that threatened existing power structures, a point to which I return later.

Halfpenny (1982) identified three main philosophical positions in classical positivism:

> a *theory of historical development* in which improvements in knowledge are both the motor of historical progress and the source of social stability . . . a *theory of knowledge,* according to which the only kind of sound knowledge available to mankind is that of science, grounded in observation . . . [and] a *unity of science thesis,* according to which all sciences can be integrated into a single natural system. (p. 15)

These can be called *scientism, empiricism,* and *naturalism,* respectively, and they form the core of classical positivism. There are also a number of supporting beliefs surrounding this core. One of these is *holism,* the belief that properties of society cannot be reduced to properties of the component individuals. In addition, classical positivism was *reformist* in that it was intended to displace authority of the Church as a main source of social stability (Halfpenny, 1982, p. 19).

The second type, *logical positivism*, was the project of the Vienna Circle. This position is the bogeyman of antipositivists, the one that engaged the critical attention of the Frankfurt School of critical theory (to which the Tübingen debater Adorno belonged). It was formulated by an interdisciplinary group of philosophers in the 1920s and 1930s who worked as a team to develop a philosophy for a new era of enlightenment.[1] They would "make all disciplines truly scientific so that they would provide the basis for rational action" (Halfpenny, 1982, p. 46). Unlike Comte, this group believed that science would probably, but not *necessarily*, lead to progress. Indeed, they hoped to purify science of all moral involvements, including its Comtean reformist trappings: Science should become a matter of pure logic (thus the "logical" part) applied to pure experience. This position leads to the most well known feature of logical positivism, the *verifiability principle of meaning*, which holds that "something is meaningful if and only if is it verifiable empirically" (Phillips, 1987, p. 39).[2] A supporting idea is *antirealism*, the belief that there is no reality independent of our experience. We cannot empirically verify that there is a reality independent of our experience (because nothing but experience could lead to such verification); thus, the idea of a reality independent of experience is meaningless.

The last type of positivism has existed on the American continent from the 1920s. When I was in graduate school, it was commonly referred to as "dustbowl empiricism," but Bryant (1985) more charitably calls it *instrumental positivism*. It is instrumental because it "confines social research to only such questions as the limitations of current research instruments allow" (p. 133). It is positivist in the sense that it aspires, through these limitations, to the standards of rigorous science. This kind of positivism, as you might expect from the name, places a lot of emphasis on the development and refinement of instrumentation. It believes in *inductivism*, the idea that general principles can be discovered by observing specific instances. It seeks these instances through a *reductionist* approach of breaking down phenomena into small components and measuring them. It values both incremental progress by teams of researchers and a strict separation of values from the research process. This position is closely allied with functionalism in organizational theory, and critiques of it are similar to those made against positivism (e.g., Putnam, 1983).

It goes without saying that I have given only the briefest review of these positions. Many books have been written about them, and any summary like this one necessarily glosses important details. But even this brief review is sufficient to show that over its approximately 175-year history, positivism has meant and continues to mean many different things. The different varieties share a certain spirit that I will discuss below, but there are important differences between varieties that typically go unacknowledged by critics. This has interesting rhetorical consequences that I turn to next.

There Is No Such Thing as a Positivist

An outcome of the long and complicated history of positivism is another point embedded in the opening story: Positivism is a straw man. Consider the following example, which I made up based on my memory of similar arguments. It may have a familiar ring.

> Positivism is bankrupt as a philosophical enterprise. First, it relies on a flawed epistemology that says observation is theory-free. Hanson (1958) has conclusively shown that there is no such thing as a disinterested observer. All observation presumes interpretation, and interpretation is inherently laden with theory and interests. Therefore, observation can never be theory-free. Second, positivism has a corrupt axiology anchored in the belief that science is *the* motor of progress, inexorably leading us toward a better future. But as everyone knows, science has produced a lot of rotten outcomes [insert here numerous examples, like nuclear weapons], and because it ignores interests (see the first point, above), it does not have the means of preventing other rotten outcomes in the future. Finally, it is based on a preposterous methodology that is obsessed with breaking phenomena into itty-bitty pieces, measuring them, and crunching the data in inscrutable computer programs. This radically decontextualizes human experience, reducing it to mere numbers, and prevents a holistic view that could be used to control those rotten outcomes (see the second point above).

Who in their right mind would subscribe to such a philosophy?

The problem is that the different kinds of positivism disagree on substantial matters. What I have done here is choose critiques that are applicable to one kind of positivism and present them as critiques of positivism in general. I have also tried to integrate the critiques by making one seem to be the root cause of the next, giving the impression of a philosophical house of cards. By eliding important differences, I am able to produce a devastating-sounding critique. Much the same situation has evolved in critiques of feminism (Buzzanell, 1994), which is ironic because many (but not all) varieties of feminism are antipositivist, and arguments like the one I caricatured are not hard to find in the feminist literature.

But the devil is in the details, and a successful critique of one kind of positivism does not indict them all. For example, my first point was an argument against the idea of theory-free observation. However, that is a belief of logical positivism, one with which the classical positivist Comte explicitly disagreed (Phillips, 2000, p. 165). The second point was a critique of reformist scientism. As I noted above, logical positivism rejected this idea, holding that science would not necessarily lead to progress. The third point about reductionism applies to instrumental positivism but not to classical positivism, which holds that there are irreducible social phenomena (Halfpenny, 1982).

When I read or hear a critique like this fictional example above, it causes me to ask: "Just *who* are they talking about" (see for example, Corman, 2000)? The beliefs being critiqued describe neither me nor anyone I know. The record shows that positivism is an *essentially* contested idea. Since shortly after its birth, classical positivism has been subject to a long series of critiques, appropriations, reappropriations, and major reformulations. The conclusion seems clear enough: There are no positivists, only postpositivists.

Principles of Postpositivism

The history of postpositivism is also quite long, a point that did not really hit home with me until I reflected on the antique auditorium. Given this long history, there is some fuzziness about the term. For example, there is divergence of opinion about what perspectives can be considered postpositivist. Under the most inclusive definition, it could be any perspective that postdates yet is not the same as classical, logical, or instrumental positivism. Using such a definition, we could classify as postpositivists the Frankfurt School and their descendants, postmodernists, feminists, and so on. This definition does not seem reasonable because it more or less just marks a point in time and encompasses positions that are both propositivist and antipositivist.

Postpositivism is better defined as a philosophy of science that respects the spirit of science in the context of fundamental reforms of positivistic principles. In other words, it is the outcome of an *appreciative* critique of the different positivisms. I am reluctant to include the notion of a "spirit" in this definition after just arguing that we cannot essentialize positivism. But in order for positivism to have the impact and staying power it has, it must have some quality that transcends its theoretical shortcomings. It must have a *spirit* or "pervading animating principle" (*Webster's New World College Dictionary*, 2001). I propose that this is the spirit of science, which values knowledge built through rigorous systematic observation. Postpositivists are people who value a scientific approach to explaining social phenomena, but who also accept many of the criticisms of the different positivisms and have developed positions that transcend them.

The remainder of this section will outline five principles that I take to be the core positions of postpositivism (for a somewhat different set see Miller, 2000). For each, I explain the issue and its background. Then, as requested by the editors, I explain how I have engaged these principles in my own research program. I also discuss how each position breaks with positivism and answers critics.

Falsificationism

Popper is a good example of an early postpositivist. He was a contemporary (though not a member) of the Vienna Circle and had sharp disagreements with its ideas. None of these was bigger than the disagreement over the verification principle of meaning. Popper believed that verification is trivial because *some* facts can always be found to support *any* plausible theory. On the other hand, no amount of verification can ever conclusively prove the truth of a theory because there could always be some future case that would come along to disconfirm it. The most important factor in scientific progress, then, is discovery of the disconfirming or *falsifying* instances. Science proceeds by a process of conjectures and refutations (Popper, 1968). It never reaches certain conclusions, yet it is the best-known process for generating reliable knowledge.

Falsificationism is clearly a uniting feature of postpositivism. It is the motivation for statistical testing, where the observed value of some statistic is tested against values of that statistic that could be observed by chance. Phillips (2000) criticizes this practice, arguing that the null hypothesis is a "bland conjecture" that is almost certain to be false (p. 150); it is a cursory rather than wholehearted attempt at falsification, and it should not be counted as a serious falsification attempt by Popper's standards. But Phillips is overstating the point. If it were as easy to reject the null hypothesis as he suggests, it would be hard to explain all the cases where I have failed to do so and all the similar failures I have read about in the course of reviewing papers or heard about in talking to other researchers.

Statistical testing is a good *minimum* standard for attempting falsification. If nothing else, statistical tests assure us that enough observation was done to make capitalizing on chance unlikely. They also ensure that the relationships researchers detect are at least stronger than the noise in their observations. That said, it is clearly desirable that there be other, more rigorous attempts at falsification of relationships discovered in research. This need not happen within the context of one study or even be done by the same researcher. For example, Hewes (1986, 1996) has proposed a socio-egocentric model of communication that, if validated, would falsify assumptions about the importance of communication in groups that have been taken for granted by researchers for decades.

My own research program can be seen as an effort to falsify the prevailing notion that communication networks, as measured, are isomorphic with communication that actually happens. In graduate school, I became interested in the subject of communication networks. At that time (mid-1980s), a hot issue in the network literature was the "informant accuracy" problem. Put simply, if you ask people to rate their network contacts using the normal methods (asking them how much or how often they interact with people) and then record their observable interaction with those same contacts, correlations between the two measures range from bad to horrible. Consensus developed among network researchers that network questionnaires measure *perceived* networks. Although these are certainly interesting phenomena in their own right, they are not straightforward reflections of communication that can be observed.

In Corman and Scott (1994a), we drew on the dualistic reasoning of Giddens (1984) to propose a theoretical model linking the two phenomena. Networks of perceived relationships are latent social structures that are activated by organizational activity to produce manifest instances of observable communication. These instances are perceived by the communicators and others, and this reproduces or perhaps modifies the perceived communication relationship network, going forward through a process of social cognition. We proposed a competitive test of two models relating networks to communication. This technique pits new models against accepted standards in explaining observed data, yielding much more than bland conjectures.

In Corman and Bradford (1993), we showed that self-reported perceived relationships are systematically biased. By comparing coded interaction in an organizational simulation with self-reports by participants, we discovered that errors of omission (where people do not report communication that occurred) are related to the communication load of the participants. Errors of commission (where people report communication that could not be observed) tended to follow and reproduce organizational structure. This research demonstrates that reports of communication have important sources of variation that are not strictly related to the communication behavior supposedly being measured.

Falsificationism is based on a *nonfoundationalist epistemology* that goes a long way toward addressing a prominent antipositivist complaint of naïveté about interpretations. Postpositivism acknowledges that interpretations "emerge from the inquirer's own grounding in a particular time and place; but that is not what is relevant when considering their status as knowledge; what is relevant is how the interpretation (or knowledge-claim) is tested and criticized" (Phillips, 2000, p. 35). Thus, postpositivism does not reject the notion of interpretation; it simply holds that interpretations must eventually be validated in some way.

Naturalism

A second unifying principle in postpositivism is a reformed naturalism. Naturalism, the belief that there is an essential unity between the social sciences and natural sciences, is one of the core principles of classical positivism. Today, few people would say that the physical and social sciences are *isomorphic*. Postpositivists accept the hermeneutical argument that human understanding plays a role in all scientific research, but they do not believe that this fact completely undermines application of scientific methods to social phenomena. As Phillips (1987) puts it, "there is much in social science that does not involve hermeneutical understanding in any central or significant way (any way that is different from the way that understanding is involved in the procedures of physics, for example)" (p. 111).

Many features of human communication and its context are influenced by obdurate characteristics of the physical world. In addition to being subjects, communicators are physical objects. They occupy space and move through it. They communicate with one another using sound and light waves, and these efforts are affected by physical circumstances (such as noise). Thus, although postpositivists do not diminish processes of interpretation and understanding, or nonscientific methods for studying them, they recognize that social behavior and social structure remain part of the natural world. They therefore "have no features that offer insuperable obstacles to the adoption of the methods of social science" (Phillips, 1987, p. 204).

My own research exemplifies this reformed naturalism. First, it acknowledges that both understanding/interpretation and physical characteristics are central to the informant accuracy problem. The first publication from my dissertation (Corman, 1990) used a field experiment to test a model of perceived communication relationships. It showed that individual-level perceptions of interpersonal attraction, positions in the organizational structure, and the physical distance separating two participants are important and independent constituents of the perceived strength of relationships.

Corman and Krizek (1993) demonstrated a hybridization of interpretive and scientific approaches. We relied on written responses, interpreted through an induced set of coding categories, to understand how people formulate responses to network questionnaires. Although the coded instances were analyzed in a statistical model, this model simply summarized individual judgments of the coders and identified categories that occurred at greater than or less than chance rates.

Corman and Scott's (1994b) digital signal processing method tries to remove human judgment from the coding of observable communication by processing sound waves people emit when they are talking to one another. The point here is not to ignore the human understanding, but to create an independent physical observation of communication behavior to which understandings can be related. Finally, in Corman, Kuhn, McPhee, and Dooley (2002), we argued strongly that it is just as important to understand the manifest content of communication as it is to understand the intentions of the author/speaker and interpretations of the reader/listener.

The naturalistic position sketched here is not without problems. Even if we grant that social phenomena are part of the natural world, we are still left with the problem that the scientists who are applying the naturalistic methods are themselves subjects. Having abandoned a foundationalist epistemology, how can postpositivism make any special claims for the validity of the knowledge produced by the scientist? This question is answered, at least to some extent, by the principle of emergent objectivity described below. Also, hermeneutics has its own problems with the active subject (Bryant, 1985) and shares with science a common problem-solving method (Popper, 1972).

Realism

A third unifying principle of postpositivism is *realism*, the belief that things (including social phenomena) have a reality that is independent of their being perceived by someone. This position is at odds with all three varieties of positivism, especially logical positivism. The positivists were *antirealist* in that they believed perceptions were *all* that mattered. For example, the Vienna Circle asserted that "there is knowledge only from experience, which rests on what is immediately given" and therefore "in science there are no 'depths'; there is surface everywhere" (cited in Bryant, 1985, p. 111). Indeed, they regarded the whole question of ontology (theory of being) to be in the realm of metaphysics, which they regarded as meaningless!

On the other hand, realism is at odds with a belief held by many antipositivists. *Relativism* can be defined as the belief that things (especially social phenomena) exist only in relation to some point of view. You could say that perspectives are to relativists what perceptions are to antirealists: Something does not exist until and unless it is interpreted from some point of view. Relativism allows that different points of view lead to different, multiple realities. A single event could, in theory, have as many realities as there are points of view to interpret it.

Postpositivists employ *transcendental reasoning* as a basis for believing that things are or are not real, focusing on what conditions must exist in order for something to be the case. Collier (1994) illustrated the application of transcendental reasoning to his Theory of Disappearing Household Objects. Why is it, he asks, that we do not believe the repeatedly proven theory that "from time to time, household objects (books, earrings, cutlery, spare parts of sewing machines, gramophone records) cease to exist without a trace" (p. 28)? The transcendental refutation of this theory is straightforward: We do not believe this theory because there are no known household conditions under which things can vanish completely without a trace. On the other hand, there are known conditions under which people lose track of things, the things become accidentally hidden from view, and so forth. These conditions are sufficient to explain the disappearance.

The reticulation theory of networks developed in Corman and Scott (1994a) is an exercise in transcendental reasoning. It asks: If perceived communication networks are not isomorphic with observable communication, then what conditions must exist in order for both to coexist in social systems? Our answer is that there must be different domains in which the two phenomena exist and processes that translate from one domain to the other. The specific nature of these domains and processes relate to the next feature of postpositivism, so I describe them below.

The realist position represents a clean break with antirealist positivism. Postpositivists believe there is more than meets the eye when it comes to studying social phenomena. As Collier (1994) pointed out, if we were *really* antirealists, we would believe the disappearing household objects theory. I would add that we would also be faced with explaining how it is that the objects, having disappeared, sometimes suddenly rematerialize. It is simply more straightforward and plausible to believe they go on existing even when we cannot see them.

A similar parsimony issue confronts relativists. Suppose groups A and B both understand the word "Earth" to mean the planet on which we live. Group A believes the Earth is flat, and group B believes the Earth is spherical. Relativists would have to say the Earth really is *both* flat and spherical at the same time. They would be faced with the task of explaining how that could be, and how the Earth could be flat even though we have observations saying that it is (only) spherical. Phillips (2000) gives another example, of one group that believes there are 3 kinds of snow and another group that believes there are 10 kinds of snow. Is it more reasonable to say there are really *both* 3 and 10 kinds of snow, or that there is really something called "snow" that is conceptualized and referenced differently by different groups? The postpositivist realist would favor the second explanation.

Transformational Models

Positivism was, if nothing else, a rejection of *metaphysics*, "the branch of philosophy dealing with a host of disparate issues that cannot be settled, in principle, by appeal to human observation or experience" (Phillips, 1987, p. 204). Positivists of all stripes rejected metaphysics as undesirable at best and meaningless at worst. Their empiricism mandated that science deal only with those things that could be experienced. Postpositivists also place a great deal of value on things that can be experienced, but they are willing to take *one step* into the metaphysical realm as long as they are securely tethered to the empirical. Specifically, they believe there can be *generative mechanisms* or systems that, while not observable themselves, are responsible for things we can observe.

Important sources of this thinking are Bhaskar and Giddens. Bhaskar (1979) proposed the *transformational model of social activity* to explain how people, who can be directly observed, relate to society, which can be only indirectly observed through the actions of people. Mechanisms of *socialization* give society influence over individuals, mechanisms of *reproduction and transformation* give individuals influence over society, and the two codetermine one another over time. Giddens (1984) uses similar dualistic reasoning in distinguishing *system* from *structure* and positing mechanisms of production and reproduction that connect them in the process of structuration.

It was this transformational idea that provided the basis for explaining perceived networks and observable communication in reticulation theory. In Corman and Scott (1994a), we distinguished a *domain of social structure* from a *domain of social interaction*, and we argued that networks exist in the former, while observable communication exists in the latter. The network influences communication by a process of *social activation*, and communication influences the network through a process of *social cognition*. Many aspects of the network are unobservable, or at least observable only by proxy in the domain of social interaction (i.e., in answers to network questions). Yet, we can believe that these networks exist because they explain regularities we can observe in the domain of social interaction.

Recently, I have concentrated on the observable side of communication. One focus finds ways to bring the content of communication into the equation, and network models are a surprisingly good fit here as well. They can be used to provide a rich abstraction of communication content, representing the essential ideas people talk about and the interconnections among these ideas (Corman, Kuhn, et al., 2002). The hope is to develop a model that integrates the physical act of communicating, the content of that communication, organizational activities, and perceived networks into one framework. Proposing this is one thing, but carrying it off presents a large number of practical problems (Dooley, Corman, McPhee, & Kuhn, 2003). At my campus, we have developed the Software Factory, a lab that does software engineering work for on-campus researchers. It also supports organizational research and is equipped for ubiquitous observation. We hope that the kind of data needed to demonstrate that networks are reproduced in communication are close at hand.

The use of transformational models is not a surprising move for postpositivists, given the affinity for transcendental reasoning described above. We must believe in things we cannot (yet) see in order to discover new things and develop the ability to see them. This position punctures yet another boundary between postpositivism and its critics. Postpositivists have repealed the prohibition on metaphysics; we just want to see it well regulated by empirical ordinances.

Emergent Objectivity

The fifth principle of postpositivism is emergent objectivity. It stands in contrast to what might be called a more absolute objectivity embedded in positivism. Starting with classical positivism, Durkheim (1895/1938) argued that there is a difference between ideas and things, and that social science ought to deal exclusively with things. Things are the stuff of sense experience, whereas ideas are either removed from them or are unconnected to them. Sticking to sense experience carries the greatest potential for agreement among observers and across cases: It is easy to get unanimous agreement or disagreement with a statement like "the walls in this room are pink" but more difficult to get agreement that "the color scheme in this room looks good." Logical positivists also believed in the purity of sense experience, and instrumental positivists thought their quantitative rigor would promote (if not guarantee) objectivity.

All these views depend on there being a way to observe things that is free from "contamination" by ideas. As noted above in the section on falsification, however, there is general agreement now that there is no such method. Bryant (1985) even questions whether Durkheim's examples supported his own arguments in the first place.

Accordingly, postpositivists have shifted the locus and domains of objectivity, without abandoning it as a goal. Even if all observation is influenced by subjective reality, this does not mean that all observations are equally good. Some observations are more influenced by the interests of the observer than are others. Therefore, what is important is that we have a good *system* for evaluating observations. Objectivity, for the postpositivist, inheres in the standards developed and enforced by a community of practice (Wenger, 1998). Objectivity is not a characteristic of individual acts of observation, but instead an *emergent property* of a system of "organized skepticism." It forces researchers to explain their methods in detail, attempts to reproduce their findings, and (following the principle of falsification) tries to find alternate explanations for them.

Postpositivism also restricts this skeptical system to a particular domain of inquiry. It is not appropriate in the *context of discovery* where, because of the nature of the task, we favor rich and unstructured methods that are influenced (even driven) by the interests of the investigator. Yet not all things discovered in this context are equally valuable or useful, and the very idea of inquiry presupposes sorting them out. For that, we rely on a *context of justification* where ideas are evaluated and objectivity (in its emergent form) is the regulative ideal. A separation between the two is justified because "processes involved in . . . the *making* of discoveries during the pursuit of a research program may not be involved—and might be counterproductive if allowed to intrude—when the discoveries are *checked* and *tested* and *critically evaluated* " (Phillips, 2000, p. 134, emphasis in original). Conversely, objective procedures of testing and evaluation are counterproductive in the creative process of discovery. Both are needed for a well-rounded approach, what Wallace (1971) called a "wheel of science."

This interaction between discovery and justification is illustrated in a research thread that grew out of reticulation theory. If perceived communication relationships are reproduced by focused activity, then how does the activity system operate? It is difficult to answer this question outside a particular organizational context, so in Corman, Stage, and Scott (1997), we engaged in a discovery exercise to describe the activity system of the typical grocery store in a chain. Based on extensive interviews and observations, we proposed a set of activity foci that interact through a network of relationships to explain observable activity at the store. This led to a computer simulation that can be used to test the model against empirical results. The model has been extended to the terrorism context (Corman, in press), but it is still a product of the context of discovery. It cannot yet be considered justified because it has not been empirically tested. Such testing is on the agenda for future research.

Once again, this postpositivist view of objectivity represents a clear break with positivism. Gone is the positivist notion that there is some pure realm, free of ideas, where science can operate safely. On the contrary, observations are so imbued with ideas that we need a special system, based on rigorous methods, specific (even tedious) definitions, and agreement between observers, to sort them out. Gone also is the elitist notion that science is the One True Path to knowledge, which alienated so many of positivism's critics. In its place, there is a formal recognition of the place of humanistic methods in the context of discovery. It is not an alternative but a complement to the context of justification, where emergent objectivity is the regulatory ideal.

Postpositivism and Other Approaches

The final point embedded in the opening story is that there is a strange tendency for people to overestimate the degree of conflict between postpositivism and competing approaches to explaining social phenomena. As with Popper and Adorno in Tübingen, a bloody fight is always anticipated, but the actual engagement rarely amounts to more than friendly sparring. What accounts for the persistent agonistic expectations? This is an interesting question that awaits some other paper. For now, I focus on why the clash does not develop.

As I emphasized in the discussion of the five principles above, postpositivism rejects the most problematic features of the different positivisms. It is not merely tinkering around the edges but a different perspective. It is also an inclusionary perspective, giving humanistic approaches a balancing position on the wheel of science, valuing them for their ability to uncover generative mechanisms and new explanations for phenomena. Thus, from the postpositivist perspective there is simply not much real competition between these different perspectives; they are useful for different purposes.

Indeed, the relationship goes beyond lacking differences to actually occupying common ground. As Phillips (1987) noted, "some of the most boisterous celebrants at positivism's wake are actually more positivistic than they realize, or have more in common with [post]positivists than they would care to admit" (p. 44). For example, the critical perspective is like postpositivism in that both proceed via a *critical method*. Claims about knowledge are argued, treated with skepticism, systematically challenged, and tested. Popper's (1972) complaint still rings true today:

> labouring the difference between science and the humanities has long been a fashion, and has become a bore. The method of problem solving, the method of

conjecture and refutation, is practiced by both. It is practiced in reconstructing a damaged text as well as in constructing a theory of radioactivity. (p. 185)

The interpretive perspective is also like postpositivism in that both assume that subjective understandings have a key impact on the scientific process. They agree that objectivity is an emergent collective interpretation rather than an inherent property of a particular observational act. Interpretive scholars have methodological concerns such as credibility (member-checking), transferability, and consistency (see Lincoln & Guba, 1985) that are strikingly similar to the reliability and validity worries of postpositivists. If I may be so bold, postmodernism can even be thought of as postpositivist in that both accept a nonfoundationalist approach to knowledge.

To be sure, there are differences between postpositivism and these perspectives as well. The point is that postpositivism pervades the context of verification and is *needed* for a well-balanced approach to understanding social phenomena. It counterweights the tendency of antipositivist approaches to make highly metaphysical claims based only on verifying examples. It is also a means for intersubjective agreement based on observables, which opposes centrifugal tendencies of the more radical approaches. Scientific methods are still "the most powerful tools available for replacing superstition and prejudice with knowledge" (Kincaid, 1996, p. xv), and their application in social research is a necessity, not an option.

Conclusion

In closing, let us revisit the points embedded in the opening story to outline an informed position on postpositivism. To begin with, postpositivism is not positivism. Positivism is a *very* old set of ideas: When you think positivism, think antique auditoriums. It got its start around the time of the U.S. Civil War, and it had peaked and faded by World War II. By the mid 20th century, scholars were arguing about what should replace positivism, not about how to preserve it. Despite this history, there is a tendency among many antipositivists to treat positivism as a going concern, assimilating anyone who favors a scientific approach to that position. It is a "straw man" that can be attacked as an easy starting point for reform.

But there are no positivists anymore. Well, OK—there could be one or two hanging around in an unexplored rain forest somewhere, but for all practical purposes positivists are an extinct species. In the wake of positivism, we have postpositivism, which values the spirit of science in the context of fundamental reforms of positivist beliefs. Postpositivists believe in falsificationism, naturalism, realism, transformational models, and emergent objectivity, significant departures from positivist beliefs. Postpositivism shares a good deal of theoretical high ground with its erstwhile competitors, and it cannot be safely relegated to the role of Third Man of this book. It is a viable perspective in its own right, one that should be respected as a valuable complement to other contemporary perspectives on organizational communication.

Notes

1. Not the old era of enlightenment, which Comte supported (Halfpenny, 1982).

2. It also could be meaningful if it is an internal logical or mathematical statement.

References

Adorno, T. W., Albert, H., Dahrendorf, R., Habermas, J., Pilot, H., & Popper, K. R. (1976). *The positivist dispute in German sociology.* New York: Harper & Row. (German language version published 1969)

Bhaskar, R. (1979). *The possibility of naturalism: A philosophical critique of the contemporary human sciences.* Atlantic Highlands, NJ: Humanities Press.

Bryant, C. G. A. (1985). *Positivism in social theory and research.* London: Macmillan.

Buzzanell, P. M. (1994). Gaining a voice: Feminist organizational communication theorizing. *Management Communication Quarterly, 7*(4), 339–383.

Collier, A. (1994). *Critical realism: An introduction to Roy Bhaskar's philosophy.* London: Verso.

Comte, A. (1970). *Introduction to positive philosophy* (F. Ferré, Trans.). Indianapolis: Bobbs-Merrill. (Original work published 1830)

Corman, S. R. (1990). A model of perceived communication in collective networks. *Human Communication Research, 16,* 582–602.

Corman, S. R. (2000). The need for common ground. In S. R. Corman & M. S. Poole (Eds.), *Perspectives on organizational communication: Finding common ground* (pp. 1–15). New York: Guilford.

Corman, S. R. (in press). Using activity focus networks to pressure terrorist organizations. *Computational and Mathematical Organization Theory.*

Corman, S. R., & Bradford, L. B. (1993). Situational effects on the accuracy of self-reported organizational communication behavior. *Communication Research, 20,* 822–840.

Corman, S. R., & Krizek, R. L. (1993). Accounting resources for organizational communication and individual differences in their use. *Management Communication Quarterly, 7,* 5–35.

Corman, S. R., Kuhn, T., McPhee, R., & Dooley, K. (2002). Studying complex discursive systems: Centering resonance analysis of communication. *Human Communication Research, 28,* 157–206.

Corman, S. R., & Scott, C. R. (1994a). Perceived communication relationships, activity foci, and observable communication in collectives. *Communication Theory, 4,* 171–190.

Corman, S. R., & Scott, C. R. (1994b). A synchronous digital signal processing method for detecting face-to-face organizational communication behavior. *Social Networks, 16,* 163–179.

Corman, S. R., Stage, C., & Scott, C. R. (1997, May). *Communication-related activity systems: An empirical description and computational organization model of activity foci in a grocery store chain.* Paper presented at the meeting of the International Communication Association, Montreal, Quebec, Canada.

Dahrendorf, R. (1976). Remarks on the discussion. In T. W. Adorno et al. (Eds.), *The positivist dispute in German sociology* (pp. 123–130). New York: Harper & Row.

Dooley, K., Corman, S., McPhee, R., & Kuhn, T. (2003). Modeling high-resolution broadband discourse in complex adaptive systems. *Nonlinear Dynamics, Psychology, and Life Sciences, 7*(1), 61–86.

Durkheim, E. (1938). *The rules of sociological method* (S. A. Solvay & J. H. Mueller, Trans.). Glencoe, IL: Free Press. (Original work published 1895)

Frisby, D. (1976). Introduction to the English translation. In T. W. Adorno et al. (Eds.), *The positivist dispute in German sociology* (pp. ix–xliv). New York: Harper & Row.

Gellner, E. (1985). *Relativism and the social sciences.* Cambridge, UK: Cambridge University Press.

Giddens, A. (1984). *The constitution of society.* Berkeley: University of California Press.

Halfpenny, P. (1982). *Positivism and sociology: Explaining social life.* London: George Allen & Unwin.

Hanson, N. R. (1958). *Patterns of discovery.* Cambridge, UK: Cambridge University Press.

Hewes, D. E. (1986). A socio-egocentric model of group decision-making. In R. Y. Hirokawa & M. S. Poole (Eds.), *Communication and group decision-making* (pp. 265–291). Beverly Hills, CA: Sage.

Hewes, D. E. (1996). Small group communication may not influence decision making: An amplification of socio-egocentric theory. In R. Y. Hirokawa & M. S. Poole (Eds.), *Communication and group decision making* (2nd ed., pp. 179–214). Thousand Oaks, CA: Sage.

Kincaid, H. (1996). *Philosophical foundations of the social sciences: Analyzing controversies in social research.* New York: Cambridge University Press.

Lincoln, Y. S., & Guba, E. G. (1985). *Naturalistic inquiry*. Beverly Hills, CA: Sage.

Miller, K. I. (2000). Common ground from the post-positivist perspective: From "straw person" argument to collaborative coexistence. In S. R. Corman & M. S. Poole (Eds.), *Perspectives on organizational communication: Finding common ground* (pp. 46–67). New York: Guilford.

Phillips, D. C. (1987). *Philosophy, science, and social inquiry*. New York: Pergamon.

Phillips, D. C. (2000). *The expanded social scientist's bestiary*. New York: Rowman & Littlefield.

Popper, K. (1968). *Conjectures and refutations* (2nd ed.). New York: Harper Torchbooks.

Popper, K. (1972). *Objective knowledge*. London: Oxford University Press.

Putnam, L. (1983). The interpretive perspective: An alternative to functionalism. In L. L. Putnam & M. E. Pacanowsky (Eds.), *Communication and organizations, an interpretive approach* (pp. 31–54). Beverly Hills, CA: Sage.

Wallace, W. (1971). *The logic of science in sociology*. Chicago: Aldine Atherson.

Webster's new world college dictionary (4th ed.). (2001). Forster City, CA: IDG Books Worldwide.

Wenger, E. (1998). *Communities of practice: Learning, meaning and identity*. New York: Cambridge University Press.

3

Social Constructionism

Brenda J. Allen

To study processes of organizing, communication scholars increasingly rely on social constructionism, a theoretical orientation to sociocultural processes that affect humans' basic understandings of the world. Scholars who take a social constructionist stance claim that anything that has meaning in our lives originates within "the matrix of relationships in which we are engaged" (Gergen & Gergen, 2000, "The Social Construction of Value and the Aging Self," ¶1). Social constructionists assert that meaning arises from social systems rather than from individual members of society. They contend that humans derive knowledge of the world from larger social discourses, which can vary across time and place, and which often represent and reinforce dominant belief systems. Social constructionists also stress the significance of language to construction processes, including its ramifications for identity development (Leeds-Hurwitz, 1995).

Social constructionism infuses my scholarly endeavors. In research and teaching, I focus a critical lens on organizational communication, with an emphasis on social identity categories such as gender, race, and social class. Social constructionism helps me identify and illuminate ways that organizational actors make, modify, and maintain meaning about social identity.

In this chapter, I explore the significance of social constructionism to engaged organizational communication scholarship. I begin by tracing origins of social constructionism and discussing its main assumptions and critiques. Next, I narrate a few personal experiences to analyze relationships between social constructionism and my development as a scholar. Then, I review social constructionist research on organizational communication. I conclude by discussing implications of social constructionism for organizational communication studies. Throughout the chapter, I refer to social identity issues to clarify or exemplify primary points.

Social Constructionism—An Overview

Social constructionism strives to understand how humans create knowledge— "anything a society holds to be true, real, and meaningful" (Hruby, 2001, p. 52). According to social constructionists, knowledge is an effect of social processes. Social constructionists maintain that humans construct the world through social practices. For example, practices such as encouraging girls to be docile or admonishing boys not to cry help to disseminate and perpetuate constructed "knowledge" about gender. This type of knowledge stems more from current connotations about femininity and masculinity (which are social constructions in their own right) than from preexisting, "natural" characteristics of human beings. Thus, social constructionists reject essentialist explanations that "certain phenomena are natural, inevitable, universal, and biologically determined" (DeLamater & Hyde, 2001, p. 10).

Social constructionism stems from, and is influenced by, diverse disciplines and intellectual traditions (Burr, 1995; Pearce, 1995). One root of contemporary approaches to social constructionism arose from late 19th-century German sociological studies on the development of intellectual or academic knowledge. From these studies branched a paradigm called "the sociology of knowledge," which delved into ways that members of scholarly communities create and agree upon what counts as scientific facts or descriptions of reality (Hruby, 2001). This new perspective challenged notions of objective reality.

The sociology of knowledge analyzed how sociocultural forces constructed knowledge, and it ascertained types of knowledge these forces produced. Scholars from various disciplines—including sociology, philosophy, anthropology, social psychology, linguistics, and communication—applied this approach to their respective fields (Burr, 1995). In 1966, sociologists Thomas Berger and Peter Luckmann published a seminal book about knowledge development titled *The Social Construction of Reality* (Berger & Luckmann, 1966). They drew upon the tradition of the sociology of knowledge as well as theoretical perspectives of social philosopher Alfred Schutz (Burr, 1995). Berger and Luckmann's treatise extended the sociology of knowledge beyond intellectual history to encompass "knowledge that guides conduct in everyday life" (p. 19). When they asserted that "the sociology of knowledge is concerned with the analysis of the social construction of reality" (p. 19), they prompted changing "the sociology of knowledge" to "social constructionism." This new conception highlighted processes of knowledge development ("constructionism"), while stressing the significance of human interaction ("social").

Assumptions of Social Constructionism

Since the late 1960s, numerous disciplines have adopted and adapted social constructionism. Within contemporary conceptions of social constructionism, several key assumptions reside (Burr, 1995). One primary assumption is "a critical stance towards taken-for-granted ways of understanding the world (including ourselves)" (Burr, 1995, p. 3). Social constructionism encourages us to be suspicious of how we understand the world and ourselves. For example, we should challenge categories of social identity such as gender and race because "the categories with which we as human beings apprehend the world do not necessarily refer to real divisions." (Ore, 2003, p. 5). We also might question why we highlight and classify some aspects of personhood and not others.

A second assumption of social constructionism stresses that all knowledge is historically and culturally specific. Labels, classifications, denotations, and connotations of social identity always are products of their times. Furthermore, processes of constructing social identities depend heavily on social, political, and historical factors, as humans rely on current ideologies to create social identity categories and their meanings. These meanings usually arise from political processes as the interests of certain groups take precedence over others.

For example, in U.S. society of the 17th and 18th centuries, discourse about sexual activity dictated that women and men should practice sexual self-control and discipline, engaging in sex only as married persons seeking to reproduce the species. This perspective on sexuality arose from religious, economic, and political concerns about increasing the population of the so-called New World. Consequently, heterosexuality was considered an abnormal manifestation of sexual appetite because it connoted sex as pleasure, and a heterosexual was defined as "an unequivocal pervert" (Katz, 1995, p. 21). In sharp contrast, contemporary positions on sexuality construct heterosexuality (or woman-to-man erotic desire) as normal.

A third assumption of social constructionism rests on the premise that social processes sustain knowledge. Among these processes, language is fundamental. We use language to produce and reproduce knowledge as we enact various roles within various contexts. Language helps us make sense of the world; it allows us to share experiences and meaning with one another. Language is a system we use to objectify subjective meanings and to internalize socially constructed meanings.

In daily interactions, we receive and repeat recurring versions of "the truth" about social identity groups. For instance, dominant discourses in the United States about aging and the elderly tend to be negative. These discourses portray aging as an undesirable state of decline. Most of us internalize those negative constructions, and we pass them on to others. When we interact with older persons, we often try to confirm our biases and ignore evidence to the contrary (Williams & Giles, 1996; also see Ng, Liu, Weatherall, & Loong, 1997).

A final assumption of social constructionism warrants that knowledge and social action are interconnected. Consider, for example, the construction of childhood. Prior to the 20th century, children were valued more for their economic worth than for emotional reasons (Fass & Mason, 2000). During the Industrial Revolution, most children in working-class families held some type of job, often engaging in monotonous, sometimes dangerous work. Children as young as 5 years of age worked in textile industries, and in 1820, nearly half of textile mill workers were children working 10-hour days (Clay & Stephens, 1996). In the 20th century, as a result of a child labor movement and the development of compulsory education, children shifted from being "economically useful" to "economically useless" but "emotionally priceless" (Fass & Mason, 2000, p. 3). Childhood became constructed as a period of "leisured growth and development" (Fass & Mason, p. 3). Thus, contemporary constructions of childhood mandate that children will go to school instead of work.

To review, four primary propositions of social constructionism are that a critical stance should be assumed toward taken-for-granted knowledge, knowledge is historically and culturally specific, social processes sustain knowledge, and knowledge and social action are interconnected (Burr, 1995). Although most social constructionists probably would agree with these tenets, some of them might disagree about aspects of social constructionism. In fact, so many differences exist among social constructionist approaches that one scholar describes them as "varied beyond hope of compatible reconciliation" (Pearce, 1995, p. 108). Although I cannot cite or discuss all those differences here, I summarize a few below.

Differences in Social Constructionist Approaches

A primary difference among social constructionists is their opinion about reality (Pearce, 1995). Although social constructionists agree that there is no such thing as objective reality, they disagree about what that means. For instance, some scholars want to understand *how* humans make things real. Consequently, they study *processes* of social construction. For example, a realist, non-objectivist position known as the coordinated management of meaning contends that "the activities performed by persons in conversations are themselves real. Persons are not only cognizing entities, we are embodied; our activities are real" (Pearce, 1995, p. 95; see Pearce, 1995, for an in-depth treatment of differences between social constructionists).

In contrast to a focus on processes of reality construction, other scholars are interested in *what* humans construct as reality. These scholars attend to *products* of social construction, such as symbolic forms, symbols, and meanings.

Another approach to dealing with reality (Lannamann, 1995) includes process *and* products. This "materialist" approach to social constructionism urges researchers to attend to details (products) of interaction (processes) because those material details influence and are influenced by sociohistorical contexts. For example, studies about gendered discourse should investigate differences in subjective worlds that women and men inhabit (Lannamann, 1995).

Numerous other differences exist among social constructionists. Scholars variously claim that social constructionism serves epistemological, ontological, and empirical purposes (Hruby, 2001). Others distinguish strong/extreme versions of social constructionism from weak/mild versions (Berger & Luckmann, 1966). They also differentiate strict constructionists from contextual constructionists (Fox, 1999). One author maps three waves of social constructionism: sociological, postmodernism, and neorealist (Hruby, 2001). Despite these differences, or maybe as a result of them, social constructionism continues to be popular in and across multiple disciplines. Of course, however, social constructionism also has its detractors.

Critiques of Social Constructionism

Some critics contest social constructionism's antirealist stance. For instance, they believe that an objective reality is the basis for human sensations. They contend that theories of knowledge and identity development should allow for material contingencies such as brain functions, bodily sensations, visceral responses, and the physical world at large (Hruby, 2001). This critique applies to "strong" versions of social constructionism which contend that *everything* is socially constructed, and which imply deep philosophical analyses about what is real. However, most social science work stems from "mild" approaches to social constructionism, which do not delve into these issues. Rather, they focus on *social* rather than physical realities and their implications (Berger & Luckmann, 1966).

Another challenge to social constructionism cites the paradox of critiquing concepts such as power relations, oppression, and domination when the concepts themselves are social constructions. Here's a summary of this viewpoint:

> The notion that there is not truth or objective reality, for example, provides a convenient objection to any claim about the (real, actual, material) existence of injustice, inequality, exploitation, and oppression. The philosophical implication is that people are not really oppressed, they just think they are. This renders the perception of injustice as just one among many equally (in)valid social constructions. (Jost & Kruglanski, 2002, p. 175)

Related to this paradox, some authors accuse social constructionism of extreme, "anything goes" relativism that can depoliticize constructs related to social (in)justice (Burr, 1995). However, social constructionism invites us to discern various conceptions and to "generate alternative understandings of greater promise" (Gergen, 1999, p. 40). These critiques do not allow that social constructionism can discover and challenge profound material consequences of constructions such as poverty conditions, joblessness, illness, mortality, and so forth. Indeed, the goal of much constructionist work is just that.

Some critics state that conceptions of social constructionism assign too passive a role to the individual by overemphasizing the power of socialization processes (Burr, 1995). They believe that such formulations overdetermine individuals by portraying them simply as entities that embody roles that society prescribes (Christensen & Cheney, 1994). Basically, this line of criticism argues that some models of social constructionism neglect to address the role of agency and individual differences in knowledge construction. However, postmodern perspectives on social constructionism stress agency. They assert that identities are fluid and subject to change. Postmodernist approaches endorse employing social constructionism to illuminate the role of sociocultural forces in creating social groups, so that individuals can imagine and enact alternative understandings (Gergen, 1999; Lewis, 2003).

The Social Construction of an Organizational Communication Scholar

As I noted earlier, I am interested in the social construction of salient categories of identity in contemporary society. Specifically, I focus on gender, race, social class, ability, sexuality, and age. I study relationships among social identity, discourse, and power dynamics. I assume a critical viewpoint on organizations as principal sites of social construction of social identities and their meanings. I seek to expose communicative practices that construct, sustain, and resist inequities based on or related to members' social identities. Moreover, I strive to detect relationships between communicative practices and dominant discourses about social identity groups and to illuminate recursive relationships between larger discourses and organizational micropractices. In addition, I try to situate analyses of these issues within the sociocultural contexts where they transpire. Educational settings particularly fascinate me.

Social constructionism is relevant to my scholarship because it encourages us to pay attention to sociocultural context, to study routine social practices and interactions, and to analyze language and discourse. Some versions of social constructionism also invite us to investigate power and control processes. This work widens the study of how humans construct knowledge to encompass power relations and the constitutive role of power. Scholarship in this vein claims that power dynamics pervade sociocultural relations and, therefore, affect social construction processes (Mumby, 1989). Included among those processes are identity constructions: "the discourses that form our identity are intimately tied to the structures and practices that are lived out in society from day to day, and it is in the interest of relatively powerful groups that some discourses and not others receive the stamp of 'truth'" (Burr, 1995, p. 55). To describe and critique these processes, researchers identify discursive practices related to the social construction of identity. They also consider influences of dominant discourses. Recall, for example, constructions of sexuality, age, and childhood that I cited earlier.

Some research construes consequences of constructions of social identity categories, such as who benefits and who suffers. For instance, work on the social construction of whiteness often refers to white privilege, invisible advantages that some people enjoy simply because they are white (McIntosh, 1995). In addition, feminist studies comprise a significant and substantive corpus of scholarship about the social construction of gender and gender inequities. Also, the ongoing debate regarding whether sexual identity is innate (essential) or socially constructed often refers to power dynamics, and it details negative implications of heteronormative ideologies (Abelove, Barale, & Halperin, 1993). These and related perspectives on social identity inspire and inform my research and teaching. Moreover, as I discuss next, numerous life experiences have led me to this area of scholarship.

As I contemplated the editors' (of this book) request that I discuss how social constructionism relates to my development as a scholar, I discerned evidence of basic tenets of social constructionism as well as critical perspectives on organizational communication. Because space constraints won't allow me to offer an in-depth treatment, I share just a few examples from two phases of my life. These examples demonstrate how sociocultural processes can affect understandings of the world. They also show how identities are co-constructed in micropractices enacted within macrosocial systems. My narrative also instantiates power dynamics, including domination, compliance, and resistance. In addition, my stories illuminate potential for social change.

My development as a scholar began at an early age as I processed gendered/raced/classed messages about who I was or could be. When I was a little girl, adults would nod approvingly when I recited my plan to be either a teacher or a nurse when I grew up. These career goals were logical in the 1950s for a "smart" Negro girl from "the projects" (government-funded housing development for low-income families).

During interactions with teachers, community members, family members, and peers, I learned that I was very intelligent. These key persons in my life always expected me to get good grades, and they affirmed me when I did.

In junior high, I was placed in the advanced track, based on IQ scores and my academic record. Although the student body was about half colored and half white, only one other colored student was in those advanced classes. Is it possible that only two colored kids (one girl and one boy) qualified, or did school administrators set a limit? Anyway, the distinction of being the only colored girl in those advanced classes helped me feel unique, exceptional, special, remarkable—well, you get my drift. Seriously, though, when teachers and others labeled me as smarter than my race peers, and when they interacted with me as if I was as capable as the white kids in my classes, they helped form the foundation for my construction as a scholar.

Although I was branded as gifted, I also experienced and internalized negative stereotypes about various aspects of my social identity. Socialization sources were the usual suspects: family members, peers, teachers, clergy, other members of my community, social service workers, and the media. From these, I absorbed implicit and explicit messages about white supremacy and patriarchy. I also learned social class ideologies. Thus, I unconsciously dealt with conflicting messages about who I was or could become.

When I went to high school, I enrolled in both college prep and office skills programs because I didn't know if I would get to go to college. Office skills seemed a logical, practical route to job security. At one point, I imagined becoming an *executive* secretary. I figured that because I was smart, I could aim high. The option of being an executive *never* crossed my mind.

Fortunately, I benefited from being in advanced classes and from interacting with my classmates. I mimicked them by registering for college entrance exams and enrolling in college prep courses. I even dared to dream of going to college. I applied for and earned a full scholarship to any college I wanted! In 1968, off I went to Case Western Reserve University, a predominantly white institution in Cleveland, Ohio.

Fast forward to Spring, 1989. I was completing my doctorate part-time while working full-time as an instructor at Howard University, a historically black university in Washington, D.C. I chose Howard University because I yearned to study with black people. (By this time, I referred to myself as "black" because that label was a source of pride and affirmation for me. "Black pride," a construction of the Civil Rights movement, was an empowering antidote to internalized oppression.) Through all my years of education, I'd never had a black teacher. Nor had I been in classes, after elementary school, with a critical mass of black students. My longing to be with racially similar others signifies the power of constructions of social identity groups in forming an individual's sense of self.

As I finished work on my dissertation, I was invited to interview for a position at the University of Colorado at Boulder (CU). A primary reason I got the interview was my race. CU was striving to (re)construct itself as a university that valued racial diversity, a result in part of accusations of racism from blacks in nearby Denver as well as negative media reports. CU also was dealing with lawsuits from female professors who claimed gender discrimination. That context proved to be a significant site for my formation as a scholar.

My social identity as an African American woman frequently seemed to affect how others interacted with me, and vice versa. Because these interactions influenced many of my decisions and behaviors, they illustrate the social constructionist tenet regarding connections between social action and knowledge construction.

From the recruiting process on, I was marked. During the interview process, my identity as an African American woman often arose or was implied. I met with a black professor (at his request) who gave me his unsolicited take on racial politics at the university. A female Asian professor offered to introduce me to eligible black men (she assumed I was heterosexual and interested in meeting a black suitor). The white male chair of the communication department warned me that people would be after me to serve on various committees related to diversity.

Once hired, I stood out on campus because I was one of only three black women in the tenure track at the university. Consequently, my experiences differed greatly from the two white women who joined the department the same time I did. Many administrators (including the president of the university), faculty, students, and community members seemed to interact with me based on their assumptions about who I was and what I could offer them as a black woman. Basically, they expected me to be an expert on race and/or gender issues.

During the first few years at CU, I created and taught undergraduate and undergraduate courses on organizational communication, and I supervised teaching assistants for the intro course. As I selected course materials, I noticed a paucity of scholarship on race and organizational communication. I expressed my concerns during a happy hour conversation with Phil Tompkins, who invited me to write a chapter on race for an organizational communication reader that he and George Cheney were compiling. That book project was never completed; however, a revised version of my chapter—titled "'Diversity' and Organizational Communication"—was published in the *Journal of Applied Communication Research* (see Allen, 1995). The publication of that article was a watershed moment in my academic career, and it became a cornerstone in my construction as a scholar. Unknowingly, I had applied a social constructionist critique of knowledge construction in organizational communication studies.

Around the same time, CU began to offer modest research funds for projects on multicultural teaching and/or research. This initiative reflected the university's continuing concerns about diversity. I applied for and earned a grant to study socialization of graduate students of color. A year or so later, I received another grant to explore socialization of faculty women of color. These projects were fundamental to eventual publications about socialization (see, for example, Allen, 1996, 1998, 2000, 2001; Allen, Orbe, & Olivas, 1999). They also accelerated my development as a scholar.

Due to these significant events and other occurrences, I changed my area of research from computer-mediated communication (CMC) to diversity right around the time I came up for tenure. The tenure review process required me to write an identity statement to indicate where I situated myself in the discipline of communication. As I constructed my statement (and my identity!), I realized that I was much more interested in diversity than in CMC. Therefore, I decided to change my area of scholarship. In other words, I chose to adopt the identity that others had assumed I embodied. Paradoxically, this conscientious decision represents what feminist-identified scholar bell hooks calls an act of resistance, in which an individual actively shapes a new identity (hooks, 1989).

Speaking of feminism, after reading about feminism when I came to CU, I proclaimed myself to be a feminist. Later, I modified that moniker to *standpoint* feminist. Later still, I christened myself a critical feminist (which some might call redundant). Later even than that, I decided I was simply(!) a critical scholar. Since I entered the tenure track, I have (re)constructed my scholarly identity based on reading, teaching, writing, talking, and thinking about various epistemologies and methodologies. By the time you read this, I may have assumed yet another identity. For now, though, I prefer social constructionist because it engages and empowers me.

I learned about social constructionism a few years ago after reviewing a course proposal on identity and communication written by Margarita Olivas, a doctoral candidate. After studying social constructionism, I incorporated it into my teaching and writing (Allen, 2004). I love to introduce my students to social constructionist thinking and to invite them to challenge taken-for-granted knowledge about social identity. However, I chose to "come out" as a social constructionist only after the editors of this book invited me to contribute a chapter. They initially asked me to write about race theory, which is not in my academic repertoire. Eager to be included in the volume, I puzzled over what I might offer. It didn't take me long to zoom in on social constructionism. In retrospect, I saw that my scholarship has always implied a social constructionist perspective. The process of writing this chapter has confirmed that for me.

In conclusion, my development as a scholar has depended greatly on interactions with key persons in my life. Those interactions occurred in varying sociohistorical-cultural contexts where social actors, including me, often exhibited but sometimes resisted influences of dominant discourses about social identity groups. Those discourses usually represented mainstream ideologies about constructs such as gender, race, class, sexuality, and intellectual ability. Furthermore, many of my decisions and behaviors related to becoming a scholar were based on socially constructed "knowledge" about numerous concepts, including work, career development, black womanhood, academia, pedagogy, intellectual identity, scholarship, feminism(s), the discipline of communication, and the field of organizational communication. Of course, the process was much, much more complex than I've described it.

Organizational Communication and Social Constructionism

A wealth of literature in organizational communication implies or explicitly employs a social constructionist framework. Most of this work contends that communicative practices of organizational members "contribute to the ongoing (and sometimes precarious) process of organizing and constituting social reality" (Mumby & Clair, 1997, p. 181). This area of study depicts organizations as socially constructed realities "that rest as much in the heads and minds of their members as they do in concrete sets of rules and relations" (Morgan, 1986, p. 131).

An emerging body of work views organizations as primary sites of identity formation where everyday practices help members construct their identities as well as their knowledge about others' identities. This area of study contends that power relations affect members' embodied identities. For instance, Stan Deetz (1992) offers a compelling theoretical perspective on how disciplinary power constitutes organization members' identities. This type of scholarship strives to understand and critique communicative practices (Trethewey, 2000). Most of these practices arise from dominant ideologies as "larger socio-historical discourses impinge upon organizational cultures and their members" (Trethewey, 2000, "Social Discourses of Power," ¶1). For instance, social discourse about gender influences gender relations within organizations, and vice versa.

Gender is by far the reigning topic in scholarship about identity and organizational communication. A significant proportion of gender studies is built upon a social constructionist framework (see, for example, Ashcraft & Pacanowsky, 1996; Buzzanell, 1994, 1995; Fine, 1993; Gayle, 1994; Gherardi, 1995; Marshall, 1993; Martin, 1990; Mumby, 1998; Trethewey, 1997, 1999). I summarize a couple of these projects later. A full review of literature on organizing, communication, and social constructionism would constitute a separate chapter, if not a book. Therefore, I've selected a small sample to display some of the topics, theories, methods, and implications that characterize these endeavors.

Some scholars focus on organizations in general as they describe and/or critique primary processes and products of organizational communication. For example, Patrice Buzzanell (1995) challenges conceptions of the glass ceiling, an invisible barrier that hinders women from advancing to higher levels in organizations. She contends that current definitions of the glass ceiling "oversimplify this discriminatory phenomenon" and "promote gender-biased research and quick-fix solutions," such as "providing opportunities to women that men routinely obtain" (p. 527). Buzzanell argues that such solutions, while logical, neglect to focus on gender as an organizing aspect of our lives. This oversight prohibits productive social action that might elicit radical transformations of gender constructions. To elicit such change, Buzzanell urges us to reframe the glass ceiling as a socially constructed process and product of how we "do gender" in organizing processes.

Dennis Mumby (1998) also discusses ways that we do gender. However, he asserts a need to study the social construction of masculinities in the workplace. He reviews a burgeoning body of literature on that topic, and he offers a comparative analysis of two organizational ethnographies (Collinson, 1992; Kunda, 1992) that provide insight about routine, everyday practices that help construct different conceptions of masculinity. Mumby maintains that a critical focus on masculinity will help male feminists to "both contribute to a critique of male power and explore possibilities for more democratic organization processes" (1998, p. 181).

Another article examines personality testing in the workplace (Nadesan, 1997). Majia Holmer Nadesan relies on a Foucauldian perspective to substantiate her claim that widespread use of personality testing reflects dominant ideologies of rationality and objectivity. Because these tests are based on values, behaviors, and attitudes typically associated with white men, they "normalize the status quo and articulate women and minorities as unruly others" (p. 216). She concludes that her analysis "illustrates how formalized communication about subjectivity affects organizational practices, and ultimately, enters into the constitution of individuals' perception of self and other" (p. 190). Nadesan encourages us to delve more deeply into implications of personality testing for organizational communication.

While the preceding authors mainly conducted meta-analyses of social constructionism, some researchers gathered data from organizational actors. For instance, Patricia Sias (1996) studied how coworkers use discourse to construct perceptions of differential treatment. Informants in her project represented a variety of organizational and occupational types and levels. Sias employed a joint conversation reconstruction method to ask dyads or groups of intact coworkers to discuss recalled conversations related to differential treatment at work. She concluded that coworker conversations help to create perceptions of differential treatment; and, they reinforce preexisting perceptions of differential treatment. Moreover, members tended to stress subordinates' roles in mistreatment rather than supervisors' roles. In addition, they often invoked equity standards to evaluate differential treatment. Sias offers numerous ideas for future research.

Sarah Tracy (2000) also studied actual employees; however, she focused on a single organization. Tracy conducted a case study of a cruise ship to observe emotion "as constructed by and managed within the constraints of interaction, communication, and local social norms" (p. 94). As an employee of the cruise line, she was a full participant observer. She conducted hundreds of formal and informal ethnographic interviews, and she studied several organizational documents. She learned that one form of managerial control was a service credo that dictated crew members' behaviors. For instance, one mandate stated, "We smile, we are on stage" (p. 107). Tracy concludes that emotion labor norms, or expectations about how workers should express or suppress their feelings, affect employee identity construction processes. She also states that emotion rules and expectations are historically contingent, which means they are susceptible to change. As Tracy observes, we can "begin to deconstruct the power structures that normalize organizational life" (p. 119).

A final example illustrates a multimethod approach to studying a single research "site." In addition, this project implies the potential for social constructionism to assess social change. A group of researchers conducted a long-term investigation of a social change program in the Peruvian Amazon (Sypher, McKinley, Ventsam, & Valdeavellano, 2002). They wanted to explore how the social system in that region was changing in response to media-sparked dialogue about reproductive health care. Specifically, they studied the social construction of a radio program, Bienvenida Salud! (Welcome to Health!). Included in their methods were focus group interviews, sustained participant observation, and a survey of listeners and nonlisteners. The research team asserts that a social constructionist perspective was the best way for them to capture the complexity of the social change process:

> The social constructionist approach in the present project demanded an understanding of local knowledge before conducting a meaningful, large-scale audience survey of radio listeners. Such local knowledge, derived from inter-preting, translating, discussing, and engaging in the lives of the study respon-dents, enhanced our understanding of the richness and peculiarities in Loreto. With an understanding of the respondents' vocabularies and engagement in their worlds, our findings are more coherent, rich, and connected. . . . A social constructionist view suggests conclusions that are reflexive and interpretively flexible regarding the effects of entertainment-education interventions. (p. 202)

They conclude that the social system is changing due to Bienvenida Salud!

The preceding examples offer a mere taste of the smorgasbord of studies about organizing and communication that take social constructionist approaches. I concede that my choices reflect theoretical and epistemologi-cal perspectives that I savor; therefore, they are not representative. However, I believe that they exemplify the value of social constructionism for the field. They also insinuate implications for future work.

Implications

Social constructionism provides a blueprint for theorizing organizational communication because it accentuates the centrality of language, and it stresses the significance of social interaction processes (Shotter & Gergen,

1994). Social constructionism also seems suited for critical projects because it enjoins us to challenge taken-for-granted knowledge and to encourage members to imagine and enact alternative realities. Social constructionism seems tailor-made for responding to these issues, given the fundamental principle that knowledge construction is specific to historical and cultural contexts. Recognizing that constructions can and do vary can empower organizational actors to work for social change.

A fitting topic for social constructionist research on organizational communication is identity. Applying a social constructionist approach can enlarge the growing body of studies on identity that concentrate on a range of constructions. This will allow us to concentrate on "how specific organizations appropriate, reproduce, and/or transform social discourses in and through everyday communicative processes that enable and/or constrain how members enact identities" (Trethewey, 2000).

Among innumerable implications of social constructionism for communication studies of organizing, one is especially prominent. Social constructionism provides a viable framework for expanding and deepening scholarship on discourse and organizations. The magnitude of this topic is eminently obvious in an essay titled "Organizations as Discursive Constructions," by Gail Fairhurst and Linda Putman (2004). These authors note an increase in research that frames organizations as discursive constructions, and they cite and explore three interpretations of this framing. One orientation views an organization as an already formed object or entity that "exists prior to discourse, remains stable over time, and has specified features or components that shape language use" (p. 9). Another viewpoint frames an organization as being in a constant state of becoming. This perspective "actively rejects the role of language as an artifact and embraces discourse as constituting the micro- and macroaspects of organizations" (p. 13). A third orientation sees organizations as grounded in action. This approach "treats action and structure as mutually constitutive. Thus, the organization never assumes the form of an identifiable entity because it is anchored at the level of social practices and discursive forms" (p. 16). Fairhurst and Putnam argue that we should recognize and understand these different orientations because they can affect how we conceive, conduct, and report research.

Organizational scholars Mats Alvesson and Dan Kärreman (2000a, 2000b) offer substantive analyses and guidance regarding research on organizations as discursive constructions. Alvesson and Kärreman distinguish between *discourse* and *Discourses* by designating the former as local practices of talk and creating texts, and the latter as general, enduring systems of thought within social systems (2000b). These conceptions correspond with social constructionist concerns about microlevel and macrolevel construction processes and products. Thus, their definitions can help scholars differentiate between these two ways of understanding discourse.

Alvesson and Kärreman also describe a linguistic turn in organizational studies that moves scholars away from perceiving language as a passive, simple medium that mirrors objective reality (2000a). The linguistic turn encourages scholars to take language as a primary subject of study, to acknowledge language as a carrier of power, and to use language as a means for clarifying social issues. Alvesson and Kärreman discuss the importance of three significant areas of language in social and organizational research: language itself, language in use, and the production of research texts. In addition, they entreat researchers to take language seriously, noting that the linguistic turn is relevant to organizational analysis at the levels of fieldwork and of analysis. They assert that "The time has come for radical rethinking. In reconsidering the way language works and operates, new research agendas emerge" (2000b, p. 155).

Lannamann (1995) also implores scholars to think about how they construct the research process and its products. He cites three questions that should be foremost in our minds:

1. Whose history does the research protocol reflect, and whose terms does the research dialogue employ?

2. How do research processes account for all participants' subject positions?

3. How do textual practices of a discipline silence voices of marginalized persons and deflect attention from actual interaction processes?

We should consider both Lannaman's questions and Alvesson and Kärreman's concerns and challenges in our pedagogy as well as our research. We also can apply them as we continue to construct the field of organizational communication. For instance, Karen Ashcraft and I contend that a foundation of whiteness undergirds textbook representations of organizational communication (Ashcraft & Allen, 2003). In a throwback to the beginnings of social constructionism, we could assess the sociology of knowledge of our field to locate areas that need to be (re)constructed to align with goals of effecting social change.

In conclusion, I have offered a few ideas for implementing social constructionism in organizational communication studies. These are mere etchings of what we might construct. I hope, however, that they suffice to encourage you to further explore the utility of social constructionism for becoming more engaged in the study of organizational communication.

References

Abelove, H., Barale, M. A., & Halperin, D. M. (1993). *The lesbian and gay studies reader.* New York: Routledge.

Allen, B. J. (1995). "Diversity" and organizational communication. *Journal of Applied Communication Research, 23*(2), 143–155.

Allen, B. J. (1996). Feminism and organizational communication: A Black woman's (re)view of organizational socialization. *Communication Studies, 47,* 257–271.

Allen, B. J. (1998). Black womanhood and feminist standpoints. *Management Communication Quarterly, 11,* 575–586.

Allen, B. J. (2000). "Learning the ropes": A Black feminist critique. In P. Buzzanell (Ed.), *Rethinking organizational & managerial communication from feminist perspectives* (pp. 177–208). Thousands Oaks, CA: Sage.

Allen, B. J. (2001). Gender, race, and communication in professional environments. In L. P. Arliss & D. Borisoff (Eds.), *Women and men communicating: Challenges and changes* (pp. 212–231). Prospect Heights, IL: Waveland Press.

Allen, B. J. (2004). *Difference matters: Communicating social identity.* Prospect Heights, IL: Waveland Press.

Allen, B. J., Orbe, M., & Olivas, M. O. (1999). The complexity of our tears: Dis/enchantment and (in)difference in the academy. *Communication Theory, 9,* 402–430.

Alvesson, M., & Kärreman, D. (2000a). On the study of organizations through discourse analysis. *Human Relations, 53,* 1125–1134.

Alvesson, M., & Kärreman, D. (2000b). Taking the linguistic turn in organizational research: Challenges, responses, consequences. *Journal of Applied Behavioral Science, 36,* 136–158.

Ashcraft, K. L., & Allen, B. J. (2003). The racial foundation of organizational communication. *Communication Theory, 13*(1), 5–33.

Ashcraft, K. L., & Pacanowsky, M. E. (1996). "A woman's worst enemy": Reflections on a narrative of organizational life and female identity. *Journal of Applied Communication Research, 24,* 217–239.

Berger, P. L., & Luckmann, T. (1966). *The social construction of reality: A treatise in the sociology of knowledge.* New York: Doubleday and Company.

Burr, V. (1995). *An introduction to social constructionism.* London: Routledge.

Buzzanell, P. (1994). Gaining a voice: Feminist organizational communication theorizing. *Management Communication Quarterly, 7,* 339–383.

Buzzanell, P. M. (1995). Reframing the glass ceiling as a socially constructed process: Implications for understanding and change. *Communication Monographs, 64,* 327–354.

Christensen, L. T., & Cheney, G. (1994). Articulating identity in an organizational age. In S. A. Deetz (Ed.), *Communication yearbook 17* (pp. 222–235). Thousand Oaks, CA: Sage.

Clay, J. M., & Stephens, E. C. (1996). Child-labor laws and the hospitality industry. *Cornell Hotel & Restaurant Administration, 37*(6), 20–26.

Collinson, D. (1992). *Managing the shop floor: Subjectivity, masculinity, and workplace culture.* New York: de Gruyter.

Deetz, S. (1992). *Democracy in an age of corporate colonization.* Albany: State University of New York Press.

DeLamater, J. D., & Hyde, J. S. (2001). Essentialism vs. social constructionism in the study of human sexuality. *The Journal of Sex Research, 35*(1), 10–19.

Fairhurst, G. T., & Putnam, L. (2004). Organizations as discursive constructions. *Communication Theory, 14,* 5–26.

Fass, P. S., & Mason, M. A. (2000). Introduction: Childhood in America: Past and present. In P. S. Fass & M. A. Mason (Eds.), *Childhood in America* (pp. 1–7). New York: New York University Press.

Fine, M. G. (1993). New voices in organizational communication: A feminist commentary and critique. In S. Perlmutter Bowen & N. Wyatt (Eds.), *Transforming visions: Feminist critiques in communication studies* (pp. 125–166). Cresskill, NJ: Hampton Press.

Fox, K. J. (1999). Learning from sociological practice: The case of applied constructionism. *American Sociologist, 30*(1), 54–74.

Gayle, B. M. (1994). Bounded emotionality in two all-female organizations: A feminist analysis. *Women's Studies in Communication, 17,* 1–19.

Gergen, K. J. (1999). *An invitation to social construction.* London: Sage.

Gergen, K. J., & Gergen, M. M. (2000). *The new aging: Self construction and social values.* Retrieved June 16, 2004, from www.swarthmore.edu/SocSci/kgergen1/web/printer-friendly.phtml?id=manu16www.swarthmore.edu/SoSci/lgergen1

Gherardi, S. (1995). *Gender, symbolism, and organizational cultures.* London: Sage.

hooks, b. (1989). *Talking back: Thinking feminist, thinking black.* Boston: South End.

Hruby, G. G. (2001). Sociological, postmodern, and new realism perspectives in social constructionism: Implications for literacy research. *Reading Research Quarterly, 36*(1), 48–62.

Jost, J. T., & Kruglanski, A. W. (2002). The estrangement of social constructionism and experimental social psychology: History of the rift and prospects for reconciliation. *Personality and Social Psychology Review, 6*(3), 168–188.

Katz, J. N. (1995). *The invention of heterosexuality.* New York: Dutton.

Kunda, G. (1992). *Engineering culture: Control and commitment in a high-tech corporation.* Philadelphia: Temple University Press.

Lannamann, J. W. (1995). The politics of voice. In W. Leeds-Hurwitz (Ed.), *Social approaches to communication* (pp. 114–134). New York: Guilford.

Leeds-Hurwitz, W. (Ed.). (1995). *Social approaches to communication.* New York: Guilford.

Lewis, Y. (2003). The self as a moral concept. *British Journal of Social Psychology, 42,* 225–237.

Marshall, J. (1993). Viewing organizational communication from a feminist perspective: A critique and some offerings. In S. Deetz (Ed.), *Communication yearbook 16* (pp. 122–143). Newbury Park, CA: Sage.

Martin, J. (1990). Deconstructing organizational taboos: The suppression of gender conflict in organizations. *Organization Science, 1,* 339–359.

McIntosh, P. (1995). White privilege and male privilege: A personal account of coming to see correspondence through work in women's studies. In M. L. Andersen & P. H. Collins (Eds.), *Race, class, and gender: An anthology* (2nd ed., pp. 76-87). Belmont, CA: Wadsworth.

Morgan, G. (1986). *Images of organization.* Beverly Hills, CA: Sage.

Mumby, D. K. (1989). Ideology & the social construction of meaning: A communication perspective. *Communication Quarterly, 37*(4), 291–304.

Mumby, D. K. (1998). Organizing men: Power, discourse, and the social construction of masculinity(s) in the workplace. *Communication Theory, 8,* 164–183.

Mumby, D. K., & Clair, R. P. (1997). Organizational discourse. In T. A. van Dijk (Ed.), *Discourse studies: A multidisciplinary introduction: Vol. 2. Discourse as structure and process* (pp. 181–205). Thousand Oaks, CA: Sage.

Nadesan, M. H. (1997). Constructing paper dolls: The discourse of personality testing in organizational practice. *Communication Theory, 7,* 189–218.

Ng, S. H., Liu, J. H., Weatherall, A., & Loong, C. F. (1997). Younger adults' communication experiences and contact with elders and peers. *Human Communication Research, 24*(1), 82–109.

Ore, T. (2003). *The social construction of difference and inequality: Race, class, gender, and sexuality.* Boston: McGraw-Hill.

Pearce, W. B. (1995). A sailing guide for social constructionists. In W. Leeds-Hurwitz (Ed.), *Social approaches to communication* (pp. 88–113). New York: Guilford.

Shotter, J., & Gergen, K. J. (1994). Social construction: Knowledge, self, others, and the continuing conversation. In S. A. Deetz (Ed.), *Communication yearbook 17* (pp. 3–33). Thousand Oaks, CA: Sage.

Sias, P. M. (1996). Constructing perceptions of differential treatment: An analysis of coworkers' discourse. *Communication Monographs, 63,* 171–187.

Sypher, B. D., McKinley, M., Ventsam, S., & Valdeavellano, E. E. (2002). Fostering reproductive health through entertainment-education in the Peruvian Amazon: The social construction of Bienvenida Salud! *Communication Theory, 12,* 192–205.

Tracy, S. J. (2000). Becoming a character for commerce: Emotion labor, self-subordination, and discursive construction of identity in a total institution. *Management Communication Quarterly, 14,* 90–128.

Trethewey, A. (1997). Resistance, identity and empowerment. A postmodern feminist analysis of clients in a human service organization. *Communication Monographs, 64,* 281–301.

Trethewey, A. (1999). Disciplined bodies: Women's embodied identities at work. *Organization Studies, 20,* 423–450.

Trethewey, A. (2000). Cultured bodies: Communication as constitutive of culture and embodied identity. *Electronic Journal of Communication, 10*(1/2). Retrieved from www.cios.org/getfile/TRETHE_V10N1200

Williams, A., & Giles, H. (1996). Intergenerational conversations: Young adults' retrospective accounts. *Human Communication Research, 23*(2), 220–250.

4

Theorizing About Rhetoric And Organizations

Classical, Interpretive, And Critical Aspects

George Cheney

With Daniel J. Lair

A s I write, the future of Iraq is still being debated. For example, what sort of regime or government will replace that of Saddam Hussein and the Baath Party? How will that new government establish and maintain legitimacy? What will be the scope of United Nations administration within this context? How will some version of democracy be constructed or imposed? What corporations will have influence over the newly managed economy? How will "reconstruction" proceed? When will it end? These are by no means all the important questions about the wake of the conflict. *The questions posed here are as much organizational as they are political: They involve dynamics within as well as between sectors. The issues involved are also rhetorical in nature and implication: They entail efforts to secure*

AUTHOR'S NOTE: Daniel Lair contributed Table 4.2 and significant portions of the categorization of organizational rhetoric.

legitimacy, to win support, and to engineer the situation (and its ultimate history) for certain interests.

On Sunday, March 23, 2003, *The New York Times* carried an interesting article on how U.S. companies were already jockeying for position in a projected postwar Iraq, *just five days into the war itself* (Oppel, Henriques, & Becker, 2003). As the article explained, there were effectively no practical or moral obstacles to the corporations "moving in." Taking the equation of democracy and Anglo-American capitalism for granted, corporations not only used their considerable material interests and clear links to officials in the G. W. Bush administration but also situated themselves rhetorically and politically in terms of the "democratization" of Iraq. Whether this mixture of private and public interests and the corresponding blurring of economic and political concerns will ever be subject to any probing media scrutiny remains to be seen, but the example is an appropriate starting point for an essay on the contributions of rhetorical theory and criticism to the study of organizational communication. In this instance, lines between various types of institutions and spheres of discourse blur, but meaning is being managed by various institutional actors so as to privilege certain interpretations of the situation and soft-pedal or suppress entirely other, alternative understandings. The management of meaning in this case both reflects and contributes to broader ideological forces, and it has implications both for the internal workings of the organizations (in this case, corporations as well as national and international government agencies) that would benefit and for the relationship between the public and private sectors writ large.

This is but one example in which insights about persuasion, in combination with other assessments of the situation, help us to see what's going on. But in a case like this, no single interpretation will do the job, just as no treatment of the symbolic without the material will account fully for the workings of power and influence. Rhetoric has its place here, however, and its heuristic value is tied to its sensitivity to *the uses and adaptations of language and other symbols, particularly as they relate to various audiences.* Let's take a closer look at the development of rhetorical approaches to the analysis of organizational communication by, first, considering the origins of organizational studies. Then we will consider the application of rhetorical theory and criticism to the study of organizational communication by looking closely at the intellectual evolution of each area, key principles and concepts, typical research efforts, and challenges to rhetorical understandings of organization. Doing so will allow us to better understand the ways in which rhetorical theory and criticism have been engaged by scholars in organizational communication.

Remembering and Reengaging the Sociological Origins of Organizational Study

Undergraduate and graduate students alike have been asking me lately, "Why do people talk about organizational communication *discovering* the larger world beyond the boundaries of organizations?" This is a good question, one that's best answered in terms of intellectual history and especially the specific development of organizational communication as a bounded area of study. As a number of review essays observe, the earliest studies of organizational *communication* examined the messages, channels, and media "inside" businesses (see, e.g., Putnam & Cheney, 1985). The subdiscipline was called "business and industrial communication" until the early 1970s (Redding, 1972). Only in certain essays (notably, one by P. K. Tompkins [1984]—a work that actually was written several years earlier) was there much consideration of the broader societal context out of which organizations arise, within which they operate, and to which they contribute. This is why movements to include *public relations* activity within organizational communication's reach (Crable & Vibbert, 1983), considerations of *power as an institutional force* (Mumby, 1997), the linkage of corporate advocacy to *legal and political matters* (Conrad, 2002; Sproule, 1990), the invocation of concepts from *cultural* studies (Carlone & Taylor, 1998), and treatments of larger processes of *organizing* (compare Taylor & Van Every, 2000; Weick, 1979) all represent efforts to push the boundaries of organizational communication beyond the old comfort zone of strictly internal affairs.

In hindsight, it's easy to dismiss early studies of organizational communication as *a-contextual* or even myopic, but they made good sense as preliminary investigations of communication phenomena internal to organizations and at the same time tried to establish the organization as a viable and theoretical important site of inquiry—somewhat independent, in fact, of management-based, psychological, and sociological studies. After all, it wasn't so long ago (the mid-1980s, to be precise) that many interpersonal scholars insisted that organizational communication was *nothing more* than the application of interpersonal study to the organizational context (e.g., that the dyad should always be the fundamental unit for building communication theory). In doing so, they effectively denied the formative role of an important domain of human interaction: work. This position still has its relevance, of course, in terms of how we examine interpersonal interaction at work and beyond (e.g., in work-home relationships), but it denies the significance of the organization as a unit of analysis and, by implication, sees the wider societal context (read: social forces and structures) as merely derivative. Such a bias is "psychologistic," individualistic, and, in a certain sense, very "American." However, it would be equally problematic to dismiss the organization by *dissolving* it into the larger cultural *milieu*, suggesting that organizations, workplaces, and other institutions are nothing but localized expressions of the broadest social trends. This theoretical bias would, in a sense, "oversocialize" the organization, denying both its ontological standing and the agency of individuals within it. Put in less theoretical language, this position would fail to recognize the practical implications of one's "moving" inside or outside an organization's very real sphere of authority, and it would work against any possibility of authentic action originating with individuals except in the most narrowly circumscribed ways.

Still, we do well to return to the sociological roots of organizational studies; by this I refer to the late 19th-century and early 20th-century commentaries on modernity by Karl Marx, Émile Durkheim, Max Weber, Georg Simmel, and others. I would add a few more theorists who wrote from the early to mid-20th century, such as George Herbert Mead, Mary Parker Follett, Harold Lasswell, and Talcott Parsons. Their theories are diverse, and I bring them together under one heading simply to stress their common concern for understanding modern institutions, distinguishing those from "premodern" ones, and observing the behavior of organizations on that landscape we call society. Weber, for example, was interested theoretically in the organization to the extent that he "needed" it to address fully his foundational question about noncoerced obedience. Organizations, after all, may be seen as spheres of authority, and all types of organizations share a concern for some degree of control over behavior and attitudes. Although Weber is called the founder of organizational studies, the other theorists mentioned offered their own perspectives on how organizations and institutions are structured, exercise power, and *express* various aspects of society— for example, the transmission of tradition. These sociological beginnings are important not only in a historical sense; they are also being revisited today as profound questions about the very nature and "progress" of our society are being explored. When we analyze organizations—and organizational communication—we come to deeper understandings of the phenomena when we simultaneously consider the status of organizations as social actors and the very processes of organizing that create, maintain, and transform those organizations. Sociology and social theory are especially helpful in keeping our examinations linked to larger questions about social structure, (re)production, agency, and authority, among other issues. What's more, sociological insights in organizational study are both suggestive of and complementary to communication-based understandings of how the organization works, as we'll see.

Engaging Organizations From the Perspective of Rhetorical Theory and Criticism

This chapter revolves around one approach—or, rather, one set of approaches—to the study of organizational communication. I refer to the influences, insights, and limitations of rhetorical theory and criticism as they define and illuminate the central phenomena of organizational communication. I have already alluded to one of the motivating questions of Weber's (1978) monumental work, *Economy and Society*: "How is it we explain uncoerced obedience?" Weber answered this question in terms of rationality (or, more precisely, rationalities) and authority (or authorities). Weber's special contribution to our understanding was in linking systems of authority (or legitimate power) to *rationalities*: logics of social action and organization. Weber offered no theory of language; he did display a deep sensitivity to the symbolic realm that was evident in how he treated our *interpretations* of the world. In an often overlooked example from *Economy and Society*, Weber argued that people's representations of organizations were "real" to the extent that these interpretations had real consequences for action. In other words, an organization's identity is meaningful to the degree that people *act like* it's meaningful. This is not a lapse into mere "nominalism"—the idea that naming anything brings it into full ontological being—but rather the notion that how people image organizations is an important object of analysis (just as it has great practical and economic significance today in the study of PR and marketing).

Here we can turn to Phillip K. Tompkins's (1987) translation of Weber's ideal types of authority and rationality in rhetorical terms. I devote attention to this connection not so much because it's an intriguing theoretical move but rather because it strikes at the heart of a rhetorical conception of organization. As Tompkins explained, Weber's ideal types can be conceptually stretched to incorporate logics of discourse and action as well as rationality writ large. In concrete terms, we can see how the *ideal/logic* of bureaucracy is at once a triumph and a limitation of modernity: in terms of how people relate to knowledge, in terms of how they treat one another, and with respect to what sorts of decisions and goals typically are envisioned and undertaken.

For example, bureaucracy institutionalizes fairness even as it disregards individual circumstance. Although bureaucracy never exists in a pure form, it can take on extreme aspects. It's one thing to examine, at the same time, the excesses of bureaucracy in cases ranging from the brutally efficient Khmer Rouge of Cambodia (1975–1979) to assembly line dehumanization in auto manufacturing in the United States and Japan. It's even more penetrating to complement social and political analyses with rhetorical ones that get down to questions of the uses of symbolic and nonsymbolic resources for persuasion in instances where more than one outcome is possible and the outcome can be effected through persuasive means. That really is the essence of the analysis of "the rhetorical situation" (compare Bitzer, 1968; Burke, 1969; Cheney & Christensen, 2001a, Tompkins & Cheney, 1985).

As for rhetorical *criticism*, as distinct from theory, we can imagine several different ways to apply the former to organizational communication. Considering domains of analysis, based on arenas of practical activity, we can critique anything from an individual message, such as an organization's name or its mission statement (see, e.g., Sharer, 2001; Swales & Rogers, 1995), to a broader discourse about organizational quality or change (see, e.g., Gorden & Nevins, 1987; Heracleous & Barrett, 2001; Zbaracki, 1998; Zorn, Christensen, & Cheney, 1999). But we can also employ rhetorical theories and concepts in a heuristic way to examine the functioning of the modern organization itself. Here we return to fundamental aspects of organization such as the individual's relationship to the organization, the organization's status as an actor, and the ongoing construction of authority. Without even trying to summarize key moments in the long debate over the nature of rhetorical criticism, let me offer this working definition for our purposes here: *Rhetorical criticism is the description, interpretation, analysis, and critique of organized persuasion—and, by extension, identification.* (See Table 4.1 for key concepts of classical and contemporary rhetoric as applied to the organizational/institutional context.) This definition is broad but useful, in that it crosses epistemological boundaries while highlighting persuasion and identification as the focus of attention (see Burke, 1969). The term "organized" directs us not only to the activities of the literal, bounded organization but also to wider institutional activities, including something like "the marketization of education" (see McMillan & Cheney, 1996), the rhetoric of health care reform (Conrad & Millay, 2000), the selling of the free market (Aune, 2001), and the "meta-messages" of public relations (Heath, 1990). As Lair (2003) has observed, there is also something of an intellectual inheritance from ideas about social-movement mobilization to organizational rhetoric (Griffin, 1952). This is most apparent in the shift from a single message (even something as large as an organizational image campaign) to broader discourse, but the connection is relevant also to the idea of collective agency and the emergence of formal organizational structure (see Table 4.2).

As McMillan (1982) explained in her analysis of various sectors, it makes good sense to look at organizations *as* rhetorical enterprises: They are fundamentally about issues of motivation, persuasion, and "sales" (writ large). Cheney and McMillan (1990) affirmed that much of organizational discourse revolves around questions of support versus lack of support; in this

Table 4.1   Some Core Concepts From the Rhetorical Tradition as Applied to
Organizations

1. **Locus** of Study: Messages and their *actual or potential effects* (Wichelns,
   1925); compare pragmatics

2. **Function** in Society: *Adjusting ideas to people and people to ideas*
   (Bryant, 1953); compare modern PR (see Crable & Vibbert, 1986)

3. "**Faculty** of observing in a given case the available means of
   persuasion"(Aristotle, 1954); compare social-psychological persuasion
   research

4. Principal **Dynamics and Excesses** of rhetoric (compare Aristotle, 1954;
   Booth, 1988; P. K. Tompkins, 1987; Weber, 1978):
   a. Speaker or source (**Ethos** or character)/"Entertainer's
      stance"/Charismatic authority
   b. Message (**Logos** or logic)/"Pedant's stance"/Rational-legal authority
   c. Audience or listeners (**Pathos** or emotional appeal)/"Advertiser's
      stance"/Traditional authority

5. The **Canons** or key principles of rhetoric (Greco-Roman traditions)
   a. **Invention,** or the sources of ideas
   b. **Arrangement,** or the organization/structure of ideas
   c. **Style,** or the use of language and other symbols
   d. **Delivery,** or the nature of the presentation of the message itself
   e. **Memory,** "the forgotten canon" (central to the oral tradition, with its
      analogues in written and electronic forms of literacy)

6. **Types or Classes of Rhetoric** (Aristotle, 1954; Perelman & Olbrechts-
   Tyteca, 1969)
   a. **Deliberative**—arriving at a decision; chiefly future-oriented
   b. **Forensic**—passing judgment; chiefly past-oriented
   c. **Epideictic**—issuing praise or blame, celebrating values, self-promotion;
      chiefly present-oriented (compare Cheney & McMillan, 1990; Cheney
      & Vibbert, 1987; Crable & Vibbert, 1983)

7. **Topoi,** topics, "commonplaces," or areas used as resources for ideas and
   claims; also, points of reference or "pools" of meaning (Aristotle, 1954;
   Karpik, 1978)

8. **Stasis,** or the status of an issue: For example, when does an issue become
   an issue—latent, active, dormant, dead? (Aristotle, 1954; Crable &
   Vibbert, 1986)

9. Central Terms
   a. Of ancient rhetoric: *persuasion* (Aristotle) or *eloquence* (Cicero, 1942)
   b. Of contemporary (post-Aristotelian, post-Marxist, post-Freudian)
      rhetoric: *identification* (Burke, 1969)

(Continued)

Table 4.1 (Continued)

---

10. **Kernel Elements** (Aristotle, 1954)
    a. The *Example*: the building block of inductive rhetorical form (compare Fisher's, 1987, narrative form)
    b. The *Enthymeme*: the building block of the deductive rhetorical form, drawing upon premises of fact or value already held by the audience to lead them toward a particular conclusion (compare Sproule's, 1988, non-enthymemic "managerial" rhetoric and P. K. Tompkins and Cheney's, 1985, "enthymeme 2" in corporate discourse)
11. The Rhetorical Situation
    a. For Aristotle: Identifiable single speaker addressing a homogeneous audience in a largely one-way manner with a discrete message
    b. For Bitzer (1968): *exigencies* (needs), *audience*, and *constraints* (parameters)
    c. For Burke (1973): *congregation* and *segregation* (in the universal human condition)
    d. In the organizational context: "Corporate" or organized bodies addressing multiple audiences, including one another, through multiple means, and in an elusive search for stable identities, within an exploding/imploding universe of communication (Cheney & Christensen, 2001a)

---

sense, a great deal of organized persuasion takes the form of "selling" of one sort or another. Hegstrom (1990) argued further that when it comes to organized persuasion, despite claims to the contrary, we often find *organizational* values superseding individual ones. In this regard, Hegstrom sees organizational rhetoric fulfilling a "mimetic condition" that serves to inhibit rather than to foster dissent. This can be seen in today's practical emphasis on "unity of voice" in the projection of an organization's identity to its publics (Christensen & Cheney, 2000; Leitch & Motion, 1998).

In his meta-analysis of research considering the different ways in which rhetoric and organizational communication intersect, Lair (2003) uses Smircich's (1983) distinction between culture as something an organization "has" versus something it "is" (again, see Table 4.2). Another way to cast this distinction would be rhetoric as a variable in, factor in, or dimension of organizations versus rhetoric as a fundamental feature of organization. The question then becomes "To what degree do we see organizations as *constituted* by rhetoric?" By extension, how does a rhetorically constitutive view of organizations differ from, or offer "added theoretical value" to, the broader social constructionism that is the received view in organizational communication

Table 4.2   Intellectual History of Organizational Rhetoric

	Rhetoric as Variable/Factor/Dimension		Rhetoric as Root Metaphor/Constitutive Activity	
	Direction/Domain of Rhetoric			
	Internal	*External*	*Internal*	*External*
Object of Analysis — TextArtifact	Cheney (1983) Pribble (1990) DiSanza & Bullis (1999)	Crable & Vibbert (1983) Seeger (1986) Benoit & Brinson (1994) Benoit (1995) Johnson & Sellnow (1995) Benoit & Lindsey (1987) Brinson & Benoit (1996) Stabile (2000) Benoit & Hirson (2001) Sellnow & Brand (2001) Livesey (2002) Boyd (2004) Rowland & Jerome (2004)	Sharer (2001) McMillan Cheney Cheney & Harrison	Goldzwig & Cheney (1984) (1982) (1991) Frenette (1993) (1995)
Object of Analysis — Discourse/"Fragments"	P. K. Tompkins, Fisher, et al. (1975) Goodall, Wilson, & Waagen (1986) Gorden & Nevins (1987) Vaughan (1988) Larkey & Morrill (1995) Salvador & Markham (1995)	Allen & Calliouet (1994) Conrad & Millay (2001)	E. V. B. Tompkins, Tompkins, & Cheney (1989) Hegstrom (1990) Peterson (1990) Heath (1990) Legge (1995) Linstead (1995) Rose (1995)	Cheney & Christensen (2001a)

(Continued)

Table 4.2 (Continued)

	Rhetoric as Variable/Factor/Dimension		Rhetoric as Root Metaphor/Constitutive Activity	
		Direction/Domain of Rhetoric		
	Internal	*External*	*Internal*	*External*
Discourse/"Fragments"	Opt (1998) Bhattacharya & Elsbach (2002)		Zbaracki (1998) Heracleous & Barrett (2001) Jordan (2003) Cheney (1992) Boyd (2001) Cheney, Conrad, & Lair Christensen, (in press)	

SOURCE: Adapted slightly from Lair (2003).

NOTE: Citations are shown in the cells of the table where they seem to fit best. In some cases, an item bridges two cells because its concerns are represented in more than one category.

today? Neither of these questions should be posed in a myopic way that neglects the material and nonnegotiable aspects of organizing (Cloud, 1994). However, examining the constitutive nature of rhetoric in organization helps us to understand the range of persuasive activities, both overt and subtle, that are inherent in any type of organization's argument for its own existence, continuance, and growth. Although the rhetorical nature of organizations is most evident in explicitly persuasive activities such as lobbying, marketing, and public relations, it applies as well to the bulk of day-to-day functioning in an organization—from employee socialization to the framing of policy statements to the presentation of "strictly informational" quarterly reports. Understanding various organizational domains and messages *rhetorically* is not an exercise necessarily divorced from lay understandings.

Sliding Into Theory Through Personal Experiences: The Organizational and the Rhetorical in Everyday Life

When guest speakers come to my organizational communication classes—whether the courses are undergraduate or graduate—one of the most common requests from students is for the speaker to explain "how you got to the point you are today."

This request has two senses. On the most pragmatic level, it asks the visitor to reveal the keys to professional success. But it has a deeper implication as well, in terms of the important moments, persons, and ideas that shaped the person—especially in terms of intellectual development. These discussions not only serve to bring to life texts and research that are ordinarily treated out of context; they also help to illustrate the *multiple* influences at work in the life of any scholar.

Sometimes situations speak to us in ways that not only invite but really demand theorizing. My interest in organizational identification and the broader issues of organized persuasion emerged directly out of a part-time job during college. While I was an undergraduate at Youngstown State University (in Ohio), in the late 1970s, I worked 20–30 hours per week at a chain store called Kinney Shoes. This store was located in a suburban shopping mall. To me, the experience was (as we say) "just a job"—something to give me some spending money beyond paying the rent. I had several friends who worked down the concourse at the Sears department store. One of them gradually *became* Sears. That is, he was so taken by the company's orientation program and so enamored of the store's policies and tradition that he would talk up Sears to the rest of our group at every opportunity. The other friends and I were amazed at the apparent merger of Tom's personality and Sears's corporate persona. This transformation in an employee's work role and manner led me to ask why and how it is that certain work and organizational relationships develop the way that they do. Why are some organizational bonds merely or chiefly instrumental, while others take on strong social or even spiritual aspects? (See Etzioni's, 1975, typology of organizational motivations; compare Galbraith, 1979). Why is the linkage of self to organization so formative and so powerful in certain cases? What is it about particular organizational symbols and messages that make them so compelling and sometimes enduring? And, when is such power abused?

At the same time in my life, an experience in the classroom gave texture and depth to these reflections. In a social psychology course, we viewed footage from Stanley Milgram's (1974) famous series of studies on *Obedience to Authority*. As you may know, Milgram was provoked by instances of egregious individual acts in line with formal authority (such as the following of orders in Nazi Germany) to investigate whether and how people would follow the wishes of authority *when the research subjects were not under great duress*. The film showed the apparent electric shocks given by "teachers" (naive research participants) to the "learners" (actually, the recorded voices of actors), each time a mistake was made in the repetition of a word list. Much to Milgram's surprise, a clear majority of the research participants took the shocks to high levels when prompted by a man in a white lab coat, even though they were warned about the dangers of the shocks to the supposed "learner," a portly, middle-aged man with a heart condition. The debriefing of the participants on the "real" study—about obedience to authority rather than cognitive learning—was traumatic for many of them. Instead of experiencing great relief, a number of them felt great shame and required counseling afterward. Milgram eventually was censured for his work, though he vigorously defended himself and the studies in the name of knowledge.

In the class that day, we took a break. We were instructed to return from the break and choose a side of the room according to how we evaluated the ethics of the research endeavor itself. Those who considered Milgram's procedures to be ethical were to sit on the right side of the room; those who did not were to be seated on the left. As I walked back into the room, I assumed that nearly everyone would choose the left side, as I did. To my surprise, more than two thirds of the class chose the right half of the room. In the subsequent discussion, most of Milgram's defenders agreed with him that the knowledge potentially gained in this case justified the use of deception in the experiments. Thus, we can see how the (in)famous studies may be considered on multiple levels, including not only the workings of obedience, authority, and power, but also the ethics of research. For me, one of the most enduring lessons is in terms of how "organized persuasion" occurs. In this instance, we can observe it within the "text" of the experiments itself but also—and very importantly—in terms of how such cases are interpreted in wider discourses about what organizations should or should not do. As I left class that day, I knew that I wanted to probe more deeply into the practical, emotional, and moral aspects of the social behavior of organizations, but it would be a little while before I had the vocabulary and the tools to do so.

Enlisting Multiple Resources in the Rhetorical Study of Organizations

For a long time, I've tried to treat education in terms of Kenneth Burke's (1969) dictum of "using all there is." Although Burke used the phrase in reference to the analysis of discourse, I mean it here in terms of taking advantage of opportunities for teaching, research, and service. By extension, we can see how organizational rhetoric engages important practical questions just as it can be used in a way that builds bridges between academic writing, pedagogy, and addressing social issues. Here I would highlight the *network nature* of knowledge, of academic disciplines, and of vocabularies of research. In fact, we can easily translate Thomas Kuhn's (1962) landmark treatise on the social epistemology of the sciences into terms readily accessed from the standpoint of persuasion: Concepts, theories, schools of thought, research traditions, and disciplines revolve around patterns of relationships— both relations between words and relations between collaborators.

I was extremely fortunate in graduate school at Purdue for two reasons. First, I had the opportunity to study closely with scholars such as Phil Tompkins, Linda Putnam, Charles Stewart, Charles Redding, Barry Brummett, Joe Turow, Brant Burleson, Steve Vibbert, Dick Crable, and Don Burks. Second, I was allowed intellectual freedom to cross subdisciplinary and disciplinary boundaries, eventually finding an "identity" that combined elements from the humanities and the social sciences. Organizational rhetoric, which was in 1980 studied by only a handful of scholars and students, mainly in the United States (see P. K. Tompkins, Fisher, Infante, & Tompkins, 1975, for perhaps the first explicit treatment of the subject), became for me one useful vocabulary and lens from which to view an array of organizational activities and messages. Through "stretching" rhetorical concepts, I found that I had license to investigate a whole array of organizational phenomena—from systems of influence and control writ large (P. K. Tompkins & Cheney, 1985) to the *epideictic* advocacy of values in society by corporations and other actors (Goldzwig & Cheney, 1984) to linkages between persuasion at the individual level to that at multiple societal levels (Cheney, 1991). In fact, the revival of epideictic rhetoric (Perelman & Olbrechts-Tyteca, 1969) has helped us to see how a long-trivialized genre of rhetoric, the rhetoric of celebration, performs numerous practical roles in social maintenance (compare Parsons, 1949), in ideological dissemination (compare McGee, 1980), and in the legitimation of "values" talk (Cloud, 1998). These are a few examples of how rhetoric has moved into the orbit of contemporary concerns.

Nevertheless, to some scholars firmly situated within the social sciences, the vocabulary of rhetoric is quaint and arcane, of relatively little relevance to the modern world, or at best is tolerated as a "precursor" to the more solid knowledge produced by scientific inquiry (Bowers, 1970). After all, the rhetoric was formed around the exemplar of the public speaker; it later was eschewed by the scientific method; and by the 19th century it was reduced to ornamentation and comparatively superficial aspects of performance. To some scholars strongly allied with critical approaches to communication, power, and institutions, rhetoric lacks the sharp teeth of a power-centered critique (see the reframing of Burke's rhetoric vis-à-vis power in Cheney, Garvin-Doxas, & Torrens, 1998). From this perspective, *why not talk about power if it is power you really want to examine?* This is, in fact, what some strongly critical theorists would argue, and it is a valid point—in fact, a point increasingly considered in the field of rhetorical studies, as in the now-blurred distinctions between *rhetorical criticism* of persuasive efforts and a *critical rhetoric* exploring how rhetoric advances the interests of power (see, e.g., McGee, 1990; McKerrow, 1989).

Beyond such efforts, however, I wish to argue here that the more traditional rhetorical concepts informing what I'd call a "rhetorical sensibility" are valuable above all for their recognition of how *discourse links individual persuasive choices with organizational resources.* That is to say, that a modified vocabulary and theoretical framework of rhetoric helps us strike to the heart of questions about how broad discourses, as well as discrete messages, accomplish action such as the establishment and maintenance of the authority of a "corporate actor." In this regard, the contributions of rhetoric to our understanding of organized persuasion and organizational communication share certain family resemblances with Foucauldian (Foucault, 1984) analyses of institutions (Wendt, 1995), approaches to organizational communication inspired by Habermas and Critical Theory (Deetz, 1992), multilevel applications of Structuration Theory (Giddens, 1984), Gramscian examinations of ideological hegemony (e.g., Mumby, 1997), critical-pragmatic studies of language in work settings (Clair, 1996), and sociolinguistic and structural-semiotic accounts of the emergence of authority in conversation (Cooren, 2000; Taylor & Van Every, 2000). In various ways, each of these types of research wrestles with the question of how communication constitutes institutions and institutionalization.

Networks of scholars, like networks of terms and concepts, help to build a discipline. In that light, I must mention the energizing roles of two pre-conferences on organizational rhetoric: in Chicago in 1988, and in San Francisco in 1989. These two gatherings of a dozen or so scholars helped to focus attention on the applications of classical and contemporary rhetorical concepts to the study of organizations and multiple forms of organizational communication. Interestingly, these groups included both social scientists and humanists; both people accustomed to studying organizations and those new to that area of the field (see, e.g., Crable, 1990; Jablonski, 1990; Peterson, 1990).

Today, we find scholars in many disciplines or interdisciplinary arenas using the terms of organizational rhetoric: public relations and issue management (e.g., Heath, 1980; Vibbert & Bostdorff, 1993), corporate *apologia* and crisis management (notably, Benoit, 1995, and his colleagues), social movements (e.g., Cloud, 1998), rhetorical critiques of economics as an institution (McCloskey, 1994), studies of rhetoric and public policy (notably,

Conrad, 2002), studies of organizational identity (Cheney & Christensen, 2001b), and studies of the diffusion of managerial knowledge (e.g., Zorn et al., 1999). What hold these areas together, to the degree that they touch each other, are a common vocabulary and a common orientation toward the workings of persuasion. In that respect, it's important to note that, in some instances, critical discourse analysis (CDA) and rhetorical criticism (RC) blend specific applications to organizations and institutions (e.g., Livesey, 2002). Although the CDA tradition revolves around the term "power" (Mumby & Clair, 1997), and rhetoric around persuasion/identification, the joining of their characteristic concepts and techniques makes for a broad and rich assessment of contemporary organizational activities—including, for example, "marketization" and its variants (Simpson, in press).

Reengaging Central Questions About Persuasion/ Identification in Modernity: Organizational Rhetoric Situated and Defined for Today

In 1995, Czarniawska-Joerges offered this conclusion from her review of the literature on organizational rhetoric: "It is probably correct to conclude that although there is (as yet) no consolidated effort at rhetorical analysis in organization studies, attempts to analyze the rhetoric of the field and the rhetoric of the discipline have been made" (p. 148). For now, let's consider the rhetoric of the "field"—meaning, the practical contexts of organizational rhetoric—and then reflect a bit on the area's "disciplinary" vocabulary and perspective below.

Lair (2003) has been writing an intellectual history of organizational rhetoric, and he offers the scheme below for organizing existing studies and considering what new ones might look like (refer again to Table 4.2). Lair's framework has two axes: one employs the terms "internal" and "external" to refer to the practical domains of organizational rhetoric, and the other characterizes the approach to analysis. Following McGee (1990), Lair employs the term "(apparently finished) text" to describe studies that examine discrete, bounded messages (such as CEO speeches, mission statements, or identifiable PR campaigns); "discursive fragments" is used to capture studies that use a variety of textual examples (perhaps including architecture and visual imagery, in addition to verbal messages) to make claims about trends (such as the total quality management movement or hype about teamwork). Thus, for Lair, the distinction between text and fragment has epistemological as well as methodological significance: To speak too much and too often about bounded texts may actually blind the critic to larger processes at work in organizational rhetoric. For example, we may miss the ideological forest for the rhetorically apparent tree. At this point, I would introduce the message-discourse distinction, thinking of a shift from an Aristotelian (Aristotle, 1954) conception of the persuasive enterprise to, say, a Foucauldian (Foucault, 1984) one, as a pair of terms parallel to Lair's. Let's look for a moment at the plotting of organizational rhetoric studies along the two axes. The horizontal axis represents a distinction between perspectives, while the vertical axis captures differences in terms of the object of analysis. Although this survey is by no means comprehensive, it does treat the bulk of published works under the explicit heading of organizational rhetoric from 1975 to 2004.

The classification scheme helps us to chart extant research, and it indicates where new research might explore further. There is a contrast or tension worth noting here: that the "text/artifact" studies of organizational rhetoric have tended to be preoccupied with *externally* directed messages and campaigns (e.g., corporate identity campaigns), while the discourse/ "fragments" studies have emphasized the *internal* domain of organizational communication (e.g., technical discourses surrounding organizational decision making). This is not surprising, given the origins of both types of research and the fact that most of the analyses of external organizational rhetoric have been inspired, directly or indirectly, by the legacies of public relations and marketing. It is now important to bring these different quadrants (octants, actually) in conversation with one another, so as to develop an identifiable body of knowledge about organizations' rhetorical nature, performance, and roles in society.

Listening to the (Good) Organization Speaking (Well)

With this section heading, I'm deliberately modifying Quintilian's (1969) shorthand account of speech-giving, which infuses it with ethical concerns. Not that such concerns were new in the late western Roman period—in fact, the relationship between Aristotle's (1980) virtue ethics and his rhetoric is often overlooked or downplayed—but the now-classic phrase "a good [person] speaking well" focuses our attention on the morality inherent in the act of communication. That idea had its various early expressions in the rhetorics of Plato, Aristotle, and Cicero, and it has its modern-day parallels in the writings of Martin Buber (1965), Jürgen Habermas (1984), and Nancy Fraser (1989), among others. All these writers have deep concerns with the inherent value-based and, therefore, ethical dimensions of the communication process—and, in their various ways, these ethically centered conceptions of communication hark back to Plato's concerns for the capacity of symbols to sway us in one direction or another. Although applied ethics in professional contexts are still evolving, we are now able to better characterize and assess moral behavior for individual employees than for collective actions in organizations. It's one thing to describe a good person speaking; it's quite another to decide upon what *is* "a good organization communicating."

As now recognized in disciplines ranging from law (Grossman, 2001) to philosophy (Werhane, 1991), we have difficulty dealing with questions of social agency, intentionality, responsibility, praise, and blame when we move our level of analysis from the individual to the organization. In the Enron et al. scandals of 2001–2002, for instance, very few commentators moved to the level of structural analysis, thereby helping to keep the discussion contained around the actions of "a few bad CEOs" (and that characterization of the discussion remains true as of this writing).

In fact, this set of problems is an implicit concern in Giddens's (1984) Structuration Theory, and it becomes even more central to the writings of James Taylor and his colleagues (e.g., Cooren, 2000; Taylor & Van Every, 2000), as they attempt to chart the linguistic emergence of collective authority in various kinds of utterances and interactions. Jill McMillan's (1982) doctoral dissertation was perhaps the first full-blown study of the nature of the "corporate actor" in public discourse, not only extending our notions of the rhetorical situation and enterprise but also probing deeply into issues of the "corporate personae." Of course, social movement studies, in both communication and sociology, have always displayed a keen interest in the processes by which agency is established for an emerging group, organization, or coalition (see, e.g., Loyal & Barnes, 2000). In most cases, however, that research has put the *issue* in the foreground rather than the unit of analysis or trans-issue processes of organizing (in both the lay and theoretical senses of the term).

I have not the space to detail various disciplinary and interdisciplinary approaches to the question of collective agency here, but I do wish to suggest that in recent years, rhetorical study has become attuned to the multiple levels by which agency is constructed and asserted. That shift can be seen in the linkages between rhetorical criticism of specific corporate artifacts and that of broader organizational discourses (Cheney, 1999; Cheney & Frenette, 1993). The relevance to the study of organizations can be found in insights about the interplay of persuasive resources within the control of the organization and beyond its boundaries. For example, the work of Czarniawska-Joerges (1995) on the changing relationship between Sweden's public and private sectors shows well how the rhetorical choices of individual agencies and companies both reflect and contribute to broader socio-economic trends regarding privatization of public activities, the withering of the welfare state, and the infusion of business models into decision making and self-representation in just about all types of organizations. At a deep level, these trends reflect changing conceptions of the public sphere; therefore, the trends have strong implications for the meanings of citizenship, participation, and governance in the future.

The real question then becomes how to assess ethical as well as practical-strategic aspects of communication by the corporate actor. Do we sidestep issues of intentionality and design, through appeals to tendencies in organizational culture (for example, in cultures that actually encourage sexual harassment or embezzlement)? Do we appeal to analogues from the field of law? Do we turn to chiefly philosophical understandings of the problem? Do we try to situate the issue within a grand theory of relationships between the activities of individual social actors and collective ones? Do we look to the micro-linguistic dimensions of a "move" from individual to organizational authority—for example, where the issue of "representation" has a connotation derived from democratic theory? These are some of the important questions with which the rhetorical study of organizations must grapple if the area is to be both practically potent and theoretically robust. These questions are far from being simply theoretical: They have enormous practical implications as well, when we consider the ongoing "investment" in the idea that individual leaders and managers have the primary responsibility (praise, blame) for the successes or failures of whole institutions (Cheney, Christensen, Conrad, & Lair, in press). Indeed, the everyday construction of agency—in cases ranging from the Enron debacle to the Roman Catholic Church's priest abuse scandal to the legitimation of new governments in the Middle East and Central Asia—desperately calls for the attention of citizens as well as scholars.

Engaging and Incorporating Critical-Modernist and Postmodernist Challenges to (Organizational) Rhetoric's Scope

I have already mentioned critiques of rhetorical conceptions of organization that come from theoretical quarters where the term "power" is more central, and I would acknowledge the force of this critique. At the same time, however, the tension between the terms "power" and "persuasion" can be a productive site of inquiry. With an emphasis on power, we are reminded of instances of brute domination (e.g., in wartime), the significance of material resources (e.g., in the statistical gap between rich and poor), and the mechanisms that subvert deliberation and persuasion (e.g., literal or figurative contracts between employees and employers that delimit the free speech and "interactive rights" of members). At the same time, however, the terminological "axis" of persuasion/identification can help to explain, for instance, how a war machine can mobilize public support through the age-old glorification of battle (i.e., we're *still* doing it!), how a wealth gap can remain acceptable for many through reaffirmation of something like "the American Dream" and mass attachment to the idea of being "middle class," and how limitations on employee behaviors can be widely tolerated when coupled with revered images of corporate and other leaders.

Where the critical-modernist perspective tends to sharpen rhetoric's explanatory edge, the postmodernist standpoint argues for a serrated or multifaceted edge. That is to say, a healthy infusion of postmodernist skepticism serves to challenge the neo-rationalist foundations of rhetoric (see, e.g., Desilet, 1999), *adds* to the uncertainties involved in rhetorical critique (applying, for instance, Derrida's, 1976, notion of "undecidability"), and accords visual images a higher status in the symbolic repertoire than that traditionally granted them by rhetoric (Cheney, 1992). Sproule (1987a, 1987b, 1988) wrote an important (but often overlooked) series of essays in the late 1980s, explaining how much of corporate rhetoric did not pass the tests of neo-rationalist (e.g., Toulminian) models of argument and debate. If the *enthymeme* were operating in much of the formal public communication of business, Sproule argued, then it was in an almost unrecognizable form. Sheer juxtapositioning of ideas and images, as we see in much of advertising, had by the 1980s come to pass for deliberation and sound argument. Thus, just as the sexy body is linked to the sleek new car, so is a corporation's image linked to patriotic practice (as in General Motors Corporation's adoption of the U.S. flag in so much of its advertising post-9/11—and it wasn't the only corporation to try this tack). In Sproule's view, a great deal of this corporate public discourse would be termed propaganda according to the definitions prevailing in propaganda studies: the presentation of a viewpoint as if it were the only legitimate viewpoint and in a way that directly obscures other active or conceivable positions. His is a neo-rationalist response to postmodern conditions of communication, one that tries to ask what democracy "looks like" within the explosion of messages and symbols today.

Although Sproule was arguing from more of a critical-modernist than skeptical-postmodernist perspective, he helped pave the way for a postmodernist point of view on organizational rhetoric. Today, rationality in organizational communication is a culturally and historically situated concept. This is not to lapse into a kind of simplistic relativism (see the critique of relativism by Rorty, 1982) but to say that rationality must be "positioned" not only vis-à-vis irrationality or nonrationality but also in terms of *how reason is accomplished in the processing of organizationally produced messages*. Public relations officers and advertisers have understood this matter implicitly for a long time, and PR as an institution benefited directly from the propaganda studies between the world wars. Today, applied research in advertising, marketing, and public relations includes surveys and focus group discussions about what makes an organization's image decline or improve.

The applied arm of that research, quite predictably, reaches for ways to help organizations polish their tarnished images, to avoid rhetorical-political failures in the first place, and to be "proactive" in setting the rhetorical stage for specific persuasive campaigns through the broader management of issues and identities. From the standpoint of rhetoric, this enterprise is one-sided and unidirectional: It is reflective of largely parochial ("private") concerns, and it does not include even a modified model of truth-seeking as a primary goal. Although Grunig and Grunig (1991) would seek to elevate public relations activity and research to a higher status than traditional models of unidirectional persuasion/rhetoric would allow (J. E. Grunig, personal communication, May, 1991), what they miss is the realities of power in the contexts within which the bulk of PR messages are produced. Despite calls for a democratic renaissance for PR, most PR activity and research remains narrowly circumscribed by institutional and market forces such that it slouches almost inevitably toward propaganda (Cheney & Christensen, 2001b).

Encountering Issues Beyond the Organizational Box: Toward the Expansion of Organizational Communication's Boundaries

Just as the boundaries of rhetoric have themselves expanded (ever since the early 1970s' "Wingspread" conferences, which helped to decouple rhetoric from exclusively historical objects of study, de-center it from great speakers, and distance it from poetics), so too has the purview of organizational communication widened. There are two risks in such a development. First, we may witness a kind of narrow disciplinary imperialism, such as is sometimes found in the debate between marketing and public relations over which profession and associated discipline lays claim to the greatest theoretical and practical territory (Grunig & Grunig, 1991). For organizational communication, the risk can become manifest if its vocabulary is imposed on other areas in a way that diminishes their own capacities for explanation, interpretation, and critique—for example, if organizational communication's central concepts are considered *robust enough* to "handle" all of the issues in, say, the study of mass media institutions or research on international development communication. The second risk, akin to one for the field of communication studies as a whole, is that organizational communication can fail to articulate and exploit a core set of theoretical and practical concerns. That is, it can lose its "self" as a network of concepts, principles, and applications. Some may say that this is no risk at all because there is no problem inherent in a discipline or a subdiscipline dissolving into a wider vocabulary and set of concepts. That may well be the case, but I would argue that the genealogy of the emphasis on organizational symbols and discourses is an important contribution to our broader understanding of work, business, and organizations today.

Within that perspective, we can see how organizational *rhetoric* has drawn attention to issues and concerns in contemporary organizational life with a focus on issues of persuasion and identification. Rhetorical theory and rhetorical criticism greatly expanded their horizons in the latter half of the 20th century with the general adoption of Burke's (1973) "post-Aristotelian," "post-Marxist," "post-Freudian" concept of identification. The application of this elastic but powerful construct allowed for considerations of rhetorical situations as diverse as a public relations officer's self-persuasion during the development of a corporate identity campaign; a project manager's identification with a new technology, such that she applies it to all organizational problems; the linkages between "professionalism," class, and success in popular books and videos (Cheney, 2004; Cheney & Ashcraft, 2003; Lair, Sullivan, & Cheney, 2003). Key principles of organizational rhetoric are presented in Table 4.3 below. Note that some of these propositions are expressed in a general, broadly theoretic way; others are explicitly contextualized in time and culture.

Conclusion: Engaging Theory, Extending Research, and Interrogating Society

With this chapter, I've sought to accomplish five interrelated purposes. First, in keeping with the larger volume, I've charted a bit of the intellectual history of rhetorical approaches to the study of organizational communication. Second, the chapter has shown how other influences—notably from

Table 4.3   Overview and Application of the Rhetorical Perspective to Organizational Communication: Key Principles

1. Rhetoric is inherent in hierarchy, differentiation/specialization, and formalization: the three main dimensions of organizational structure. Just as division suggests the need for cooperation, so does hierarchy entail mystery and the need for collective action. Bureaucracy itself may be examined rhetorically for its rational ethos.

2. Much of contemporary communication involves organizations "speaking," thus invoking the traditional rhetorical situation: speaker → message → audience. Moving from the individual to the collective level of analysis, of course, greatly complicates questions of the source, which may be decentered; the message, which may not be discrete or bounded at all; and the audiences, which may be multiple and heterogeneous.

3. Organizations in all sectors engage in a variety of persuasive functions or activities, from recruitment to socialization to leadership to advertising to identity management. This observation is as true of nonprofit organizations and governmental agencies as it is of private corporations.

4. To consider the workings of power and authority is also to move into the realm of rhetoric: that is, any situation or context where persuasion and identification can help to bring about one outcome rather than another (e.g., in public discussion of an environmental impact statement but perhaps not as much in application of a corporation's contract with a city for land development once signed).

5. Many forms of persuasion (within and outside organizational life) are subtle and even ironic: for example, the expression of one's "uniqueness" by association with a profession, employer, or brand.

6. Especially in the modern industrialized world (and in postmodern society), a great deal of persuasion is tied up with issues of identity (i.e., at the levels of groups, organizations, professions, "classes," etc.).

7. Communication-centered activities and professions (i.e., advertising, public relations, marketing, employee relations, labor-management negotiations, and much of organizational consulting) have each developed over time according to a specific "logic" (e.g., PR originally as a defensive strategy).

8. Particularly since the mid-1970s, organizations in a variety of sectors have engaged in promoting values, issues, and identities—sometimes much more than they have featured their products, services, and activities.

9. Recently, a number of internal and external organizational communication activities have become blurred—both with the practical consolidation of functions and with various kinds of messages having effects on multiple (external and internal) audiences.

10. In the 1990s, the marketing function came to be dominant, as all sectors tried to be both responsive to customers/clients and proactive in shaping their wants and preferences.

11. The communication predicament today is how to design symbols that will be part of, yet stand out from, "the crowd."

12. The dynamics of mass-mediated communication in a cluttered environment are such that yesterday's mission statement often becomes today's empty, overused slogan (e.g., "green marketing").

sociology and social theory—have intermingled with the rhetorical analysis of organizations and in some cases helped to sharpen its critical focus. Third, with the benefit of almost a quarter-century of hindsight, I've been able to identify key moments, concepts, and persons in the development of organizational rhetoric. Fourth, (à la Lair's, 2003, review) this chapter has helped to classify extant studies in the area according to their general theoretical orientations and objects of study. Fifth, I've concluded with a summary of key principles in the study of organizational rhetoric.

Like any area of study that's still alive, organizational rhetoric has the opportunity to consider new concepts, methods, and objects of study even as scholars try to augment rhetorical analysis of organizations with theories and strategies from other areas and approaches. Given the multiple ways in which organizations and networks are configured today, as well as the changing roles of all major sectors of society, there will be pressing questions to consider. Perhaps the most important contribution that the study of organizational rhetoric can offer is assistance in understanding the nexus of persuasive activity where polity, economy, and culture meet. Issues of globalization, citizen participation, consumerism, civil rights, religious fundamentalism, military hegemony, environmental stewardship, and corporate responsibility are the key arenas where much of the rhetorical "action," as well as the most overt uses of power, will be seen. The ambiguities surrounding these terms, as with notions of "freedom," "justice," and "equality," will provide the territory and the tools for the defining rhetorical contests of our age.

References

Allen, M. W., & Caillouet, R. H. (1994). Legitimation endeavors: Impression management strategies used by an organization in crisis. *Communication Monographs, 61*, 44–62.

Aristotle. (1954). *The rhetoric* (W. R. Roberts, Trans.). Cambridge, MA: Modern Library.

Aristotle. (1980). *The Nichomachean ethics.* Oxford, UK: Oxford University Press.

Aune, J. A. (2001). *Selling the free market.* New York: Guilford.

Benoit, W. L. (1995). *Accounts, excuses, and apologies: A theory of image restoration strategies.* Albany: State University of New York Press.

Benoit, W. L., & Brinson, S. L. (1994). AT&T: "Apologies are not enough." *Communication Quarterly, 42*(1), 75–88.

Benoit, W. L., & Hirson, D. (2001). *Doonesbury* versus the Tobacco Institute: The smoker starters' coupon. *Communication Quarterly, 49*(3), 279–294.

Benoit, W. L., & Lindsey, J. J. (1987). Argument strategies: Antidote to Tylenol's poisoned image. *Journal of the American Forensic Association, 23,* 136–146.

Bhattacharya, C. B., & Elsbach, K. D. (2002). Us versus them: The roles of organizational identification and disidentification in social marketing initiatives. *Journal of Public Policy & Marketing, 21*(1), 26–36.

Bitzer, L. F. (1968). The rhetorical situation. *Philosophy and Rhetoric, 1*(1), 1–14.

Booth, W. C. (1988). *The vocation of a teacher.* Chicago: University of Chicago Press.

Bowers, J. W. (1970). *Designing the communication experiment.* New York: Random House.

Boyd, J. (2001). Corporate rhetoric participates in public dialogue: A solution to the public/private conundrum. *Southern Communication Journal, 66,* 279–292.

Boyd, J. (2004). Organizational rhetoric doomed to fail: R. J. Reynolds and the principle of oxymoron. *Western Journal of Communication, 68,* 45–71.

Brinson, S. L., & Benoit, W. L. (1996). Dow Corning's image repair strategies to the breast implant crisis. *Communication Quarterly, 44*(1), 29–41.

Bryant, C. D. (1953). Rhetoric: Its functions and its scope. *Quarterly Journal of Speech, 39,* 401–424.

Buber, M. (1965). *The knowledge of man: A philosophy of the interhuman* (M. Friedman, Ed.). New York: Harper & Row.

Burke, K. (1969). *A rhetoric of motives.* Berkeley: University of California Press.

Burke, K. (1973). The rhetorical situation. In L. Thayer (Ed.), *Communication: Ethical and moral issues* (pp. 263–275). London: Gordon & Breach.

Carlone, D., & Taylor, B. (1998). Organizational communication and cultural studies: A review essay. *Communication Theory, 8*(3), 337–367.

Cheney, G. (1983). The rhetoric of identification and the study of organizational communication. *Quarterly Journal of Speech, 69,* 143–158.

Cheney, G. (1991). *Rhetoric in an organizational society.* Columbia: University of South Carolina Press.

Cheney, G. (1992). The corporate person (re)presents itself. In E. L. Toth & R. L. Heath (Eds.), *Rhetorical and critical approaches to public relations* (pp. 165–184). Hillsdale, NJ: Lawrence Erlbaum Associates.

Cheney, G. (1999). *Values at work: Employee participation meets market pressure at Mondragón.* Ithaca, NY: Cornell University Press.

Cheney, G. (2004). *Discourses of professional ethics in an age of careerism, consumerism, and contingency.* Unpublished manuscript, University of Utah.

Cheney, G., & Ashcraft, K. L. (2003, November). *The many faces of "the professional."* Paper presented at the annual meeting of the National Communication Association, Miami Beach, FL.

Cheney, G., & Christensen, L. T. (2001a). Organizational identification: Linkages between internal and external communication. In F. M. Jablin & L. L. Putnam (Eds.), *The new handbook of organizational communication: Advances in theory, research, and methods* (pp. 231–269). Thousand Oaks, CA: Sage.

Cheney, G., & Christensen, L. T. (2001b). Public relations as contested terrain. In R. L. Heath & G. Vasquez (Eds.), *The handbook of public relations* (pp. 167–182). Thousand Oaks, CA: Sage.

Cheney, G., Christensen, L. T., Conrad, C., & Lair, D. J. (in press). Corporate rhetoric as organizational discourse. In D. Grant, C. Hardy, C. Oswick, N. Phillips, & L. L. Putnam (Eds.), *Handbook of organizational discourse.* London: Sage.

Cheney, G., & Frenette, G. (1993). Persuasion and organization: Values, logics, and accounts in contemporary corporate public discourse. In C. Conrad (Ed.), *The ethical nexus* (pp. 49–73). Norwood, NJ: Ablex.

Cheney, G., Garvin-Doxas, K., & Torrens, K. (1998). Kenneth Burke's implicit theory of power. In B. Bock (Ed.), *Kenneth Burke for the 21st century* (pp. 133–150). Albany: State University of New York Press.

Cheney, G., & McMillan, J. J. (1990). Organizational rhetoric and the practice of criticism. *Journal of Applied Communication Research, 18*(2), 92–114.

Cheney, G., & Vibbert, S. L. (1987). Corporate discourse: Public relations and issue management. In F. M. Jablin, L. L. Putnam, K. H. Roberts, & L. W. Porter (Eds.), *Handbook of organizational communication* (pp. 165-194). Newbury Park, CA: Sage.

Christensen, L. T., & Cheney, G. (2000). When organizations talk about identity: Self-absorption and self-seduction in the corporate identity game. In M. Schultz, M. J. Hatch, & M. H. Larsen (Eds.), *The expressive organization* (pp. 246–270). Oxford, UK: Oxford University Press.

Cicero. (1942). *De Oratore: Books I, II & III* (E. W. Sutton & H. Rackham, Trans.). Cambridge, MA: Harvard University Press.

Clair, R. P. (1996). The political nature of the colloquialism, "A real job": Implications for organizational socialization. *Communication Monographs, 63,* 249–267.

Cloud, D. (1994). The materiality of discourse as an oxymoron: A challenge to critical rhetoric. *Western Journal of Communication, 58,* 141–163.

Cloud, D. (1998). *Control and consolation in American culture and politics: Rhetoric of therapy.* Thousand Oaks, CA: Sage.

Conrad, C. (2002, March). *Organizational discourse as strategic action: The "corporate" actor, public messages, and organizational (non)rationality.* Paper presented at the Western Communication Association Convention, Long Beach, CA.

Conrad, C., & Millay, B. (2001). Confronting free market romanticism: Health care reform in the least likely place. *Journal of Applied Communication Research, 29*, 153–170.

Cooren, F. (2000). *The organizing property of communication.* Amsterdam: John Benjamins.

Crable, R. E. (1990). "Organizational rhetoric" as the fourth great system: Theoretical, critical, and pragmatic implications. *Journal of Applied Communication Research, 18*(2), 115–128.

Crable, R. E., & Vibbert, S. L. (1983). Mobil's epideictic advocacy: "Observations" of Prometheus-bound. *Communication Monographs, 50*, 380–394.

Crable, R. E., & Vibbert, S. L. (1986). *Public relations as communication management.* Edina, MN: Bellwether.

Czarniawska-Joerges, B. (1995). Rhetoric and modern organizations. *Studies in Cultures, Organizations, and Societies, 1*, 147–152.

Deetz, S. (1992). *Democracy in an age of corporate colonization.* Albany: SUNY Press.

Derrida, J. (1976). *Of grammatology* (G. C. Spivak, Trans.). Baltimore: Johns Hopkins University Press.

Desilet, G. (1999). Physics and language—Science and rhetoric: Reviewing the parallel evolution of theory on motion and meaning in the aftermath of the Sokal hoax. *Quarterly Journal of Speech, 85*, 339–360.

DiSanza, J. R., & Bullis, C. (1999). "Everybody identifies with Smokey the Bear": Employee responses to newsletter identification inducements at the U.S. Forest Service. *Management Communication Quarterly, 12*(3), 347–399.

Etzioni, A. (1975). *A comparative analysis of complex organizations* (Rev. ed.). New York: Free Press.

Fisher, W. R. (1987). *Human communication as narration.* Columbia: University of South Carolina Press.

Foucault, M. (1984). *The Foucault reader* (P. Rabinow, Ed.). New York: Pantheon.

Fraser, N. (1989). *Unruly practices.* Minneapolis: University of Minnesota Press.

Galbraith, J. K. (1979). *The new industrial state* (3rd ed.). Boston: Houghton Mifflin.

Giddens, A. (1984). *The constitution of society.* Berkeley: University of California Press.

Goldzwig, S., & Cheney, G. (1984). The U.S. Catholic bishops on nuclear arms: Advocacy, role redefinition, and rhetorical adaptation. *Central States Speech Journal, 35*, 8–23.

Goodall, H. L., Wilson, G. L., & Waagen, C. L. (1986). The performance appraisal interview: An interpretive assessment. *Quarterly Journal of Speech, 72*, 74–87.

Gorden, W. I., & Nevins, R. J. (1987). The language and rhetoric of quality: Made in the U.S.A. *Journal of Applied Communication Research, 15*(1–2), 19–34.

Griffin, L. M. (1952). The rhetoric of historical movements. *Quarterly Journal of Speech, 38*, 184–188.

Grossman, R. L. (2001). Ending corporate governance. In D. Ritz (Ed.), *Defying corporations, defining democracy: A book of history and strategy* (pp. 23–34). New York: Apex.

Grunig, J. E., & Grunig, L. A. (1991). Conceptual differences in public relations and marketing: The case of health-care organizations. *Public Relations Review, 17*(3), 257–278.

Habermas, J. (1984). *A theory of communicative action.* Boston: Beacon.

Harrison, M. I. (1995). Organizational rhetoric and collective action in a medical association. *Studies in Cultures, Organizations, and Societies, 1,* 209–230.

Heath, R. L. (1980). Corporate advocacy: An application of speech communication skills and more. *Communication Education, 29,* 370–377.

Heath, R. L. (1990). Effects of internal rhetoric on management response to external issues: How corporate culture failed the asbestos industry. *Journal of Applied Communication Research, 18*(2), 153–167.

Hegstrom, T. G. (1990). Mimetic and dissent conditions in organizational rhetoric. *Journal of Applied Communication Research, 18*(2), 141–152.

Heracleous, L., & Barrett, M. (2001). Organizational change as discourse: Communicative actions and deep structures in the context of information technology implementation. *Academy of Management Journal, 44*(4), 755–778.

Jablonski, C. (1990). Introduction. *Journal of Applied Communication Research, 18*(2), 88–91.

Johnson, D., & Sellnow, T. L. (1995). Deliberative rhetoric as a step in organizational crisis management: Exxon as a case study. *Communication Reports, 8*(1), 54–60.

Jordan, J. W. (2003). Sabotage or performed compliance: Rhetorics of resistance in temp worker discourse. *Quarterly Journal of Speech, 89*(1), 19–40.

Karpik, L. (1978). *Organizations and environment: Theory, issues and reality.* London: Sage.

Kuhn, T. S. (1962). *The structure of scientific revolutions.* Chicago: University of Chicago Press.

Lair, D. J. (2003, April). *Organizational rhetoric(s): Towards a framework situating rhetorical approaches to organizational communication.* Unpublished manuscript, University of Utah.

Lair, D. J., Sullivan, K., & Cheney, G. (2003, November). *The rhetoric and ethics of personal branding.* Paper presented at the annual meeting of the National Communication Association, Miami Beach, FL.

Larkey, L., & Morrill, C. (1995). Organizational commitment as symbolic process. *Western Journal of Communication, 59,* 193–213.

Legge, K. (1995). *Human resource management: Rhetoric and realities.* Basingstoke, UK: Macmillan.

Leitch, S., & Motion, J. (1998). Public relations on the edge of puzzlement: A defence of scholarly research. *Australian Journal of Communication, 25*(2), 161–169.

Linstead, S. (1995). After the autumn harvest: Rhetoric and representation in an Asian industrial dispute. *Studies in Cultures, Organizations, and Societies, 1,* 231–251.

Livesey, S. M. (2002). Global warming wars: Rhetorical and discourse analysis approaches to Exxon Mobil's corporate public discourse. *The Journal of Business Communication, 39*(1), 117–148.

Loyal, S., & Barnes, B. (2000). "Agency" as a red herring in social theory. *Philosophy of Social Sciences, 31,* 507–524.

McCloskey, D. (1994). *Knowledge and persuasion in economics.* Cambridge, UK: Cambridge University Press.

McGee, M. C. (1980). The "ideograph": A link between rhetoric and ideology. *Quarterly Journal of Speech, 66,* 1–16.

McGee, M. C. (1990). Text, context, and the fragmentation of contemporary culture. *Western Journal of Speech Communication, 54,* 274–289.

McKerrow, R. E. (1989). Critical rhetoric: Theory and praxis. *Communication Monographs, 56,* 91–111.

McMillan, J. J. (1982). *The rhetoric of the modern organization.* Unpublished doctoral dissertation, The University of Texas at Austin.

McMillan, J., & Cheney, G. (1996). The student as consumer: Implications and limitations of a metaphor. *Communication Education, 45,* 1-15.

Milgram, S. (1974). *Obedience to authority.* New York: Harper Torchbooks.

Mumby, D. K. (1997). The problem of hegemony: Rereading Gramsci for organizational communication studies. *Western Journal of Communication, 61,* 343–375.

Mumby, D. K., & Clair, R. P. (1997). Organizational discourse. In T. A. van Dijk (Ed.), *Discourse as social interaction* (Vol. 2, pp. 181–205). London: Sage.

Oppel, R. A., Jr., Henriques, D. B., & Becker, E. (2003, March 23). Who will put Iraq back together? *The New York Times,* sec. 3, p. 1.

Opt, S. K. (1998). Confirming and disconfirming the American myth: Stories within the suggestion box. *Communication Quarterly, 46*(1), 75–87.

Parsons, T. (1949). *The structure of social action.* New York: Free Press.

Perelman, C., & Olbrechts-Tyteca, L. (1969). *The new rhetoric: A treatise on argumentation.* Notre Dame, IN: University of Notre Dame Press.

Peterson, T. R. (1990). Argument premises used to validate organizational change: Mormon representations of plural marriage. *Journal of Applied Communication Research, 18*(2), 168–184.

Pribble, P. T. (1990). Making an ethical commitment: A rhetorical case study of organizational socialization. *Communication Quarterly, 38*(3), 255–267.

Putnam, L. L., & Cheney, G. (1985). A critical review of research traditions in organizational communication. In M. S. Mander (Ed.), *Speech communication in the 20th century* (pp. 206–224). New York: Praeger.

Quintilian. (1969). Institutio oratoria. In T. W. Benson & M. H. Prosser (Eds.), *Readings in classical rhetoric* (pp. 143–148). Bloomington: Indiana University Press.

Redding, W. C. (1972). *Communication within the organization: An interpretive review of theory and research.* New York: Industrial Communication Council.

Rorty, R. (1982). *The consequences of pragmatism.* Minneapolis: University of Minnesota Press.

Rose, D. (1995). Private democracy: On corporate theories of persuasion in public life. *Studies in Cultures, Organizations, and Societies, 1,* 153–173.

Rowland., R. C., & Jerome, A. M. (2004). On organizational apologia: A reconceptualization. *Communication Theory, 14,* 191–211.

Salvador, M., & Markham, A. (1995). The rhetoric of self-directive management and the operation of organizational power. *Communication Reports, 8*(1), 45–53.

Seeger, M. W. (1986). C.E.O. performances: Lee Iacocca and the case of Chrysler. *The Southern Speech Communication Journal, 52,* 52–68.

Sellnow, T. L., & Brand, J. D. (2001). Establishing the structure of reality for an industry: Model and anti-model arguments as advocacy in Nike's crisis communication. *Journal of Applied Communication Research, 29*(3), 278–295.

Sharer, W. B. (2001). The persuasive work of organizational names: The Women's International League for Peace and Freedom and the struggle for collective identification. *Rhetoric Review, 20*(3–4), 234–250.

Simpson, M. (in press). *The marketisation of ageing services in New Zealand.* Unpublished doctoral dissertation, The University of Waikato, Hamilton, NZ.

Smircich, L. (1983). Concepts of culture and organizational analysis. *Administrative Science Quarterly, 28,* 339–358.

Sproule, J. M. (1987a). Ideology and critical thinking: The historical connection. *Journal of the American Forensic Association, 24*(1), 4–15.

Sproule, J. M. (1987b). Propaganda studies in American social science: The rise and fall of the critical paradigm. *Quarterly Journal of Speech, 73*(1), 60–78.

Sproule, J. M. (1988). The new managerial rhetoric and the old criticism. *Quarterly Journal of Speech, 74,* 468–486.

Sproule, J. M. (1990). Organizational rhetoric and the rational-democratic society. *Journal of Applied Communication Research, 18*(2), 192–240.

Stabile, C. A. (2000). Nike, social responsibility, and the hidden abode of production. *Critical Studies in Media Communication, 17*(2), 186–204.

Swales, J. M., & Rogers, P. S. (1995). Discourse and the projection of corporate culture: The mission statement. *Discourse & Society, 6*(2), 223–242.

Taylor, J. R., & Van Every, E. (2000). *The emergent organization: Communication as its site and surface.* Mahwah, NJ: Lawrence Erlbaum.

Tompkins, E. V. B., Tompkins, P. K., & Cheney, G. (1989). Organizations as arguments: Discovering, expressing, and analyzing the premises for decisions. *Journal of Management Systems, 1*(2), 35–48.

Tompkins, P. K. (1984). The functions of communication in organizations. In C. Arnold & J. Bowers (Eds.), *Handbook of rhetorical and communication theory* (pp. 659–719). New York: Allyn & Bacon.

Tompkins, P. K. (1987). Translating organizational theory: Symbolism over substance. In F. M. Jablin, L. L. Putnam, K. H. Roberts & L. H. Porter (Eds.),

Handbook of organizational communication: An interdisciplinary perspective (pp. 70–96). Newbury Park, CA: Sage.

Tompkins, P. K., & Cheney, G. (1985). Communication and unobtrusive control in contemporary organizations. In R. D. McPhee & P. K. Tompkins (Eds.), *Organizational communication: Traditional themes and new directions* (pp. 179–210). Beverly Hills, CA: Sage.

Tompkins, P. K., Fisher, J. Y., Infante, D. A., & Tompkins, E. L. (1975). Kenneth Burke and the inherent characteristics of formal organizations: A field study. *Speech Monographs, 42,* 135–142.

Vaughn, M. A. (1988). Interpretive research in organizational communication and the rhetorical critic. *Communication Reports, 1*(2), 68–75.

Vibbert, S., & Bostdorff, D. (1993). Issue management and the "lawsuit crisis." In C. Conrad (Ed.), *The ethical nexus* (pp. 103–120). Norwood, NJ: Ablex.

Weber, M. (1978). *Economy and society* (2 vols.) (G. Roth & C. Wittich, Trans.). Berkeley: University of California Press.

Weick, K. E. (1979). *The social psychology of organizing* (2nd ed.). Reading, MA: Addison-Wesley.

Wendt, R. F. (1995). Women in positions of service: The politicized body. *Communication Studies, 46*(3 & 4), 276–296.

Werhane, P. H. (1991). *Adam Smith and his legacy for modern capitalism.* New York: Oxford University Press.

Wichelns, H. A. (1925). The literary criticism of oratory. In A. M. Drummond (Ed.), *Studies in rhetoric and public speaking in honor of James A. Winans.* New York: Century.

Zbaracki, M. J. (1998). The rhetoric and reality of total quality management. *Administrative Science Quarterly, 43,* 602–636.

Zorn, T. E., Christensen, L. T., & Cheney, G. (1999). *Do we really want constant change?* (Beyond the Bottom Line no. 2). San Francisco, CA: Berrett-Koehler.

5

Critical Theory

Stanley Deetz

Concepts from critical theory have been widely used to support studies
of the structures, social relations, and practices in work organizations.
Many studies have identified systems and practices of inappropriate control
and distorted decision making and have detailed the costs of these for
people, organizations, and host societies. Other studies have provided models to foster the development of wider and more democratic participation in
organizational decision making, hoping to make organizations more representative of the different interests of workers and other stakeholders and
more responsible to the wider community. Critical studies range in focus
from macro (relations to the larger society) to micro (practices internal to
specific organizations and situated in contexts). Of central concern have
been efforts to understand the relations among power, language, social/cul-
tural practices, and the treatment and/or suppression of important conflicts
as they relate to the production of individual identities, social knowledge,
and social and organizational decision making (for reviews, see Alvesson &
Deetz, 1996; Mumby, in press). Fundamentally, critical work encourages
the exploration of alternative communication practices that allow greater
democracy and more creative and productive cooperation among stakeholders through reconsidering organizational governance and decision-
making processes.

Traditional critical analyses showed that work organizations have often
been guilty of economic exploitation of workers and have created social and
environmental harm. Various reproduced ideologies have been shown to

make it difficult to see and discuss such exploitations. In most of the more recent critical work, however, decisional asymmetry has more often been conceptualized as the subtle arbitrary, power-laden manners of constituting the world, the self, and others, requiring no structure of exploitation or ideological cover. Communication is core to these constitutive practices. With such a conceptual shift, contemporary critical analyses more often focus on systems that develop organizational members' active roles in producing and reproducing domination and their exclusion from decision making. Fostering more democratic communication in these terms must look to the formation of knowledge, experience, and identity, rather than merely to their expression.

Critical work in organizations has included many different theoretical approaches. Critical studies include a large group of researchers who differ in theory and conception but who share important discursive features in their writing. They include Frankfurt School critical theorists (see Alvesson & Willmott, 1995, 2003; Czarniawska-Joerges, 1988; Mumby, 1988), conflict theorists (Benson, 1977; Dahrendorf, 1959), some structurationists (Banks & Riley, 1993; Giddens, 1984, 1991; Howard & Geist, 1995), some versions of feminist work (e.g., Ashcraft, 1998; Benhabib, 1992; Calás & Smircich, 1991; Ferguson, 1984, 1994; Martin, 1990), some Burkeans (Barker & Cheney, 1994; Tompkins & Cheney, 1985), and many labor process theorists (Braverman, 1974; Burawoy, 1979; Knights & Willmott, 1990), postmodern/poststructuralist scholars (Burrell, 1988; Cooper, 1989; Holmer-Nadesan, 1996), and race and postcolonial theory (Ashcraft & Allen, 2003; Prasad, 2003). Most of these perspectives are covered in detail in other places in this volume.

"Critical studies of organizations" has a broad meaning and includes all works taking a basically critical or radical stance on contemporary society, with an orientation toward investigating exploitation, repression, social injustice, asymmetrical power relations (generated from class, gender, or position), distorted communication, and misrecognition of interests. Many people in communication, sociology, economics, and management schools do "critical" work. Here, I focus on critical theory proper as a specific part of this mix. Critical theory is most often given a more restricted meaning, referring to organization studies drawing concepts primarily, though not exclusively, from the German Frankfurt School, where many of these concepts were developed beginning in the 1920s (see Alvesson & Willmott, 2003). Although many if not most scholars doing critical work draw on critical theory, very few simply do critical theory work.

Various critical works share many of the same roots and history, and they have influenced and transformed each other in their articulations and development. My own work, as well as that of most others, clearly mixes and draws from other critical approaches in a variety of ways (see Deetz, 1996). Critical theory conceptions focus on or offer a slant to a specific set of more general critical concerns. Understanding it is a part of a larger critical agenda.

My Development as a Critical Scholar

My personal biography is clearly represented in my critical scholarly work and interventions in actual organizations. My reconstruction and presentation of critical theory here inevitably reveals biography. I grew up relatively poor on a dairy farm in a small, rural, isolated community in Indiana. The emphasis there was on the community, family, and church as central institutions giving meaning and direction to life. The "simple life" was a core moral theme: taking only what you needed, giving back as much as you could. Decision making guided by the health of the community, driven by consensus and the need to endlessly live together, was an everyday reality. Farm work is very lonely and contemplative but also cooperative and collaborative. The extended illness, and finally the death, of my sister accentuated and deepened these cultural properties and heightened my sense that the world was filled with both injustices and beauty, some of which you can do something about and some not.

Coming from such a community, even casual external contact reminds you that you are "other," marginal, and outside the mainstream. You're a "hick," you don't speak or dress well, your life is quaint, your community sense is naive. Although most of my peers stayed behind to either decry, or in some cases to quickly embrace, the growing encroachment of the newly structured secular world focused on consumption and white middle-classness, I was much more unsettled and ambivalent. I was in a "red" state caught at the very beginning of the "cultural wars" to come.

College brought a much larger world, a different kind of reflection, and the realization that there are lots of ways of being "other." My feelings—awkwardness, being scrutinized, not belonging, caught between, being in the wrong battle rather than on the wrong side of it—were hardly unique. Blacks, women, laborers, those from non-European ethnic traditions, ecologists, individuals with different sexual orientations, and native peoples throughout the world suffered a variety of exclusions. Not only are specific groups of people left out, but so are parts of ourselves. Although the types and depths of exclusion were far different from and much greater than mine (I could learn to "pass"), all shared ways that their hopes, values, and very sensibilities found little way of expression or representation in the decisions and development of the community. Their exclusion both led to their disadvantage and limited the development of the wider society.

Only in contact with the various outsides does the seamlessness and even idealized nature of my farm story disappear. It is not only marginal, it also marginalizes. My own endless uneasiness and confusions growing up couldn't find expression or even become organized as thoughts. Feelings of being trapped, frustrations with reoccurring compromises, the sequestering of the feminine, discussion of the communally shared anger toward the "gover'-ment" and the outside society, the pain and fear of those I now know as gay friends—all were pushed to the margins and rendered voiceless and invisible. Critical theory reminds us that self-reflection cannot get to that; we must reach out to others rather than in to ourselves to understand. All cultures have a tendency to produce themselves as *the* culture, *the* world as nature intended, but in contact with others we know each is only *a* culture and begin to understand its oppressions.

College and this growing awareness were the 1960s to me. The year 1968, for me and many others, brought the first personal and general social sense that significant groups of people, and aspects of each of us, lacked a voice. The lack was not just of the opportunity to speak (this limitation was already known); we were becoming aware that the real restriction was on our ability to form and represent our own experience in our own terms—a much more radical idea. Freedom of speech was a necessary but not sufficient condition; a politics of experience preceded a politics of expression, and the personal already was political. I was drawn to political action and social philosophy, but I lacked the conceptual tools to understand very deeply. I was nineteen, life was simpler, I was a pre-law/econ major, and the complexity and richness of the idea of "voice" and the politics of experience were lost in a world conveniently divided into oppressors and oppressed. A more complex exploration of the processes of social constitution was lost to me in a world where an oppressed group's opinion of how things worked became fact, and all of everyday life's difficulties were simply attributed to some powerful person's fault somewhere. I reacted in the world but rarely could act on it.

My graduate work focused on phenomenology and hermeneutics, I suspect implicitly to understand how social worlds come to be constructed as they are and to understand more richly those worlds that are different from my own. To be honest, all this seems cleaner and clearer in retrospect. More properly, it was fragmented and random. I bumped into great teachers, I read things that showed me a world I had never considered, and I got hooked on books as well as action. I began to think about and act in systems at a deeper, more complex level.

My philosophical studies in graduate school, especially through the works of Edmund Husserl, Martin Heidegger, and Hans-Georg Gadamer, provided a radically different way to understand and explore the social construction of reality and fed a growing suspicion that the dominant psychological conceptions of people and the nature of their experience not only missed much but was finally oppressive (see Deetz, 2003b; Rose, 1990). The gradual development in these works of the "linguistic turn" placed language and communication as core to any understanding of social construction and political exclusion (see Deetz, 1973, 2003c). Communication replaced consciousness as the core human and political concern. With this, communication became a central mode of description and explanation of organizational life rather than simply a phenomenon in it (Deetz, 1994, 2001).

The application to the study of organizations arises, for me, out of an awareness that practices and decisions made inside organizations actively colonize other potentially alternative meaning-giving institutions such as the family, church, and community and the public political process. Furthermore, these practices colonize our feelings and relations among the many parts of our lives both in and outside the workplace. This colonization both produces and reproduces forms of domination and exclusion. And, although organizational decisions are inevitably value-laden, they are most often justified by single-dimension logics (of profitability and rational, value-free decision making), thus distorting choices and precluding the creative accomplishment of different social interests (Deetz, 1995b, 2003a). Our own lives come to mirror that one-dimensionality. This was finally summarized in my book *Democracy in an Age of Corporate Colonization* (1992). The attempt was not to valorize other social institutions with their own forms of domination and exclusion (their own monoculturalisms) but to enable other institutions to have a less colonized development and, hence, put them in a more balanced and dynamic relation with each other. Social life is considered as an ongoing social construction that may be openly developed, reflecting many different conflicting needs, or it can be one-sided and skewed, reflecting dominant interests alone. Neither I nor critical theory has an easy vision of how we should develop, but critical theory provides some understanding of how a wider variety of interests might be brought into the process of choices and development. In some sense, critical theory seems obvious rather than radical. Once we understand that our world, our cultural life, is a social construction, we should know by whom and to what ends it was constructed in this way and have some choice in the matter.

Critical theory, as I express it, is somewhat different from that expressed by those who come to it from class politics or labor processes. Critical theory is expressed differently by a white male farm kid than by a person of color, woman, or child of factory laborers. Our biographies, as they are constituted by larger social-historical processes, enable differences to be brought to the larger discussion, both limiting and helping enable a fuller discussion. My focus here differs from that of other critical works: My focus is more on meaning and personal identities, the micropolitical processes by which these are formed is emphasized over class politics and radical structural change, who is in power is of less concern than people's inclusion in processes by which decisions are made, understanding the processes of exclusion is complemented by a desire to make decisions together, and concern with communication distortion is emphasized over false consciousness as a key element of nonrepresentative and socially irresponsible decisions. The tenor is different. I work more to figure out how to include diverse interests rather than to complain about the injustice of exclusion. I suspect that everyone coming to critical theory has some degree of anger at social injustice and some love of the potential in human sociality. I lean to the latter.

Critical Theory as a Way of Living

Critical theory offers a different way of thinking about theory and its relation to knowledge, life, and action. I would be remiss if I treated critical theory as just another school of thought out there to be summarized and studied. Critical theory is as much a way of living as a "theory" in the more traditional, everyday sense.

The social constructionism of critical theory suggests that theory is not well thought of as an abstract mirror or reflection of an external world (see Deetz, 1992, Chap. 3; Rorty, 1979). Explicitly presented theories do not differ fundamentally in form or effect from the implicit theories that direct our everyday seeing and choices. All theories are particular ways of being directed to and engaged with the external world, driven by various desires and tasks. As a way of seeing/thinking/talking, they lead to the constitution of a particular world and action options.

To the extent that the particular lenses (vocabulary, constitutive practices) that we bring to bear on the world are socially constructed, we inevitably enact the power conditions in their production in the very act of seeing. Theories are not neutral; they are always value laden. Concern with representational fidelity alone fails to account for the more practical and political issues in prior constitutive practices (Deetz, 2000, 2001). Theories focused only on prediction and control lack a consideration of other motives for understanding people as well as a moral justification for their use on other people.

We need to ask questions like "What kind of person will I become?" or "What kind of society will this make?" if I approach the world in this way. Critical theory thus asks us to critically examine our theories and processes of knowledge construction in the light of a moral commitment to inclusion and shared decision making (Deetz, 1995a, 1999). Critical theory asks for a personal courage to identify and challenge assumptions behind ordinary ways of perceiving, conceiving, and acting, and for recognition of the influence of history, culture, and social positioning on perceptions, meanings, and actions.

Furthermore, critical theory has an activist dimension. Critical theory, with its concepts, implicitly purports to be a better, more interesting, and useful way to engage the world. It is not enough to understand the world: One must act in it. This is developed as "praxis"—a theoretically informed engagement in life choices. The politically astute student is given an active role in the production of an enlightened understanding. The hope is to provide forums and voice so that different segments of the society and different human interests can be part of a better, more moral, historical dialogue, so that each may contribute equally to the choices in producing a future for all.

Almost all critical work assumes that power and authority relations and their impact on decision making are real, gendered, classed, institutionalized, and evoked/enforced by specific others in specific ways. But critical theory also holds out a reformist hope that is often absent or less explicit in other critical work. Power is neither simply centralized nor monolithic. People are not condemned to its logic; there are lots of different ways to feel/conceptualize/act in specific situations. The available options are different for each of us in a situated way, but we also (at least implicitly) choose (or have chosen for us) different ways of engagement that make our understanding of our circumstances, action choices, and anticipated responses different.

Power and authority act differently on different people partly by situation but also partly in how power is framed or encountered. Enlightenment and conceptual tools, as well as radical action, can change our choices and power to act. A critical theorist holds out hope that power/authority relations can be at least momentarily transcended or partly set aside for a more productive interaction, all the while not forgetting about power differences and how sneaky and intrusive they are. With this hope come efforts to create communicative contexts where power is suspended or held in check so that more creative and representative decisions can be made (Deetz & Simpson, 2004). Some of the critical work has focused almost exclusively on how such safe, democratic places can be created (Deetz & Brown, 2004; Forester, 1989, 1999; Zoller, 2000).

The Emergence of Critical Theory in Organizational Studies

Critical theorists position their work in regard to four specific developments in Western thought. The way they respond to and partly use mixes of these developments accounts for many of their differences. These developments are (a) the power/ knowledge relation arising with Friedrich Nietzsche's perspectivalism; (b) a nondualistic, constructionist account of experience and language arising with phenomenological hermeneutics and structural linguistics; (c) a historically based social conflict theory arising from Karl Marx; and (d) a complex human subject arising from Sigmund Freud.

The first posed a challenge to any possible foundations for knowledge located in the external world: All knowledge claims are relational, referencing social communities filled with specific power relations and processes of knowledge production rather than simply representing an essential external world. The second situated all perspectives within specific social/historical/ linguistic contexts; intersubjectivity precedes any subjectivity or objectivity as structured in specifiable ways. The third removed the innocence of social/ historical/linguistic perspectives by positioning them within materially produced social divisions and denied any smooth unitary historical development. The fourth provided for a complex, conflict-ridden, and often mistaken *subject* in place of a knowing, unitary, autonomous *person*, thereby challenging any claim to simple rationality and a clear and fixed identity.

Together, people, realities, language, and social relations become nonessential constructions, developing under specific conditions of power and contestation, and filled with opacities, contradictions, and conflict suppression. These different concepts provide the historically specific tools for encountering the dominant discourses of the time.

Critical theory's development as philosophy occurred over a rather long period of time, roughly from the mid-1920s to the present. Nonetheless, until the late 1970s and early 1980s, conceptions from critical theory rarely appeared in studies of organizations. Most of the critical focus was at the societal level. The primary concern was with the rise of mass media and the ways the general society had moved to a focus on consumption, guided by values rarely openly developed by the public, values clearly benefiting some at the expense of others (e.g., Theodor Adorno and Herbert Marcuse). If organizations were of concern at all, it was in regard to the general economic forces producing social inequalities and closing off the possibility of public discussion and choice.

The late 1970s witnessed a crisis in business organization thinking in the United States and Europe. Economic difficulties and competition from Japan and economically developing countries challenged business models and increased the interest in the "human/cultural" side of organizational life. Much of the change provided just a wider set of management tools focused on cultural management, but it also provided a space for scholars trained in more radical theories to advocate a more fundamental rethinking of organizational structures and practices. Much of this was an attack on bureaucracy and what was called "modernist" and masculine approaches to organizational theory and practice (Ferguson, 1984).

The term "modernist" draws attention to the instrumentalization of people and nature through the use of scientific/technical knowledge (modeled after positivism and other "rational" ways of developing safe, robust knowledge) to accomplish predictable results measured by productivity and technical problem solving (Fischer, 1990). Organizational improvements were supposed to lead to the "good" economic and social life, defined primarily by accumulation of wealth by investors and consumption by consumers. Modernism in organizational literature of the early 20th century represented emancipation from myth, authority, and traditional values, through knowledge, reason, and opportunities based on heightened capacity. Although writings in human relations, quality of work life, and (later) cultural studies would continue to claim a place for traditional values and norms with their particular logics, each would be "strategized" and used to aid further rationalization of work for the sake of convenience, efficiency, and direction of the work effort (Reed, 1996).

In particular, critical theory showed how modernism itself was based on myths, had acquired an arbitrary authority, subordinated social life to technological rationality, and protected a new dominant group's interests (Alvesson, 1987; Deetz & Kersten, 1983; Horkheimer & Adorno, 1947/ 1972). The old conflict between modern and traditional discourse, where the modern laid claim to all the positive terms, was suddenly displaced by a new set of conflicts, those arising from the problems of modernity itself. Critical theorists see their work as a response to specific social conditions. As a result of science, industrialization, and communication/information technologies, contemporary society has developed positive capacities but also dangerous forms of domination (Deetz, 2003b).

The critical theorists, especially Habermas (1984, 1990), focus on the development of the positive potential remaining in the enlightenment. Different forces have utilized their power and advantages to force new forms of tutelage, often based in a contrived consent by organizational and societal members. As will be discussed in regard to organizational studies, critical theorists have focused on the skewing and closure of the discussion about choices through reification, universalization of managerial interests, domination of instrumental reasoning, and specific forms of hegemony. In different ways, critical theorists hope to recover more open discussions and choices through understanding social/historical/political constructionism, developing broader conceptions of rationality, including more groups in social choice making, and overcoming systematically distorted communication. Central to this is the critique of domination and the ways those subjugated actively participate in their own subjugation.

Researchers based in critical theory thus, in general, see organizations and their structures and practices as social-historical creations accomplished in conditions of struggle and usually unequal power relations. Organizations are largely described as political sites dominated by some values at the expense of others; thus, general social theories and especially theories of decision making in the public sphere are seen as appropriate. Organizations could be positive social institutions providing forums for the articulation and resolution of important group conflicts over the use of natural resources, distribution of income, production of desirable goods and services, the development of personal qualities, and the direction of society. Instead, various forms of power and domination have led to skewed decision making and fostered social harms and significant waste and inefficiency. Either explicit or implicit in critical theorists' presentation is a goal of demonstrating and critiquing forms of domination, asymmetry, and distorted communication through showing how reality can become obscured and misrecognized. Such insights help produce forums where the conflicts can be reclaimed, openly discussed, and resolved with fairness and justice.

Research, as well as organizational interventions, aims at reclaiming hidden or suppressed conflicts and providing forums for and models of discussion to aid in the building of more open consensus. Of special concern are forms of ideology, consent, systematically distorted communication, routines, and normalizations that produce partial interests and keep people from genuinely understanding or acting in their own interests. Studies have focused both on (a) the relation of organizations to the wider society and their possible social effects of colonization (rationalization of society) and domination or destruction of the public sphere (Deetz, 1992) and on (b) internal processes in terms of domination by instrumental reasoning, discursive closures, and consent processes (e.g., Alvesson, 1987; Clair, 1993; Forester, 1989; Mumby, 1987, 1988; Thackaberry, 2004). Critical theorists tend to enter their studies with a priori theoretical commitments that aid them analytically in ferreting out situations of domination and distortion (Deetz, 2001). Two principal types of research can be identified in organization studies: Ideology critique and communicative action.

Ideology Critique

Most of the critical work has focused on ideology critique. The term *ideology* is used here to denote the presence of implicit values directing thinking and action—values that remain unknown and closed off from discussion. Analyses of ideologies show how specific interests fail to be realized because of people's inability to understand or act in their own interests. Some identified ideologies are group-specific, and others are held by people in technological-capitalist society in general. Ideological critique is guided by a priori researcher conceptions and aims at displaying implicit values with the hope of recovering value conflicts, making them discussable and enabling people to choose more clearly in their own interests. For example, our personal wants may seem spontaneous and chosen but can, at times, be shown to be socially produced and opposed to our own interests (Lukes, 1974). Critical theory in such cases reopens our processes of exploration, discussion, and choice.

Karl Marx offered the earliest ideology critiques of the workplace. In his analyses of work processes, he focused primarily on practices of economic exploitation through direct coercion, and structural differences in work relations between the owners of capital and the owners of their own labor. However, Marx also described the manner in which the exploitative relation is disguised and made to appear legitimate. This is the origin of ideology critique. Marxist-inspired analyses have largely disappeared owing to social-historically different conditions and layers of misunderstanding and abusive uses. Still, the themes of domination and exploitation by owners and later by managers have been central to ideology critique of the workplace for much of the past century (see works as varied as Braverman, 1974, Clegg and Dunkerley, 1980, and Edward, 1979). These later analyses became less concerned with class-based coercion and economic explanations and more focused on why coercion was so rarely necessary and on how systemic processes produce active consent (e.g., Burawoy, 1979; Czarniawska-Joerges, 1988; Deetz & Mumby, 1990; Gramsci 1929–1935/1971; Knights & Willmott, 1989; Mumby, 1997). Ideology produced in the workplace would supplement ideology present in the media, as well as the growth of the consumer culture and the welfare state, as accounting for workers' and other stakeholders' failure to act on their own interests (DuGay, 1997).

Four themes recur in the numerous and varied writings about organizations working from such a perspective: (a) Concern with reification, or the way a socially/historically constructed world would be treated as necessary, natural, and self-evident; (b) the suppression of conflicting interests and universalization of managerial interest; (c) the eclipse of reason and domination by instrumental reasoning processes; and (d) the evidence of consent.

Reification

In *reification*, a social formation is abstracted from the ongoing conflict-ual site of its origin and treated as a concrete, relatively fixed, entity. The illusion that organizations and their processes are "natural" (as if given in this form by nature) protects them from examination as produced under spe-cific, potentially temporary, historical conditions and out of specific power relations. For example, the managerial prerogative in decision making is his-torically recent and based largely on specific early 20th-century ownership and investment conditions quite different from our contemporary ones. Ideological critique demonstrates the arbitrariness of presumed "natural/ neutral objects" such as decisional routines, accounting practices and bureau-cracy, and the power relations that result and sustain these forms. For exam-ple, Hopwood (1987) showed how standard accounting practices are anything but standard. They are outcomes of heavily value-laden, political choices. Jacques (1996) showed how the idea of an "employee" historically arose and became naturalized in organizational discourse and practices. Critique hopes to reclaim conflict over the values embedded in these forms, initiate discussions about these formations, and discover the remaining places of possible choice.

Universalization of Sectional Interests

Lukács (1971), among many others (see Giddens, 1979), has shown that particular sectional interests are often *universalized* and treated as if they were everyone's interests, thus producing a false consensus. In contemporary organizational practices, managerial groups are privileged in decision mak-ing and research. *The* interests of organizations frequently are equated with management's interests. For example, worker, supplier, or host community interests can be interpreted in terms of their effect on organizational—that is, universalized managerial—interests. As such, these groups' interests are only occasionally considered in decisions, usually reactively, and are often represented as simply economic commodities or "costs"—for example, the price the "organization" must pay for labor, supplies, or environmental clean-up (Deetz, 1995b). Central to the universalization of managerial inter-ests is the reduction of the multiple claims of ownership to financial owner-ship. In ideology critique, managerial advantages can be seen as produced historically and reproduced actively through ideological discursive practices in society and in organizations themselves (see Bullis & Tompkins, 1989; Deetz, 1992; Mumby, 1987). Those working from critical theory joins other recent theorists in arguing for the representation of the full variety of orga-nizational stakeholders (see Deetz, 2003a).

Dominance of Technical Rationality

Habermas (1971, 1984, 1987) has traced the social-historical emergence of *technical rationality* over competing forms of reason. Habermas described *technical reasoning* as instrumental, tending to be governed by the theoretical and hypothetical, and focusing on control through the development of means-ends chains. The natural opposite to this, Habermas conceptualizes as a *practical interest*. Practical reasoning focuses on the process of understanding and mutual determination of the ends to be sought rather than control and development of means of goal accomplishment. But in the contemporary social situation, the form and content of modern social science and the social constitution of expertise align with organizational structures to produce the domination of technical reasoning (see Alvesson, 1987; Fischer, 1990; Mumby, 1988; Stablein & Nord, 1985). To the extent that technical reasoning dominates, it lays claim to the entire concept of rationality, and alternative forms of reason appear irrational. To a large extent, studies of the "human" side of organizations (climate, job enrichment, quality of work life, worker participation programs, and culture) have each been transformed from alternative organizational objectives into new means to be brought under technical control for extending the dominant group interests of the organization's leadership group (Alvesson, 1987; Wendt, 1994). The productive tension between the two becomes disregarded or overlooked for the sake of the efficient accomplishment of often unknown but surely "rational" and "legitimate" organizational goals.

Consent

Early critical theorists focused primarily on bureaucracies and other means of direct control and domination. As the work has developed and these forms have declined, more sophisticated conceptions of power have arisen. Various forms of indirect control have become of greater concern (see Bullis, 1991; Burawoy, 1979; Edward, 1979; Lukes, 1974). Many of these forms of indirect control involve active "consent" of those controlled. *Consent* processes occur through the variety of situations and activities in which someone actively, though often unknowingly, accomplishes the interests of others in the faulty attempt to fulfill his or her own.

People are oppressed but are also enticed into activities that create complicity in their own victimization (for examples, see Brunsson, 1989; Deetz, 1998; Pringle, 1988). As a result, rather than being open, discussions are foreclosed, or there appears to be no need for discussion. The interaction processes reproduce fixed identities, relations, and knowledge, and the variety of possible differences is lost. Thus, important discussions do not take place because there appears to be no reason for them. Consent often appears in direct forms as members actively subordinate themselves to obtain money, security, meaning, or identity—things that should result from the work process rather than subordination. In fact, both the subordination and the requirement of it hamper the accomplishment of these work goals.

Critical organizational communication research during the past 20 years includes a rather wide body of studies describing hegemonic processes whereby specific standard practices and commonsense understandings become organized and reproduced (e.g., Alvesson, 1987; Deetz, 2003b; Mumby, 1997). Other researchers have shown how normative, unobtrusive, or concertive control processes develop in organizations and subvert employee participation programs (see Barker, 1993, 1999; Barker & Cheney, 1994; Bullis, 1991; Bullis & Tompkins, 1989; Ezzamel & Willmott, 1998; Papa, Auwal, & Singhal, 1995).

Communicative Action

Whereas earlier critical studies focused on distortions of consciousness, thought, and meanings, Habermas's work since the late 1970s has concentrated on distortions in communication processes (Habermas, 1979, 1984, 1990). This project retains many of the features of ideology critique, including the ideal of sorting out constraining social forms from those grounded in reason, but it envisages procedural ideals rather than substantive critique and thus becomes quite different from traditional ideology critique. It also introduces an affirmative agenda, not based on a utopia, but on a hope of how we might reform institutions along the lines of morally driven discourse in situations approximating an "ideal speech situation" (Deetz, 1992, 1999; Habermas, 1979).

Organizational communication scholars have developed these ideas to support more participatory communication and decision making in organizations and to display power-based limitations on organizational democratization (Cheney, 1995; Deetz, 1992; Forester, 1989). From a participation perspective, communication difficulties arise from communication practices that preclude value debate and conflict, that substitute images and imaginary relations for self-presentation and truth claims, that arbitrarily limit access to communication channels and forums, and that then lead to decisions based on arbitrary authority relations (see Deetz, 1992, for development).

Basically, Habermas (1984, 1990) argued that every speech act can function in communication by virtue of common presumptions made by speaker and listener. Even when these presumptions are not fulfilled in an actual situation, they serve as a base of appeal as failed conversation turns to argumentation regarding the disputed validity claims. As a basic overriding presumption, we expect symmetrical opportunities to speak and make claims. Further validity claims arise out of our shared domains of reality: the external world, human relations, and the individual's internal world. The claims raised in each domain are, respectively, truth, rightness (propriety), and truthfulness (sincerity). Each competent, communicative act thus makes three claims: (a) asserting a knowledge proposition, (b) establishing legitimate social relations, and (c) disclosing the speaker's socially-historically positioned personal experience. If any of these claims cannot be brought to open dispute, we are likely to have systematically distorted communication. The ideal speech situation is to be recovered to avoid or overcome such distortions.

The ideal speech situation, thus, describes four basic guiding conditions as necessary for free and open participation in the resolution of conflicting claims. First, the attempt to reach understanding presupposes a symmetrical distribution of the chances to choose and apply speech acts that can be heard and understood. This would specify the minimal conditions of skills and opportunities for expression, including access to meaningful forums, media, and channels of communication. Minimally, forums would be available for discussion and decision making, and no individual or group would be excluded arbitrarily from the opportunity to participate.

Second, the understanding and representation of the external world needs to be freed from privileged preconceptions or authority relations in the social development of "truth." Ideally, participants have the opportunity to express interpretations and explanations with conflicts resolved in reciprocal claims and counter-claims without privileging particular epistemologies or forms of data. The freedom from preconception implies an examination of any ideology that would privilege one form of discourse, disqualify certain possible participants, and universalize any particular sectional interest. Knowledge is to be understood as always positional; thus, knowledge claims are always open to productive contestation (Harding, 1991). As Martin (1995) demonstrated, knowledge construction—often even in professional settings—can be highly distorted based on a number of institutional and structural configurations.

Third, participants need to have the opportunity to establish legitimate social relations and norms for conduct and interaction. The rights and responsibilities of people are not given in advance by nature nor by a privileged, universal value structure, but are negotiated through interaction. The reification of organizational structures and their maintenance without possible dispute and the presence of managerial prerogatives are examples of potential immorality in organizational discourse.

Finally, interactants need to be able to express their own interests, needs, and feelings as they are experienced in their own social-cultural context. This would require freedom from various coercive and distorted processes by which the individual is unable to form experience openly, to engage the individual's own social positioning, to develop and sustain competing identities, and to form expressions presenting them.

The most frequent objections to Habermas, and those who have followed this work, is that he has overemphasized reason and consensus and has only a negative view of power that hampers ways to conceive of social change (see Benhabib, 1990; Lyotard, 1984). What Habermas does well is give an arguable standard for normative guidance to communication as a critique of domination, even if his position is distinctly Western, intellectual, and male (see, Benhabib, 1992, and Fraser, 1987, for a discussion of these problems and ways of recovering the critical hopes of his work).

The participative conception of communication describes the possibility and conditions for mutual decision making and also provides a description of communication problems and inadequacies. In general, most strategic or instrumental communicative acts have the potential to assert the speaker's opinion over the attempt to reach a more representative consensus. In such cases, an apparent agreement precludes the conflict that could lead to a new position of open mutual assent. In cases where the one-sidedness is apparent, usually the processes of assertion/counterassertion and questions/answers reclaim a situation approximating participation.

Critical theorists have been very effective in showing the invisible constraints to mutual decision making in organizations. In many workplaces today, strategy and manipulation are disguised and control is exercised through manipulations of the natural, neutral, and self-evident. Critical work has both demonstrated the presence of ideological domination and processes of "discursive closure" and "systematically distorted communication" (Deetz, 1992, Chap. 7; Deetz, MacDonald & Heath, in press; Markham, 1996; Thackaberry, 2004). Although Habermas has been criticized for focusing too much on consensus at the expense of conflict and dissensus, implicit in his analyses is the recovery of conflict as an essential precursor to a new consensus and the perpetual critique of each new consensus as interaction continues.

The theory is further weakened by the failure to carefully document the various forms of resistance to domination that are present in organizations. Although dominant discourse in organizations may be skewed, critical work has also shown that organization members often operate critically in their own attempts to have control and a space for their own accomplishments, and not all of this is negative, ineffective, or co-opted (Collinson, 1992, 1994; Kassing, 2001; Murphy, 1998; Pringle, 1988; Trethewey, 1997).

Critical Theory as a Way of Being a Scholar

In the last section, critical theory was examined as an explicit theory, and theoretical objections and evaluations were made. But it is also a way of life needing to be assessed as it engages concrete life situations. In order to provide an assessment of critical theory in that light, I need to make a brief detour to provide a context for evaluation. I wish to build a critical studies metatheory to provide a basis for assessment. For the sake of space, I will not here try to ground this metatheory but only give some sense of how it might be done.

From a critical standpoint, a fully engaged human being operates in three tension-filled modes—being filled with care, thought, and good humor. Each of these has a strong and a weak version. A theory provides a less adequate attention to and response to people and life events when the weaker version is chosen or one mode dominates over the others. Allow me to develop these modes and return the attention to assessing critical theory.

Being Filled With Care

To be filled with care, for our purposes, means to be directed to, totally occupied by, or centered by the outside and others. The weak version of this provides a kind of sympathy, a caring about. This is most completely manifest in a feeling for others in tragedy, in their disadvantage, and in their losses as well as positively in their joys and successes. Conceptually, this is grounded in humanistic psychology as based in underlying, presumably shared, human qualities that transcend our differences. We see this manifest in helping behaviors, descriptive "colonial" ethnographies, and many documentaries. These evoke feelings but neither entail risk of our self-definition or culturally based understandings nor aid understanding of others in their difference. A constructionist would argue that this mode contains a self-deception in that although the outside—the other—is the target of the sympathy, the attention, feeling, and responses arise out of an unexplored set of culturally based scripts and values held by the observer. In the case of U.S. society, these tend to be liberal white middle-class sensibilities that overlook and deny important differences of the other. The other is felt about but understood in one's own, though presumed to be universal, terms.

Heidegger, as his work is developed through Gadamer and others, provided a much more fundamental notion of care. In this conception, the person is pulled out of his or her self by the demand of the outside (see Deetz & Simpson, 2004). Others are to be understood in their own terms. Although this is inevitably incomplete, to the extent that it happens the self can never be the same. One's own values become exposed as partial and incomplete, and the injustice, even violence, of applying them to another becomes exposed. In Benhabib's (1992) sense, the other is a concrete specific other, irreducible to one's own concepts and preconceptions, a "thou" in Buber's and Gadamer's sense. This type of care requires a self-abandonment and creates a risk in the face of the easy surface caring. The other is truly other, filled with understandings and responses to the world that are not one's own, potentially distasteful and uneasy. Being filled with care in this sense is to attend to the difference of the other, the parts that seem absurd or don't make sense, things that challenge one's own sense of how the world works. The other complicates our easy thoughts and emotions; none of it is so simple as we might believe.

Being Filled With Thought

If care is a mode of being directed to the outside and unknown, thought is directed from existing, known concepts. Thought involves a critical reflection and pulling back. The other becomes "categorized and generalized" rather than "specific and concrete." The political agenda becomes focused on groups and classes of people.

In its weak sense, thought becomes criticism and the application of rules and procedures. Its mode of working tends to be oppositional, and the world is seen as filled with relatively fixed interests set in conflict. In its conservative mode, it decries ignorance, deviance, and disruption, applying its critical glance to groups of individuals who don't fit or fulfill dominant social norms. In its liberal version, it is critical of existing processes and institutions, seeing individual circumstances as outcomes of social inequality and inadequate social institutions and processes. Criticism is based on theories *of* existing social contexts. For example, the focus might be on specific outcomes of managerial decision making.

In thought's strong mode, reflection is to the larger social-historical processes by which groupings and interests arise. The interest focuses on the more subtle, less visible, and deeper ways that inequality occurs. Critique, rather than criticism, focuses on theories *about* social contexts. Consent, rather than domination, is seen as a more central organizational problem. Thought thus requires the invention of a language to draw our attention to hidden systems, and to focus on and bring to articulation the social processes through which dominant institutions and practices were formed. For example, the attention might well be on the processes by which a managerial prerogative in decision making was produced and is sustained.

Being Filled With Good Humor

In contrast to the seriousness and centered quality of care and thought, good humor recognizes the random, ironic, incongruent aspects of life. Good humor smiles at the human contradictions, the mistakes, and the best plans gone astray. It is a bemusement about ourselves. Despite all we know, all that we are capable of, all the energy and seriousness we put into life, nature tricks us, our own emotions surprise us, our pride bruises easily, and life is filled with unintended consequences and rude awakenings.

In its weak form, good humor becomes mere cynicism. The joke is on us. No commitment is finally worth it. Because the *Titanic* is going down anyway, I might just as well book first class and party. Or, "how can I bring children into a world so frightening, filled with folly, unpredictable, and ultimately doomed?" We are all filled with contradictions, and that is okay.

The stronger version works toward the acceptance of the lack of certainty and the awareness that we make it up as we go. Vocabulary and answers are not final but rather are "resting places" ("time-outs" on our worldly engagement) as we move into worlds where they no longer work, where their partiality is shown, where a different response is needed. The righteousness and pretense are gone, and we must act without knowing for sure. The grand narratives are dead, but there is meaning and pleasure in the little ones. The pleasure embarrasses us but also gives us energy and a smile at ourselves. Personal contradictions are not just there but provide the disruption of any attempt to simply center and give endless tasks of resolution.

Balance and Assessing Critical Theory

Both following the weaker version of each of these modes or emphasizing one at the expense of the others creates characteristic difficulties. For example, individuals (especially students) who are upset with the general social/political/economic climate may discover critical theory in a weak sense emphasizing criticism of existing institutions. The criticisms are often abstract, elitist and polemical, lacking connection with actual human beings in actual situations, lacking depth in understanding how institutions function, and lacking the complexity and grace that comes with humor. This can happen in academic work, where the reading is merely political (e.g., Wendt, 1994). It also can happen with political movements focusing on things like equality and justice. Class and gender politics can stand out as easy cases of oppression without an understanding of the nature and exercise of power in institutions. Anecdotes about oppression, mythically carried by groups, often substitute for detailed description, careful analysis, and engagement in concrete people's lives and their choices. Such passion-filled movements lacking genuine thought, care, or humor plug into the oppositional roles prescribed by the game of more dominant systems rather than acquiring the insights, concepts, or complexity of positive social action. Scholars in such a mode at best become journalists. Finally, alienation, frustration and, cynicism replace any effective political involvement.

Care without thought can focus local action but cannot detail the social/historical/institutional context constituting the personal and institutional choices. Political engagement is personal, local, and isolated without effect. Thought without care becomes arid, distant, elitist, and abstract. The political agenda is clear but often at the expense of insights into the complexities of everyday people's lives. The specific individual can be reduced to generalized fodder for the intellectual cannons of others. Humor without care and thought becomes merely ironic, playful but with a political practice.

Even theories that take on the strong forms of each of these modes can have limitations. Different theories have propensities to fail in different ways. Critical ethnographies can be filled with too much care. Postmodernists can be filled with too much humor. Critical theory, along with some feminist and labor process theories, more often emphasizes thought at the expense of care and humor. When this occurs, the focus turns to the endless interpretation and reinterpretation of theoretical texts. The conceptions become too grand and abstract, lifeless and lacking grounding in everyday experience or organizational life. This is to take nothing away from the need for conceptual precision, for without it significant differences collapse into seeming similarities. Nor am I overlooking the difficulty of rethinking everyday life in new terms—terms that may seem difficult because thinking differently is difficult. Still, the contribution of critical theory is weakened when it becomes unbalanced. Critical theory has been at its best when it begins with deep care but doesn't end there, explores social-historical constructionism without forgetting the concrete other, and makes general claims without becoming smug, pretentious, or simplistic. Much of contemporary social life oscillates between a life world reduced to 1960s-style humanism and a system world guided by consumption. Critical theory offers a better set of tensions.

The Future of Critical Theory in Organization Studies

Critical theory is far less interested in predicting the future than in making it. Here, at the end, I wish to reflect more on what critical theory could do than even begin to guess what it will do. What it will do is based in choices you and I are yet to make. First, let me return to the beginning and bring back the idea that critical theory in no way stands alone. Critical theory is part of a complex interrelated critical project composed of many other groups, including cultural, feminist, postmodern/poststructuralist, race, labor process, and postcolonial scholars. Critical theory does not have an independent trajectory. It will shape and be shaped by others. But here is a future.

1. Critical theory will continue to be relevant, thrive, and develop to the extent that it provides useful and interesting ways for people to attend to and think about their historically situated dissatisfactions in and suspicions about contemporary social institutions. These dissatisfactions and suspicions arise from strains and reduced productivity in the work experience itself, the quality of organizational decisions, and the relation of organization life to the development and sustaining of a rather singularly directed consumption-based social value system. The relationship of critical theory to this larger social context will be more important than specific new theoretical developments.

2. Critical theory will continue to be relevant, thrive, and develop to the extent that its insights and concepts affect (though without co-optation) more traditional concerns and ways of thinking in communication and organization studies. If critical theory can help make productive already present tensions internal to organizations such as that between profitability and social good, or technological deskilling and human skill development, it may become a dominant theoretical perspective. The development of critical accounting studies (Power, 1994), critical human resource development studies (Deetz, 2003b), and so forth are evidence of the consequences of critical theory for the consideration of a variety of organizational processes (see Alvesson & Willmott, 2003).

3. Critical theory will continue to be relevant, thrive, and develop to the extent that the studies of specific organizations continue to become more detailed and empirical. This needs to include continued development of research methods suited to critical work, including theoretically informed ethnographies, critical discourse analysis, and participatory action research (Alvesson & Deetz, 2000; Fairclough, 2001). Positive work will (a) detail the nature of resistance and change more carefully; (b) move beyond studies based in assumed class or other group differences and pay greater attention to how groupings are formed, how they intersect, and the complexities and varieties in and among groups; and (c) look more to communicative processes of dissensus and consensus production, and identify more carefully forms of discursive closure and conflict suppression (Thackaberry, 2004).

4. Critical theory will continue to be relevant, thrive, and develop to the extent that it becomes more affirmative and future directed. Much of the contemporary work still primarily engages in critique without doing much to propose positive alternatives and put them in place. Looking at relations of stakeholder involvement and organizational governance or communication in participation processes provides the possibility of pilot programs and positive change efforts to compete with those that are managerially directed.

References

Alvesson, M. (1987). *Organizational theory and technocratic consciousness: Rationality, ideology, and quality of work.* New York: de Gruyter.

Alvesson, M., & Deetz, S. (1996). Postmodernism and critical approaches to organizations. In S. Clegg, C. Hardy, & W. Nord (Eds.), *Handbook of organization studies* (pp. 191–217). London: Sage.

Alvesson, M., & Deetz, S. (2000). *Doing critical management research.* London: Sage.

Alvesson, M., & Willmott, H. (1995). *Making sense of management. A critical analysis.* London: Sage.

Alvesson, M., & Willmott, H. (Eds.). (2003). *Studying management critically.* London: Sage.

Ashcraft, K. L. (1998). "I wouldn't say I'm a feminist, but . . .": Organizational micropractice and gender identity. *Management Communication Quarterly, 11,* 587–597.

Ashcraft, K. L., & Allen, B. J. (2003). The racial foundation of organizational communication. *Communication Theory, 13,* 5–33.

Banks, S., & Riley, P. (1993). Structuration theory as an ontology for communication research. In S. Deetz (Ed.), *Communication yearbook 16* (pp. 167–196). Thousand Oaks, CA: Sage.

Barker, J. (1993). Tightening the iron cage—Concertive control in self-managing teams. *Administrative Science Quarterly, 38,* 408–437.

Barker, J. R. (1999). *The discipline of teamwork: Participation and concertive control.* Thousand Oaks, CA: Sage.

Barker, J., & Cheney, G. (1994). The concept and the practice of discipline in contemporary organizational life. *Communication Monographs, 61,* 19–43.

Benhabib, S. (1990). Afterword: Communicative ethics and current controversies in practical philosophy. In S. Benhabib & F. Dallmayr (Eds.), *The communicative ethics controversy* (pp. 330–369). Cambridge, MA: MIT Press.

Benhabib, S. (1992). *Situating the self: Gender, community and postmodernism in contemporary ethics.* New York: Routledge.

Benson, K. (1977). Organizations: A dialectical view. *Administrative Science Quarterly, 22,* 1–21.

Braverman, H. (1974). *Labor and monopoly capitalism.* New York: Monthly Review Press.

Brunsson, N. (1989). *The organization of hypocrisy: Talk, decisions and action in organizations.* New York: John Wiley & Sons.

Bullis, C. (1991). Communication practices as unobtrusive control: An observational study. *Communication Studies, 42,* 254–271.

Bullis, C., & Tompkins, P. (1989). The forest ranger revisited: A study of control processes and identification. *Communication Monographs, 56,* 287–306.

Burawoy, M. (1979). *Manufacturing consent.* Chicago: University of Chicago Press.

Burrell, G. (1988). Modernism, postmodernism and organisational analysis 2: The contribution of Michel Foucault. *Organization Studies, 9,* 221–235.

Calás, M., & Smircich, L. (1991). Voicing seduction to silence leadership. *Organization Studies, 12,* 567–602.

Cheney, G. (1995). Democracy in the workplace: Theory and practice from the perspective of communication. *Journal of Applied Communication Research, 23,* 167–200.

Clair, R. (1993). The use of framing devices to sequester organizational narratives: Hegemony and harassment. *Communication Monographs, 60,* 113–136.

Clegg, S., & Dunkerley, D. (1980). *Organization, class and control.* London: Routledge and Kegan Paul.

Collinson, D. (1992). *Managing the shop floor: Subjectivity, masculinity and workplace culture.* New York: de Gruyter.

Collinson, D. (1994). Strategies of resistance. In J. Jermier, D. Knights, & W. Nord (Eds.), *Resistance and power in organizations* (pp. 25–68). London: Routledge.

Cooper, R. (1989). Modernism, postmodernism and organisational analysis 3: The contribution of Jacques Derrida. *Organization Studies, 10,* 479–502.

Czarniawska-Joerges, B. (1988). *Ideological control in nonideological organizations.* New York: Praeger.

Dahrendorf, R. (1959). *Class and class conflict in industrial society.* Stanford, CA: Stanford University Press.

Deetz, S. (1973). An understanding of science and a hermeneutic science of understanding. *Journal of Communication, 23,* 139–159.

Deetz, S. (1992). *Democracy in an age of corporate colonization: Developments in communication and the politics of everyday life.* Albany: State University of New York Press.

Deetz, S. (1994). The future of the discipline: The challenges, the research, and the social contribution. In S. Deetz (Ed.), *Communication yearbook 17* (pp. 565–600). Thousand Oaks, CA: Sage.

Deetz, S. (1995a). Character, corporate responsibility and the dialogic in the postmodern context. *Organization: The Interdisciplinary Journal of Organization, Theory, and Society, 3,* 217–25.

Deetz, S. (1995b). *Transforming communication, transforming business: Building responsive and responsible workplaces.* Cresskill, NJ: Hampton Press.

Deetz, S. (1996). Describing differences in approaches to organizational science: Rethinking Burrell and Morgan and their legacy. *Organization Science, 7,* 191–207.

Deetz, S. (1998). Discursive formations, strategized subordination, and self-surveillance: An empirical case. In A. McKinlay & K. Starkey (Eds.), *Foucault, management and organizational theory* (pp. 151–172). London: Sage.

Deetz, S. (1999). Multiple stakeholders and social responsibility in the international business context: A critical perspective. In P. Salem (Ed.), *Organization communication and change: Challenges in the next century* (pp. 289–319). Cresskill, NJ: Hampton Press.

Deetz, S. (2000). Putting the community into organizational science: Exploring the construction of knowledge claims. *Organization Science, 11,* 732–738.

Deetz, S. (2001). Alternative perspectives in organizational communication studies. In F. Jablin & L. Putnam (Eds.), *The new handbook of organizational communication* (pp. 3–46). Thousand Oaks, CA: Sage.

Deetz, S. (2003a). Corporate governance, communication, and getting social values into the decisional chain. *Management Communication Quarterly, 16,* 606–611.

Deetz, S. (2003b). Disciplinary power, conflict suppression and human resource management. In M. Alvesson & H. Willmott (Eds.), *Studying management critically* (pp. 23–45). London: Sage.

Deetz, S. (2003c). Taking the "linguistic turn" seriously. *Organization: The Interdisciplinary Journal of Organization, Theory, and Society, 10,* 421–429.

Deetz, S., & Brown, D. (2004). Conceptualising involvement, participation and workplace decision processes: A communication theory perspective. In D. Tourish & O. Hargie (Eds.), *Key issues in organizational communication* (pp. 172–187). London: Routledge.

Deetz, S., & Kersten, A. (1983). Critical models of interpretive research. In L. Putnam & M. Pacanowsky (Eds.), *Communication and organizations* (pp. 147–172). Beverly Hills, CA: Sage.

Deetz, S., MacDonald, J., & Heath, R. (in press). On talking to not make decisions: Models of bridge and fish markets. In F. Cooren (Ed.), *Interacting and organizing: Analysis of a board meeting.* Mahwah, NJ: Lawrence Erlbaum.

Deetz, S., & Mumby, D. (1990). Power, discourse, and the workplace: Reclaiming the critical tradition in communication studies in organizations. In J. Anderson (Ed.), *Communication yearbook 13* (pp. 18–47). Thousand Oaks, CA: Sage.

Deetz, S., & Simpson. J. (2004). Dialogic open formation and organizational democracy. In R. Anderson, L. Baxter, & K. Cissna (Eds.), *Dialogic approaches to communication* (pp. 141–158). New York: Lawrence Erlbaum.

DuGay, P. (1997). *Production of culture, culture of production.* London: Sage.

Edward, R. (1979). *Contested terrain: The transformation of the workplace in the twentieth century.* New York: Basic Books.

Ezzamel, M., & Willmott, H. (1998). Accounting for teamwork: A critical study of group-based systems of organizational control. *Administrative Science Quarterly, 43,* 358–396.

Fairclough, N. (2001). Critical discourse analysis as a method in social scientific research. In R. Wodak & M. Mayer (Eds.), *Methods of critical discourse analysis* (pp. 121–138). London: Sage.

Ferguson, K. (1984). *The feminist case against bureaucracy.* Philadelphia: Temple University Press.

Ferguson, K. (1994). On bringing more theory, more voices and more politics to the study of organizations. *Organization: The Interdisciplinary Journal of Organization, Theory, and Society, 1,* 81–100.

Fischer, F. (1990). *Technocracy and the politics of expertise.* Thousand Oaks, CA: Sage.

Forester, J. (1989). *Planning in the face of power.* Berkeley: University of California Press.

Forester, J. (1999). *The deliberative practitioner: Encouraging participatory planning processes.* Cambridge, MA: MIT Press.

Fraser, N. (1987). What's critical about critical theory? The case of Habermas and gender. In S. Benhabib & D. Cornell (Eds.), *Feminism as critique* (pp. 31–55). Cambridge, MA: Polity.

Giddens, A. (1979). *Central problems in social theory.* London: Macmillan.

Giddens, A. (1984). *The constitution of society.* Berkeley: University of California Press.

Giddens, A. (1991). *Modernity and self-identity: Self and society in the late modern age.* Stanford: Stanford University Press.

Gramsci, A. (1971). *Selections from the prison notebooks* (Q. Hoare & G. N. Smith, Trans.). New York: International. (Original work published 1929–1935)

Habermas, J. (1971). *Knowledge and human interests* (J. Shapiro, Trans.). Boston: Beacon.

Habermas, J. (1979). *Communication and the evolution of society* (T. McCarthy, Trans.). Boston: Beacon.

Habermas, J. (1984). *The theory of communicative action: Vol. 1. Reason and the rationalization of society* (T. McCarthy, Trans.). Boston: Beacon.

Habermas, J. (1987). *The theory of communicative action: Vol. 2. Lifeworld and system* (T. McCarthy, Trans.). Boston: Beacon.

Habermas, J. (1990). *Moral consciousness and communicative action* (C. Lenhardt & S. W. Nicholsen, Trans.). Cambridge, MA: MIT Press.

Harding, S. (1991). *Whose science? Whose knowledge?* Ithaca, NY: Cornell University Press.

Holmer-Nadesan, M. (1996). Constructing paper dolls: The discourse of personality testing in organizational practice. *Communication Theory, 7,* 189–218.

Hopwood, A. (1987). The archaeology of accounting systems. *Accounting, Organizations and Society, 12,* 207–234.

Horkheimer, M., & Adorno, T. (1972). *Dialectic of enlightenment* (J. Cumming, Trans.). New York: Herder and Herder. (Original work published 1947)

Howard, L., & Geist, P. (1995). Ideological positioning in organizational change: The dialectic of control in a merging organization. *Communication Monographs, 62,* 110–131.

Jacques, R. (1996). *Manufacturing the employee: Management knowledge from the 19th to 21st centuries.* Thousand Oaks, CA: Sage.

Kassing, J. (2001). From the looks of things. *Management Communication Quarterly, 14,* 442–470.

Knights, D., & Willmott, H. (1989). Power and subjectivity at work: From degradation to subjugation in social relations. *Sociology, 23,* 535–58.

Knights, D., & Willmott, H. (Eds.). (1990). *Labour process theory.* London: Macmillan.

Lukács, G. (1971). *History and class consciousness* (R. Livingstone, Trans.). Cambridge, MA: MIT Press.

Lukes, S. (1974). *Power: A radical view.* London: Macmillan.

Lyotard, J.-F. (1984). *The postmodern condition: A report on knowledge* (G. Bennington & B. Massumi, Trans.). Minneapolis: University of Minnesota Press.

Markham, A. (1996). Designing discourse: A critical analysis of strategic ambiguity and workplace control. *Management Communication Quarterly, 9,* 389–421.

Martin, J. (1990). Deconstructing organizational taboos: The suppression of gender conflict in organizations. *Organization Science, 1,* 339–359.

Martin, J. (1995). The organization of exclusion: The institutionalization of sex inequality, gendered faculty jobs, and gendered knowledge in organizational theory and research. *Organization: Interdisciplinary Journal of Organization, Theory, and Society, 1,* 401–431.

Mumby, D. (1987). The political function of narrative in organizations. *Communication Monographs, 54,* 113–127.

Mumby, D. (1988). *Communication and power in organizations: Discourse, ideology, and domination.* Norwood, NJ: Ablex.

Mumby, D. K. (1997). The problem of hegemony: Rereading Gramsci for organizational communication studies. *Western Journal of Communication, 61,* 343–375.

Mumby, D. (in press). Discourse, power, and ideology: Unpacking the critical approach. In D. Grant, C. Hardy, C. Oswick, N. Phillips, & L. Putnam (Eds.), *The handbook of organizational discourse.* London: Sage.

Murphy, A. G. (1998). Hidden transcripts of flight attendant resistance. *Management Communication Quarterly, 11,* 499–535.

Papa, M. J., Auwal, M. A., & Singhal, A. (1995). Dialectic of control and emancipation in organizing for social change: A multitheoretic study of the Grameen Bank in Bangladesh. *Communication Theory, 5,* 189–223.

Power, M. (1994). The audit society. In A. Hopwood & P. Miller (Eds.), *Accounting as social and institutional practice* (pp. 299–316). Cambridge, UK: Cambridge University Press.

Prasad, A. (2003). *Post-colonial theory and organizational analysis.* New York: Palgrave/Macmillan.

Pringle, R. (1988). *Secretaries talk.* London: Verso.

Reed, M. (1996). Organizational theorizing: A historically contested terrain. In S. Clegg, C. Hardy, & W. Nord (Eds.), *Handbook of organization studies* (pp. 31–56). London: Sage.

Rorty, R. (1979). *Philosophy and the mirror of nature.* Princeton, NJ: Princeton University Press.

Rose, N. (1990). *Governing the soul: The shaping of the private self.* London: Routledge.

Stablein, R., & Nord, W. (1985). Practical and emancipatory interests in organizational symbolism. *Journal of Management, 11,* 13–28.

Thackaberry, J. A. (2004). Discursive opening and closing in organizational self study: Culture as the culprit for safety problems in wildland firefighting. *Management Communication Quarterly, 17,* 319–359.

Tompkins, P. K., & Cheney, G. (1985). Communication and unobtrusive control in contemporary organizations. In R. D. McPhee & P. K. Tompkins (Eds.), *Organizational communication: Traditional themes and new directions* (pp. 179–210). Beverly Hills, CA: Sage.

Trethewey, A. (1997). Resistance, identity, and empowerment: A postmodern feminist analysis of clients in a human service organization. *Communication Monographs, 64,* 281–301.

Wendt, R. (1994). Learning to "walk the talk:" A critical tale of the micropolitics at a Total Quality University. *Management Communication Quarterly, 8,* 5–45.

Zoller, H. (2000). A place you haven't visited before: Creating the conditions of community dialogue. *Southern Communication Journal, 65,* 191–207.

6

Postmodern Theory

Bryan C. Taylor

I dedicate this chapter to Leonard C. Hawes, whose voice may be heard throughout.

*P*ostmodernism is an umbrella term that is used in different ways by different speakers. As a result, this term defies easy summary. Typically, however, speakers invoking "postmodernism" are committed to exploring the complex relationships of power, knowledge, and discourse created in the struggle between social groups. Additionally, postmodernism is intertwined with several other perspectives that challenge the conduct of business as usual. These traditions include feminism (Mumby, 1996), neo-Marxism, poststructuralism (Parker, 1995), and postcolonialism. Because many of these perspectives are covered elsewhere in this volume—e.g., chapters 4 (rhetorical theory), 5 (critical theory), and 7 (feminist theory)—I encourage you to refer to these chapters and explore their intersections.

My charge is to review for you the relationship between postmodernism and organizational communication. I'm game, but to do this I'll need to make some strategic choices. Generally, I proceed by mapping this relationship as a convergence of several phenomena. I'll construct and evaluate this map in six sections.

First, I'll examine the terms *modernity* and *postmodernity* as descriptors of *the contemporary period* characterized by dramatic changes in global politics, economics, and culture. These changes have also been described as *postmodernism*. Second, I'll examine how these changes have shaped—and been shaped by—recent changes in *postindustrial* organizations. These developments have also been described as creating *postmodern* organizations. Third, I'll review key assumptions and critical applications of postmodernism as *an intellectual resource* for theorizing and studying organizational communication. Fourth, I'll review what are commonly noted as the strengths and weaknesses of this perspective. Fifth, I'll discuss a specific case from my own research program. In this discussion, I'll show how postmodern theory can help us to better understand communication in—and about—organizations that have produced nuclear weapons for the United States during the Cold War. I also discuss here my own journey in discovering this topic, and in developing its relationships with postmodern theory. In this section, I hope to illustrate how organizational communication research is both a personal and a professional activity that joins the abstractions of theory with the messy, sensuous, and improvisational qualities of life as it is actually lived. Finally, I conclude this chapter with some questions for your own reflection. In an important sense, postmodernism invites you—and your fellow organizational members—to take over "writing" this chapter at that point.

Converging Elements of Postmodernism and Organizational Communication

Modernity, Postmodernity, and Postmodernism

The term "postmodernism" is an object of celebration and scorn, both in intellectual discourse and in cultural vernacular. Through repeated use and enduring controversy, it has assumed several forms, including a powerful theoretical resource (e.g., used to analyze self-conscious cultural forms), a political lightning rod (usually struck by the Right to discredit the Left), and a cultural cliché (a catch-all to describe anything that seems unfamiliar, innovative, or transgressive). The ambiguity of this term stems partly from the *enormous* work that we ask it do. That work involves adequately conceptualizing and engaging the phenomena of *postmodernity*. This term is used to describe the historical period that has, presumably, succeeded *modernity*.

Modernity, in turn, describes a global historical epoch spanning the 16th to mid-20th centuries. Modernity is often characterized as the heir to—and fulfillment of—the Enlightenment triumph of Truth and Reason over medieval-era superstition and ignorance (Berman, 1982). Modernity is characterized by several dominant elements. These include

- The development of mechanical and electrical technologies, and the associated industrialization of production;
- Theoretical revolutions in the physical and social sciences, many of which reflected positivist faith in achieving objective knowledge of phenomena;
- Large-scale demographic upheaval, including cataclysmic urban migration that disrupted rural, agrarian, and communal traditions;
- The growth of consumer capitalism;
- The rise of multinational corporations and the internationalization of markets;
- The normalization of "instrumental" rationality (i.e., narrow means-end reasoning) and bureaucracy as paradigms for social life;
- The development of powerful mass media systems that enable both totalitarian control of publics and their fragmentation into markets and audiences;
- The growth of nation-states projecting ideological influence and military force throughout the globe; and finally,
- A drastically fluctuating world economy that binds the fates of nation-states through international trade and loans.

Needless to say, the experience of modernity for its affected groups has been marked by fluctuation and contradiction. These experiences include *transformation* (e.g., following the destruction of traditions and the sensing of new possibilities for identity), *organization* (e.g., recruitment, integration, and compulsory performance within institutions), *differentiation* (e.g., the simultaneous management of multiple commitments to various groups), and *reflection* (e.g., nostalgia and hope created by differences between the status quo and actual or imagined alternatives).

Postmodernism, in turn, describes a series of breaks *and* continuities between modern and contemporary conditions. Although the relationship between modernity and postmodernity is often cast as a dichotomy, this image is not helpful. It implies that each entity is independent and monolithic, when in fact both are marked by contingency and variety. For example, observers have categorized varieties of postmodernism that differ based on their proponents' reaction to changing conditions. Some postmodernists, for example, *affirm* and embrace change (although critics have noted that this stance has been appropriated for questionable ends, as in the "creative destruction" of organizational re-engineering). Other postmodernists are more *skeptical*, seeking to direct change toward the subversion of modern rationality. In this way, it's best to think of modernism and postmodernism as existing in a mutually constitutive relationship (Mumby, 1997). Neither form of life is separate or total; each contains the seeds and residues of the other. In fact, each *requires* the continued existence of the other in order to appear—through opposition—distinct and coherent.

In their recent survey of postmodernism, Best and Kellner (2001) argue that "the transition to a postmodern society is bound up with fundamental changes that are transforming pivotal phenomena from warfare to education to politics, while reshaping the modes of work, communication, entertainment, everyday life, social relations, identities, and even bodily existence and life-forms" (p. 2). This is obviously a very broad field to survey. Some of its most famous explorers (many of whom are European) include Baudrillard (1994), Bhaba (1994), Deleuze and Guattari (1987), Derrida (1976, 1978), Foucault (1972, 1973a, 1973b, 1979), Gergen (1991), Jameson (1983), Laclau and Mouffe (1985), Lyotard (1984), Rorty (1989), and Said (1983). These primary commentators—and their numerous followers and interpreters—have consistently noted particular conditions that bridge the 20th and 21st centuries (Foster, 1983). These include

- The disintegration of colonial systems historically ruled by imperial nation-states, and the subsequent dispersal of people, traditions, information, and commodities at accelerated rates across geopolitical boundaries (e.g., through immigration). One consequence for U.S. organizations of this globalization involves the "offshoring" of corporate jobs and functions to international subsidiaries and contractors (e.g., located in India).

- The decline of industrial capitalism and the rise of a transnational, information-age economy. The imperatives of corporate survival in this economy include relentless consolidation and/or expansion of markets; rapid exploitation of temporary opportunities for improved production, distribution, and marketing created by innovations in computing and telecommunication technologies; and the commodification of symbols (e.g., as brands) and knowledge (e.g., as innovation).

- The rise of global media systems whose continuous operations collapse traditional boundaries of space and time. In their cumulative effects, the programs circulated by these systems collapse important distinctions that traditionally have shaped modern cultural identities (e.g., between "high art" and "popular culture," "public" and "private," and "surface" and "depth"). These systems create a rapidly shifting phantasm of fragmented, decontextualized *information*, in which people are encouraged to view themselves as the audience of a flickering spectacle (e.g., the Las Vegas "strip") that relentlessly stimulates their impulses. This stimulation does not, however, necessarily produce *knowledge* or *wisdom*, but rather *hyper-realities* with no "real" referents. These environments are populated by simulations, models, and copies of *something else* that has no single, original, "real" source.

- The rise of new creative and artistic practices (e.g., in literature and television). These practices reject artistic modernism's reliance on linearity, coherence, realism, and internal consciousness as frameworks for creating plots and characters. Instead, they recycle old cultural forms to create new-but-partly-familiar forms (*pastiche*), and they combine elements from diverse cultural media and genres in new and unexpected ways (bricolage).

- Increasing suspicion and rejection of "foundational" narratives that traditionally have authorized the dominant institutions of modern Western culture (e.g., religion, politics, and science), including positivism, patri-archy, liberal democracy, and Christianity. What is common across these challenges is critical disenchantment with the promise of grand stories to provide absolute, permanent, and universal Truth for their audiences. Alternately, contemporary cultures increasingly embrace the "small" sto-ries of local, situated, and temporary experience. These stories often are produced by marginalized cultural members (e.g., gays and lesbians) and challenge hegemonic values (e.g., of heteronormativity). As they circulate and multiply in culture, these narratives of *diversity* form potential resources for new and liberating forms of "identity politics" (e.g., the prac-tice of informal "tactics" in everyday struggle against oppression). This form of politics is characterized less by participants' pursuit of strategic goals than by their continuous, reflective—and serious—"play." As a result, traditional relationships between dominant, subordinate, and sub-versive voices in culture have become less formal and predictable. Powerful groups have had to rethink their traditional strategies for maintaining their positions as they respond to challenges posed by other interests using spontaneous, intuitive, dispersed, and theatrical modes of resistance (e.g., the Internet).

- The erosion of traditional identities premised on stability and essence. For example, "the individual" has long dominated modern psychology and philosophy as a figure believed to "author" original thought and then express it as intentional speech or writing. Alternate, postmodern models of identity (e.g., the schizophrenic, the cyborg) are characterized by ambiguity, fluidity, fragmentation, partiality, and simultaneity. Personal identity is not viewed as the *author* or the *referent* of communication. Instead, it is the *effect* of discourses that construct and enforce preferred narratives for under-standing the self, other, and world. It is one potential form of *subjectivity*.

If you have found this list disorienting or disturbing, you're not alone. Postmodernism is, maddeningly, both urgent and playful. It uses the strategies of blankness, irony, and reflexivity to heighten our awareness of paradox, ambiguity, uncertainty, emergence, and difference. It works like a virus to disrupt the tendencies of modernist thinking that "turn verbs into nouns, process into structure, relationships into things . . . and constructs into concrete (reified) objects" (Chia, 1995, p. 589). It reminds us that our knowledge and identities—all of the taken-for-granted elements of human *organization*—might have been, and might yet be, *otherwise*. These elements, which we may have viewed as total, transcendent, or permanent, are suddenly *vulnerable* (Mumby, 1997). They are "problematized"—recovered for the purposes of interrogation, critique, and transformation.

Postindustrialism

Let's turn now to the ways that contemporary organizations have both shaped and been shaped by postmodernism. One of the first scholars to analyze this process was American sociologist Daniel Bell (1973), who argued that modern industry was being rapidly transformed by the computerization of information. Bell concluded that this transformation would lead to the decline of the manufacturing sector and the rise of a new class of technicians and professionals known as "knowledge workers." Because knowledge is inherently abstract and symbolic, and is exchanged through communication systems, this argument was especially relevant for organizational communication scholars. Many of Bell's predictions were correct. Since the 1970s, organizations have increasingly adopted new structures and cultures described alternately as "postindustrial," "post-Fordist," and "postmodern." Several commentators have surveyed these changes (Cheney & Carroll, 1997; Chia, 1995; Clegg, 1990; Hatch, 1997, pp. 24–27; Horsfield, 2000; Parker, 1992). They note the following characteristics:

• Where *modern* organizations favor centralized authority and hierarchy, *postmodern* organizations favor decentralized authority, lateral relationships within and between units, and localized autonomy in employee decision making. Networks replace pyramids as the dominant icon of organizational structure. Dynamic, collaborative "team talk" (Donnellon, 1996) replaces the cybernetic drone of authoritarian "command and control."

• Where *modern* organizations favor mass markets, consistent goals, and predictable strategies, *postmodern* organizations favor fragmented (niche) markets, evolving goals, and improvised strategies.

- Where *modern* organizations favor bureaucratic structures that formalize roles, rules, and procedures, *postmodern* organizations favor democratic processes that are informal, emergent, and based on consensus. In this process, authority that is traditionally tied to rank and position is rearticulated with personal or group possession of situationally relevant knowledge.

- Where *modern* organizations favor differentiation of units, identities, and functions, *postmodern* organizations favor *de*-differentiation of those elements. In this process, they create multiskilled employees and holistic, flexible work processes. Traditional boundaries—such as those between suppliers, competitors, and customers—become more permeable and unstable (e.g., in the contexts of joint ventures and industry-wide integration of quality standards).

- Where *modern* organizations favor standardized systems of reward and punishment (e.g., those tied to job descriptions and performance contracts), *postmodern* organizations favor general and continuous *empowerment* enabling employees to be *proactive* (i.e., successfully anticipate and respond to change).

- Where *modern* organizations favor employee conformity to goals and policies, *postmodern* organizations favor complex, negotiated relationships in which employees cultivate dedication, reflexivity, and creativity in the service of organizational performance (e.g., by recognizing and innovating ineffective procedures). In this process, externally imposed *organizational* discipline is replaced by internally sustained *self*-discipline.

- Where *modern* organizations favor unity and similarity, *postmodern* organizations favor diversity and difference as resources for increasing useful knowledge and effective performance.

- Where *modern* organizations favor technologies designed for routine, mass production, *postmodern* organizations favor sensitive and interactive technologies enabling customized, certified production. Paradigms of quality and innovation replace the brute benchmarks of output rate and volume. Competitiveness and efficiency, however, are sustained as "new" values of service and responsiveness (e.g., in the organizational imposition of quotas for and monitoring of phone calls processed by employees of customer service centers).

- Where *modern* organizations favor coherent cultures grounded in stability, tradition, and custom, *postmodern* organizations favor "agile" cultures that unfold dynamically in conditions of paradox and uncertainty. Employees gain new flexibility—and responsibility—in fashioning consistent identities amid controlled chaos (e.g., as "entrepreneurial" change agents).

Although this list is not comprehensive, it suggests how the organizational and cultural conditions of postmodernism are related (Carlone & Taylor, 1998). Specifically, we see that the experience of speed, flux, image, style, emergence, connection, and ambiguity cuts across these two spheres. In organizational theory, postmodernists pit these experiences against the reassuring verities of functionalism. They note that organizational communicators must find shared grounds of meaning even as conditions conspire to question cherished certainties, and to offer replacements that are alternately compelling, dubious, and exhausting.

We can conclude this section with two caveats. The first is to recall that although it may be useful to identify exemplars of modern or postmodern organizational communication (Horsfield, 2000; Pacanowsky, 1988), these forms and processes typically *coexist* in organizations *as tendencies*. The pure type is probably the exception, not the rule. If for no other motivation than to seem current with their competitors, for example, most contemporary organizations reflect *some* postmodern tendencies.

The second point is that these changes create ambiguity surrounding the term "postmodern organizational communication." One meaning for this term is "communication occurring in postindustrial organizations." We have partly characterized these forms and processes in this section. A second meaning, however, is "theories and studies of organizational communication that are produced using postmodernism as an intellectual resource." This meaning emphasizes how postmodernist scholars view and engage organizational communication. It implies that "postmodern organizational communication" is *not* necessarily tied to postindustrial organizations. One might conduct, for example, a postmodernist study of a thoroughly modern organization (e.g., in challenging its preferred history by recovering suppressed narratives; Boje, 1995), or vice versa. As a result, to avoid misunderstanding, we can recall this distinction when we are using this term.

Postmodernist Theory: Key Assumptions and Critical Applications

We arrive now at our main focus: how scholars make use of postmodernism to theorize and study organizational communication. Understanding this process requires, first, a brief history of how organizational studies assimilated postmodernism.

Intensive discussion of postmodernism in organizational studies flowered shortly after the field's adoption of interpretivism (e.g., as the "organizational culture" movement) during the 1980s (see Putnam & Pacanowsky, 1983). Crucial here was a series of articles published in the international journal *Organization Studies* by Gibson Burrell (1988) and Robert Cooper (1989) (see also Cooper & Burrell, 1988) that reviewed the relevance of postmodern figures and theories for organizational research. The appearance of these primers was accompanied by an explosion of related activities: formal discussion of postmodernism at the meetings of professional groups such as the Academy of Management; the creation of informal networks among dedicated postmodern scholars, such as those attending the Alta (Utah) Conferences on Organizational Communication; special journal issues (Boje, 1992); authored (Clegg, 1990) and edited (Boje, Gephart, & Thatchenkery, 1996; Hassard & Parker, 1993) volumes devoted to postmodernism; and the uncoiling of arguments between organizational scholars about its significance and consequences (e.g., Chia, 1995; Feldman, 1997; McSwite, 1997; Parker, 1992). As investments of scarce professional resources (e.g., conference panel slots, journal pages), these developments indicated the emergence of a new theoretical "market."

Because it is a multidisciplinary field, organizational communication has always been sensitive to intellectual sea changes. As a result, its scholarly forms and practices (e.g., dissertations and conference panels) increasingly reflected and reinforced this trend. Landmark works appearing during this period include Browning and Hawes's (1991) analysis of "consulting" as exemplary postmodern organizational communication; Deetz's (1992) analysis of postmodern theories of representation, subjectivity, and power; May's (1993) review of the implications of postmodernism for organizational theories of subjectivity, textuality, and audiences; Mumby's (1987, 1988) exploration of connections between neo-Marxist and Foucauldian theories of narrative, ideology and power; and Smircich and Calas's (1987) deconstruction of discourses about organizational culture. By the turn of the millennium, discussion of postmodernism had been normalized—if not legitimated—in the field, demonstrated by its inclusion in canonical texts such as undergraduate textbooks (Eisenberg & Goodall, 1993) and disciplinary handbooks (Jablin & Putnam, 2001).

Let's proceed by discussing five claims that have proven central to organizational communication scholars as they work through the implications of this perspective.

Organizations Are (Inter-)Texts

Postmodernists take discourse to be central and primary to all organizational processes. They view all human understandings and relationships to be constituted and mediated by language. This has led them to adopt the metaphor of *(inter-)text* to study organizational communication.

In this process, postmodernists extend traditional usage of the metaphor *organization-as-"text"* by interpretivists (Westwood & Linstead, 2001). Historically, interpretivists have invoked this metaphor to study organizational culture as-if the symbolic document of a structured life-world, and its communicative reproduction. This metaphor has legitimated the use of hermeneutic methods to unravel the nature and significance of communication by focusing on its modes of production and interpretation. In this view, *textualization* occurs as organizational members use discourse to define, clarify, and manage the conditions of their organizational lives. In this process, they draw upon cultural ideologies that prescribe the use of particular norms, values, and beliefs as resources for sensemaking and expression. Organizational communication, subsequently, can be "read" as a text whose "surface structure" (its stable, conventional patterns of action and understanding) reflects traces of determination by "deep structure" (core organizational rules and metaphors). This metaphor extends the significance of organizational communication beyond its immediate, situational reference and productivity. It allows scholars to reconstruct how subjectivity and social reality are (re-)produced in the organizational milieu. It foregrounds how dominant organizational interests invite participation in systems of discourse that nonetheless constrain the expression of experience. In this process, distinctions between "meaning" and "politics" collapse (Brown & McMillan, 1991; Taylor, 1990).

Postmodernists extend this metaphor in several ways. Most importantly, they argue that, although organizational texts are collaboratively authored, they are not singular, stable, or consensual. Rather, the potential meaningfulness of organizational texts is both precarious and prolific. This position reflects a postmodernist view that texts are situated in a continuous "infinite intercourse" (Cheney & Tompkins, 1988) of discourse. It alerts us to the presence of multiple and competing narratives (e.g., of subcultural experience) within organizations that are hierarchically distributed and moralized (e.g., as "official" vs. "illegitimate"). It suggests that organizational members are simultaneously oriented *to* and *by* multiple discourses. Communicators use these discourses in both prescribed and unofficial ways to make meaning (e.g., in supplementing their reading of official corporate statements with participation in systems of gossip and rumor).

As a result, organizational communication can be viewed as *intertextual*. Postmodernists use this metaphor to conceptualize organizations as fluid entities that are situated within a broader cultural "economy" of textual interaction (e.g., between popular-cultural images of work, and the actual performance of work in organizational settings). In this metaphor, organizational communication is meaningful because it is variously configured with other cultural and historical discourses—such as when employees are constructed using the language of "character" (Jacques, 1996) and "enterprise" (du Gay, 1996). Postmodern scholarship examines how these potential relationships between texts are constructed. Organizational cultures are viewed, subsequently, as entangled textualities (Carlone & Taylor, 1998; Taylor, 1999).

It is important to note that postmodernist use of this metaphor differs from that of interpretivists. Specifically, while those theorists interpret organizational texts to reveal the concealed truths of domination, postmodernists defer such claims. Instead of generating single or final claims about truth, they prefer to juxtapose and relativize competing organizational texts, focusing on how their relationships destabilize taken-for-granted claims and reveal the dynamic interaction of domination and resistance (Boje, 1995).

Organizational Cultures and Identities Are Fragmented and De-centered

Postmodernists argue that organizations are marked by irony, ambiguity, contradiction, and paradoxes that oppress their members by prematurely foreclosing options for (self-)understanding and action (Trethewey, 1999; Wendt, 2001). As a result, postmodernists adopt the image of *fragmentation* to characterize some organizational cultures and identities (Martin, 1992).

This condition is presumed to result from several factors. One is that organizational members are subject to dominant narratives promoting modernist values (e.g., of efficiency and rationality) as imperatives for performance. Although these narratives—and their associated identities—are at least partly effective, they are nonetheless constructed "fictions" that are arbitrarily imposed on the chaos of organizational life. In their ongoing activities, organizational members continually register the gap between these ideals and their actual situations (e.g., in confronting unsolvable problems). In this process, they alternately accept and reject preferred identities, and they form competing interpretations. As these interpretations proliferate, "fragmentation results from multiple voices and interpretations that separate rather than coalesce into a consensus" (Putnam & Fairhurst, 2001, p. 114).

Although this condition may sound dire, it is not necessarily so. By taking fragmentation seriously, we are better able to appreciate the skillful efforts (the *artfulness*) of organizational members as they coordinate their actions and create shared meaning—however fleeting these accomplishments may be. We may cheer for identity entrepreneurs who overcome objectification and reclaim their potential for self-determination.

Postmodernists use a related term, *de-centered*, to challenge modernist theories of identity and agency. These theories generally assume that individuals are the original source of their intentions and actions, that they exercise these capacities through free will, and that identity is co-extensive with the material body (i.e., as a unique "personality"). Alternately, postmodernists—particularly those affiliated with the theory of *poststructuralism*—argue that human experience (including that of the self and the body) is never direct, pure, or immediate. Instead, it is always already structured by language. This is because the structure of language (e.g., syntax and semantics) creates a cultural technology that is utilized by institutions to shape the processes of human development. In this process, *potential* human subjectivity is structured through discursive operations as an *actual* orientation (or *interpellation*) of the knowing subject toward Self, Other, and the World *as objects*. Because language is the medium for the reproduction of ideology, this process also means that the particular identities (or *subject positions*) we are "hailed" to assume by organizational discourses are prestructured to facilitate actions that are ideologically productive. For example, the discourse of "professionalism" hails organizational consultants to assume identities whose corresponding performances may include advising corporate clients on "effectively" communicating the results of their downsizing decisions to affected employees.

When, finally, we note that *multiple* ideologies operate simultaneously and unpredictably to *overdetermine* organizational identities, then we have grasped the postmodernist view. In this view, the organizational subject is fragmented, partial, and discontinuous. He or she is the site of struggle between often-conflicting ideological narratives seeking to reproduce their associated interests through the interpellation of subjectivity. In this process, the subject continually draws upon discursive resources to interact with others, and to reflect upon those actions. He or she continually shifts between multiple, discontinuous, and scripted voices that have been internalized and assimilated—stitched together—*as* the self. Significantly, this view assumes there is *no* original, transcendent "person" standing behind or outside discourse to accomplish these actions. *All* identities spring from the capacities of language to organize subjectivity. In affirming this "death of the subject," Calas and Smircich (1987, p. 4) conclude, "We are nothing but the discourses through and in which we live. In a sense, we are nothing more than transgressing points in networks of discourses."

Postmodernists subsequently focus on how particular discourses of identity inevitably constitute their coherence and effectiveness by marginalizing alternate discourses. In this view, the apparently unified subject is a productive—but potentially dangerous—entity. Organizational members act repeatedly in ways that are familiar, consoling, and at least partly or temporarily effective. They lack, however, a memory of their own contingency that would open them to alternatives producing different outcomes. They "do what is called for," but they are not always aware of *who* is "calling," or how. Again, although this condition may sound dire, it is not necessarily so. While postmodernism is sobering in identifying discourse as the means of ideological reproduction, it also locates the potential for personal and organizational transformation in the micro-practices of mundane interaction. As we help each other to reflect on the costs and consequences of our complicity in organizational identification, we gain a new sense of alternatives—forms of identity that, while never finished, might nonetheless be *other-wise* (Hawes, 1998).

Organizational Knowledge, Power, and Discourse Are Inseparable; Their Relations Should Be Deconstructed

The literature on organizational power and control is vast indeed (Hardy & Clegg, 1996; Mumby, 2001). Postmodernists draw heavily in their orientation to these topics on the work of French philosopher and historian Michel Foucault. Foucault's arguments were complex and counterintuitive, and they evolved significantly over the course of his career. They centered consistently, however, on the relationships between knowledge, power, discourse, and identity (Burrell, 1988; Marsden, 1993). Generally, Foucault was committed to rejecting visions of history that emphasized coherence and progress. Instead, his histories (e.g., of human sexuality) emphasized the role of ruptures and repetitions in the development of social life. They argued that apparent truth was the contingent product of systems of discourse. Additionally, he was committed to de-centering the dominant images of subjectivity that were produced by institutions and theories.

Foucault focused on diagnosing the relationships between power, knowledge, and the body. He argued that, throughout modernity, indirect and subtle *discipline*—in which individuals internalized customs of speech and deportment—had replaced direct, coercive *punishment* as the dominant system of organizational and cultural power. Under regimes of discipline, Foucault argued, individuals adopt "technologies of the self" (e.g., programs of diet, exercise, and time management) to reflectively manage their potential productivity (e.g., their sexuality and labor). Although individuals may experience these acts of subordination as voluntary and empowering, Foucault argued that they are not necessarily or completely so. This is partly because individuals subsequently mobilize their productivity in ways that are not in their interests (e.g., in working longer hours to maintain the apparent freedom and privilege of working *as* consultants; Deetz, 1998). This is also true because the forces of discipline are systematically coordinated between multiple institutions. Even though they appear to be diverse, institutions are commonly invested in channeling and exploiting human productivity in particular ways. One example of this type of research is Barker and Cheney's (1994) analysis of apparently progressive, peer-based systems of team management. Ironically, those systems can lead team members to develop increasingly "concertive" control practices (i.e., those that are indirect, implicit, and focused on the development of premises for decision making).

Foucault's work holds several implications for studying organizational communication. First, it means that, instead of residing in specific organizational positions or actors, power is pervasive and fluid. It "resides in the discursive practices and formations themselves" (Deetz, 2001, p. 35). In this view, power circulates multilaterally and unpredictably throughout organizations. By successfully enlisting the self as an agent of its reproduction, "power reaches into the very grain of individuals, touches their bodies and inserts itself into their actions and attitudes, their discourses, learning processes and everyday lives" (Foucault, quoted in Marsden, 1993, p. 117). Power is manifest in the capacity of organizational discourse to produce and maintain distinctions that produce identities and differences that form the objects of power relations (e.g., surrounding "productive" vs. "unproductive" employees). Instead of focusing on the relative power of groups (e.g., reflected in their possession of resources), postmodernists argue that we should study how their distinctions are produced in and through discourse.

Secondly, this view emphasizes that knowledge is inextricably tied to power. This is because it is inevitably produced through, and serves the interests of, *discipline.* For postmodernists, the organizational production of knowledge (e.g., of technologies, regulations, clients) is a central, normalized practice through which particular groups establish their authority and legitimacy over other groups. As a result, facile organizational claims to objectivity, neutrality, and consensus (i.e., when it is characterized as the undistorted alignment and voluntary resolution of individual wills) are no longer tenable. Instead, through its capacities to objectify phenomena and normalize those very objectifications, knowledge serves power by shaping the boundaries of what may legitimately be thought and spoken in organizational settings (Fletcher, 1992).

Against the organizational nexus of power-knowledge-discourse, postmodernists pose the technology of *deconstruction.* This term formally describes the literary-critical process of disassembling a text and uncovering its tensions, contradictions, absences, and paradoxes. In this view, meaning is not *contained in* the superficial content of the text, but *dispersed throughout* various relationships activated by its component signs. These relationships include those between textual signs and their multiple connotations, between the text and all other texts from which it draws its significance (i.e., its *intertextuality*), and between the text and its readers, created as they apply differing frameworks of interpretation that are shaped by their relationships to the text's encoded ideologies (a condition known as *polysemy*). The goal of deconstruction is to reveal arbitrary patterns of language use and to open the text to alternative interpretations that are otherwise hidden by dominant meanings.

In one example, Calas and Smircich (1991) provide a vivid deconstruction of conventional discourse about organizational leadership. Their reading is controversial because it reveals a suppressed *homosocial* dimension in that discourse. Specifically, they argue that leadership is shaped by images of communication as "seduction" practiced between male and male-identified members. Leadership may thus be viewed as sexualized interaction, in which potent male authority figures "arouse," "probe," and "satisfy" the desires of feminized subordinates for direction and coherence. This analysis is shocking to many readers, and for Calas and Smircich this reaction is exactly the point. By simultaneously evoking and denying this imagery, they argue, leadership discourse accomplishes several outcomes: It mystifies leadership, normalizes the arbitrary relationship between male sexuality and organizational authority, and legitimates itself as an account of that mystery. Although it is apparently rational, leadership discourse is nonetheless shadowed by visceral, sexualized imagery.

Additional examples of deconstruction may be found in Boje (1997), Holmer-Nadesan (1997), Martin and Knopoff (1997), and Mumby and Putnam (1992). These studies demonstrate that "deconstruction is used not to abolish truth, science, logic, and philosophy, but to question how these concepts are present in texts and how they are employed to systematically exclude certain categories of thought and communication" (Kilduff, 1993, p. 15).

Organizational Communication Involves Complex Relations of Power and Resistance

Postmodernists view organizations as sites of intersection between two modes of power. The first mode involves strategic systems that seek control over bodies, thoughts, and voices to ensure their conformity and productivity. The other mode emerges in relation to the first. It arises from the fact that, although organizational members are recruited to actively consent to their domination, that consent is often grudging, partial, inauthentic, and temporary. As a result, organizational hegemony is precarious, and in continuous need of refreshment. It inevitably provokes tactical exploitation by organizational members of system paradoxes and vulnerabilities (e.g., those associated with discretionary role performances and the formation of alliances). This resistance is often local, subtle, ambiguous, and micro-practical (Trethewey, 1997). It is performed by organizational members to increase their margins of freedom, dignity, and pleasure. In this process, they seek to open up the indeterminacy of meaning and action that is foreclosed by organizations in their quest for certainty, progress, and control.

There are two counterintuitive implications that follow from this argument. The first is that power is not neatly mapped or conducted in ways that conform to organizational hierarchies (e.g., which imply that senior staff are always *more* powerful than junior staff). Instead, postmodernists assume that potential modes of power in organizations are multiple and widely distributed, rather than singular and narrowly bounded. As a result, organizational superiors may find themselves subject to ironic and unanticipated disruptions that exceed their official scripts for interaction. It does not follow from this argument, however, that inversions of power relationships will always or totally determine the outcomes of interaction. They are equally likely to be temporarily and partially effective. Instead, the argument alerts us to the simultaneity and unpredictability of *actual* power flows within the circuits of organizational communication.

Secondly, this perspective reminds us that "powerful" and "powerless" are not binary states that occur discretely in organizational communication. Indeed, as Deetz and Mumby (1990) and Shorris (1978) have demonstrated in their analyses of embattled middle managers, organizational figures can experience *both* states simultaneously and multilaterally. They can exercise agency even as they are being subjected to organizational control—either within a single relationship or across multiple relationships. Indeed, the exercise of power by organizational members does not necessarily spring *from* a single identity. It may instead result from the subjective articulation of *multiple* identities whose unpredictable interaction produces the conditions for new forms of action (e.g., through contradiction; Holmer-Nadesan, 1996).

This argument is controversial because we are often encouraged to view the use and experience of power by organizational actors through discrete, limited, and moralized categories—viewing those actors, for example, as "heroes," "villains," "oppressors," and "victims." Each of these cultural frames possesses an accompanying script that specifies the amount, legitimacy, and consequences of power-use by their associated figures. Indeed, supporting or challenging organizational members who adopt these identities for themselves and attribute them to others in contested events forms a significant act of organizational power.

Thus, postmodernism encourages us to examine the complex and conflicted relations that organizational members *actually* have with power. At a basic level, this analysis focuses on the messy, evolving choices that organizational members make in accepting, negotiating, and resisting domination. At a more complex level, it examines *how* those choices and identifications have been shaped historically by discursive processes (e.g., of organizational socialization). In experiencing these processes, we discover, organizational members come to believe that *some* choices (but not others) are *possible, effective,* and *legitimate.* The questions then become, *How did this happen? Why those choices? How would things be different if we made other choices?* Potentially, this analysis focuses on how organizational members "hear" converging disciplinary voices (e.g., of family, education, religion, *and* formal organization) in key moments of interaction. In this process, we can distinguish between asking members to be *accountable* for their participation in organizational power, and *blaming* them. We can accept *responsibility* for changing the undesirable conditions that bind our selves with others.

Knowledge of Organizational Communication Is Representational; as a Result, Communication Should Be Reflexive

Postmodernism rejects so-called "reference" theories of language that assume symbols have naturally corresponding and preexisting objects. Instead, it focuses on how knowledge is produced as *an effect* of discourse's ability to constitute *relationships* between subjects and objects—for example, in oral storytelling, written memos, or theatrical skits enacted at staff retreats. One theme in this process involves analyzing organizational "language games" (e.g., meeting talk) that are structured according to particular rules and conventions. Becoming aware of how these elements shape our claims about organizational communication can make us skillful players in these games. Instead of narrowly insisting on the objective accuracy of organizational stories, for example, we can realize how these stories—*as discourse*—activate particular games and produce particular effects (e.g., by reinforcing preferred identities and relationships).

This theme is closely related to the theme of organizational (inter-)textuality discussed above. The connection lies in the postmodern argument that *all* depictions of organizational communication—particularly scholarly ones—are *always-already* shaped by prior texts, and by their encoded logics, procedures, and methods. Under this condition (which has been described as a *crisis of representation*; Clifford & Marcus, 1986), we accept that we cannot know a total, final truth about organizational communication—or, for that matter, *any* truth about it—*except* through contingent representations such as fieldnotes, interview transcripts, and questionnaires. As a result, we become more sharply attuned to the *poetics* and *politics* of these representations. The term "poetics" here refers to the presence and operation of rhetorical elements in these representations (e.g., metaphors). "Politics" refers to the ability of these representations to produce normalized effects (e.g., organizational identities such as "welfare client") that reproduce and transform existing power relations. As a result, postmodernists encourage audiences of these representations to continuously reflect on—and potentially challenge—the means by which their knowledge is constituted through specific conventions of writing, speech, and performance (Jeffcutt, 1993).

In organizational communication scholarship, some researchers have attempted to achieve this goal by producing *postmodern ethnographies* (Taylor and Trujillo, 2001, pp. 174–181; Van Maanen, 1995). These qualitative studies of organizational communication are uniquely reflexive, improvisational, and *dialogic*. In completing them, researchers strive to *collaborate* with organizational members as coproducers of situated, embodied knowledge. They incorporate diverse voices in their research narratives not only to demonstrate the plurality of organizational sensemaking but also to relativize their authority as researchers and narrators. Instead of "capturing" a single, preexisting organizational reality, these representations *evoke* multifaceted qualities of organizational experience—the whole beautiful, exciting, boring, and horrifying mess. In this process, they remind audiences about the contingency of all such discourse. Prominent examples include Pacanowsky's (1983) experimental account of a police officer's unfolding reaction to posttraumatic stress, Brown and McMillan's (1991) "synthetic" narrative of a new employee's socialization in a nursing home, and Goodall's (1989) hilarious and disturbing depictions of organizational and community life in the New South.

Evaluation: Advantages and Disadvantages

This may be a good point to stop and assess your own reactions so far to this chapter. Do you find postmodern theory exciting, confusing, or outrageous? If so, you're not alone. This body of theory has generated considerable controversy (Parker, 1995). I'll review here three of these arguments, beginning with the associated critique and following with its defense.

The first—and most frequent—charge is that postmodernism's radical critique of ontology and epistemology creates a condition in which "anything goes," and therefore no interpretation should assume priority over an alternative. Crucial activities of judgment and evaluation are, as a result, paralyzed by postmodern analysis. Closely associated with these attacks is a spirited defense of modernist communication theory, and particularly elements such as the role of intention in the production of meaning, and the continuous accomplishment by individuals—despite the instability of signification—of shared meaning in their interaction. In this argument, faddish, cult-like, and misguided postmodernists have "fire[d] up the semiosis machine" (Ellis, 1991, p. 223), emphasizing abstract textual contingencies at the expense of appreciating actual and successful language use.

Although these charges have enormous visceral appeal, the adequacy with which they depict the breadth of postmodern theory is questionable (e.g., some of them caricature the category rather than examine specific studies). One might reply, for example, that postmodernism does *not* deny that meaning is possible—indeed, it emphasizes that meaning is accomplished continuously. Instead, postmodern theory reminds us that meaning is *never* universal, total, neutral, or permanent. It questions *how* particular meanings are produced in the situated, arbitrary, and interested fixing of relations between signifiers, as well as how those configurations might be changed. Also relevant here is a comment (attributed to Foucault) that postmodern studies are "anti-humanist, but not inhumane." These studies, in other words, may challenge dominant images of human identity, but this does not preclude their appreciation of the experience and creativity of organizational members as they negotiate their ongoing relationships with power. Indeed, by abandoning our unreflective faith in abstract sources of certainty, we may turn anew to each other and gain a renewed appreciation for our interdependency in the ongoing production of meaning—one turn at a time. The postmodernist concession, "I do not know anything, including who I am, *for certain*," may mark the beginning of a liberating—even if painful—journey.

Second, students initially exposed to postmodern theory often wonder how the theory is supposed to be "practical" or "useful." Postmodernists typically respond by observing that the point of this theory is precisely to subject these entrenched, modernist criteria to reflection and critique. Joanne Martin (2002) summarizes this defense as follows:

> The purpose of a social science theory is not to comfort managers with promises of relatively easy solutions but to capture and perhaps even construct organizational experiences, in all their discomforting complexity, conflict, ambiguity, and flux. . . . An oversimplified theory, however comforting and appealing, is not likely to be useful if it ignores important complexities in the world it attempts, imperfectly, to represent. (p. 9)

This response is acceptable, of course, to the extent that one is willing to revise one's expectations. You may or may not, for example, believe that it is "useful" (or even possible!) to interrupt the dominant power-knowledge regime operating in your organization in order to recover suppressed values. But in reflecting on your response to this invitation, you may learn more about how you are *already* aligned with various ideologies circulating in organizations. You may sharpen your sense of the malleability of organizational power—for example, its openness to indirect, improvisational, and tactical resistance. You may become more aware of how you are already doing this.

Finally, it is not clear in this perspective if and how organizational communication research is supposed to contribute to theory—particularly if "theory" is understood in its traditional, positivist sense as a valid, generalizable explanation of the objective world. One solution to this dilemma involves revising our understanding of "theory" as representations of organizational communication that—now matter how local or specific their scope—support relationships and structures that we feel create positive, rather than negative, consequences for organizations and society. Our criteria for developing postmodern organizational theory, then, would include "intelligibility" and "usefulness," but only to the extent that these can be developed in an accountable, ethical dialogue between groups holding a stake in the outcome (Hassard, 1993).

Case Study: Postmodernism, Communication, and the Nuclear Weapons Organization

As one example of how postmodern theory can be applied in the study of organizational communication, I now turn to a brief discussion of my own research on nuclear weapons organizations.

Let me begin by disclosing what many communication scholars know but rarely have a chance to say: Our relationship with theory is part of our biography. It is tied up in the specifics of the places and times we have lived and studied, the texts we have read, the lectures we have heard, the students we have taught, the studies we have conducted, and the personal and professional relationships we have developed. Over time, theory merges—at least partly—with our ambitions, our hopes, our questions, and our fears. As we use it, it uses us. It is possible in narratives like this to sift a relationship with theory out of the totality of one's life. But it is no longer clear that such a ruse is necessary, or even useful.

As a result, a mildly scandalous confession: I am not a "true" organizational communication scholar who "chose" postmodernism. Instead, I am a cultural studies scholar whose encounter with postmodernism led me—with some ambivalence—to affiliate with the goals and projects of organizational communication. I am, in other words, either a convert or a poacher, depending on whom you ask.

Some context will make this clearer. At the University of Utah during the 1980s, many of the graduate faculty in the Department of Communication embraced the interpretive and critical "turns" in theory. Space does not permit discussion of the associated figures or events. Suffice it to say that in this intellectual climate, graduate students were permitted to pursue problems and explore connections in an entrepreneurial fashion. Because my life experience had sensitized me to the relationships between violence and voice (see Taylor, 1997a), I became increasingly interested in rhetoric surrounding the history of U.S. nuclear weapons development.

As I tried to conceptualize this topic, I quickly came to appreciate the role played by organizations in shaping knowledge of that history. This mediation occurred in at least three forms. The first involved the basic condition that nuclear weapons are organizational *products*, manufactured through rational and mundane processes of communication. Adequate understanding of this history required sensitivity to the interrelated organizational scenes of laboratories, government agencies, and factories. The second form involved the historical influence of official agencies such as the Atomic Energy Commission in shaping accounts of nuclear weapons development, and its consequences for public health, worker safety, and the environment. As a result, the organizational history surrounding nuclear weapons development is highly contested between officials and affected stakeholders (Taylor, 1993b, 1997c; Taylor & Freer, 2002). Adequate understanding of this history involved sensitivity to organizations as the corporate authors and audiences of discourse. A final mediation involved the role played by nuclear weapons organizations—such as the wartime Los Alamos (New Mexico) Laboratory, where the atomic bombs dropped on Japan were developed—as *significant symbols* in historical narratives. That is, I came to understand that organizations like Los Alamos were not just the recurring *topic* of popular-cultural texts, but that they also functioned as "portals" that textual producers could use to organize audience understanding of the highly complex and ambiguous relationships between the signs of figures, events, policies, institutions, and technologies that constitute the material of nuclear history (Taylor, 1993a, 2002). These organizations, in other words, had been appropriated as *narrative devices*.

In this way, I began to think about nuclear weapons as phenomena that *simultaneously* involved both *organizational culture* and *cultural organization.* The first process involved the role played by systems of ideology (e.g., involving secrecy, elitism, and patriotism) in shaping the experience and expression of nuclear-organizational members (Taylor, 1990). The second process involved the development of cultural rules and traditions—a discursive *apparatus*—for representing that organizational activity (e.g., in museum exhibits). What is at stake in both processes, I came to believe, was the possibility of undistorted and democratic deliberation concerning the consequences of nuclear weapons development in post–Cold War culture (Taylor, 1996, 1997b).

This recounting is a little deceptive in making it seem like these impressions emerged fully formed (they didn't). But I hope it helps to show how this conceptualization of the research "problem" was shaped by my growing familiarity with postmodern theory. What I did not anticipate was the way in which the assimilation of postmodernism within organizational communication (described above) would *fuel* my research, leading me to make deeper and broader connections with the literature of organizational culture and power as ways of explaining what I was "seeing." Along with some practical career advice from a mentor, this connection led me to market myself in my first job search *as* an "organizational communication scholar." Recounting the consequences of that decision would require another narrative. More important is to note how my career demonstrates the opportunities both for bridging fields of study and for expanding traditional conceptualizations of "true" and "real" organizational communication research that were created by the field's assimilation of postmodernism. I have benefited from— and, I hope, contributed to—the work of my mentors and colleagues who blazed this trail.

Conclusion

In the spirit of postmodernism, I'll conclude this chapter not by summarizing its content, but by evoking its implications. These implications include whether—and how—you might choose to further engage postmodern theory in your practice and study of organizational communication. To stimulate your reflection, I'll suggest these choices by posing the questions below. These questions are not designed to have "right" or "wrong" answers. When, where, and with whom you respond to them is up to you—you, that is, and all the others who participate in your ongoing organization.

• How willing are you to consider that your "self" is not a unique, coherent individual, but a fragmented collection of multiple, diverse, and competing "voices"? If you are willing to engage in this reflection, consider *whose* voices you speak. Where and when do they come from? Where and when do you speak them? Do *they* ever speak *you*?

- How willing are you to examine the various texts and discourses on which your organizational communication depends (e.g., for its coherence, authority, and legitimacy)? How might recognizing and questioning these dependencies be useful for you?

- How willing are you to consider your different relationships to organizational power and knowledge? In what ways are you power*ful* in your organization? In what ways are you power*less*? How has your communication with others created and maintained these conditions? How could changes in your communication transform these conditions?

- How willing are you to reflect on the ways your organizational communication forecloses alternate voices and interpretations? How willing are you to reopen that communication to consider these alternatives? What would you risk in this process? What might you gain?

References

Barker, J. R., & Cheney, G. (1994). The concept and the practices of discipline in contemporary organizational life. *Communication Monographs, 61,* 19–43.

Baudrillard, J. (1994). *Simulacra and simulation.* Ann Arbor: University of Michigan Press.

Bell, D. (1973). *The coming of post-industrial society: A venture in social forecasting.* New York: Basic Books.

Berman, M. (1982). *All that is solid melts into air: The experience of modernity.* New York: Simon and Schuster.

Best, S., & Kellner, D. (2001). *The postmodern adventure: Science, technology, and culture at the third millennium.* New York: Guilford.

Bhaba, H. K. (1994). *The location of culture.* New York: Routledge.

Boje, D. M. (Ed.). (1992). Postmodernism and organizational change [Special issue]. *Journal of Organizational Change Management, 5*(1).

Boje, D. M. (1995). Stories of the storytelling organization: A postmodern analysis of Disney as "*Tamara*-land." *Academy of Management Journal, 38,* 997–1035.

Boje, D. M. (1997). Restorying reengineering: Some deconstructions and postmodern alternatives. *Communication Research, 24,* 631–668.

Boje, D. M., Gephart, R. P., & Thatchenkery, T. J. (1996). *Postmodern management and organization theory.* Thousand Oaks, CA: Sage.

Brown, M. H., & McMillan, J. (1991). Culture as text: The development of an organizational narrative. *Southern Communication Journal, 57,* 49–60.

Browning, L. D., & Hawes, L. C. (1991). Style, process, surface, context: Consulting as postmodern art. *Journal of Applied Communication Research, 19*, 32–55.

Burrell, G. (1988). Modernism, post modernism and organizational analysis 2: The contribution of Michel Foucault. *Organization Studies, 9*, 221–275.

Calas, M. B., & Smircich, L. (1987, June). *Post-culture: Is the organizational culture literature dominant but dead?* Paper presented at the Third International Conference on Organizational Symbolism and Corporate Culture, Milan, Italy.

Calas, M. B., & Smircich, L. (1991). Voicing seduction to silence leadership. *Organization Studies, 12*, 567–602.

Carlone, D., & Taylor, B. C. (1998). Organizational communication and cultural studies: A review essay. *Communication Theory 8*, 337–367.

Cheney, G., & Carroll, C. (1997). The person as object in discourses in and around organizations. *Communication Research, 24*, 593–630.

Cheney, G., & Tompkins, P. K. (1988). On the facts of the text as the basis of human communication research. In J. Anderson (Ed.), *Communication yearbook 11* (pp. 455–481). Newbury Park, CA: Sage.

Chia, R. (1995). From modern to postmodern organizational analysis. *Organizational Studies, 16*, 579–604.

Clegg, S. (1990). *Modern organizations: Organization studies in the postmodern world.* Newbury Park, CA: Sage.

Clifford, J., & Marcus, G. E. (Eds.). (1986). *Writing culture: The poetics and politics of ethnography.* Berkeley: University of California Press.

Cooper, R. (1989). Modernism, post modernism and organizational analysis 3: The contribution of Jacques Derrida. *Organization Studies, 10*, 479–502.

Cooper, R., & Burrell, G. (1988). Modernism, postmodernism and organizational analysis: An introduction. *Organization Studies, 9*, 91–112.

Deetz, S. (1992). *Democracy in an age of corporate colonization.* Albany: SUNY Press.

Deetz, S. (1998). Discursive formations, strategized subordination and self-surveillance. In A. McKinlay & K. Starkey (Eds.), *Foucualt, management and organization theory* (pp. 151–172). London: Sage.

Deetz, S. (2001). Conceptual foundations. In F. Jablin & L. Putnam (Eds.), *The new handbook of organizational communication* (pp. 3–46). Newbury Park, CA: Sage.

Deetz, S., & Mumby, D. K. (1990). Power, discourse, and the workplace: Reclaiming the critical tradition. *Communication yearbook 13* (pp. 18–47). Newbury Park, CA: Sage.

Deleuze, G., & Guattari, F. (1987). *A thousand plateaus: Capitalism and schizophrenia* (B. Massumi, Trans.). Minneapolis: University of Minnesota Press.

Derrida, J. (1976). *Of grammatology* (G. C. Spivak, Trans.). Baltimore: Johns Hopkins University Press.

Derrida, J. (1978). *Writing and difference* (A. Bass, Trans.). Chicago: University of Chicago Press.

Donnellon, A. (1996). *Team talk: The power of language in team dynamics*. Boston: Harvard Business School Press.

du Gay, P. (1996). *Consumption and identity at work*. Thousand Oaks, CA: Sage.

Eisenberg, E., & Goodall, H. L. (1993). *Organizational communication: Balancing creativity and constraint*. New York: St. Martin's.

Ellis, D. G. (1991). Post-structuralism and non-sense. *Communication Monographs, 58*, 213–224.

Feldman, S. P. (1997). The revolt against cultural authority: Power/knowledge as an assumption in organizational theory. *Human Relations, 50*, 937–956.

Fletcher, J. K. (1992). A poststructuralist perspective on the third dimension of power. *Journal of Organizational Change Management, 5*, 31–38.

Foster, H. (Ed.). (1983). *The anti-aesthetic: Essays on postmodern culture*. Port Townsend, WA: Bay Press.

Foucault, M. (1972). *The archaeology of knowledge*. New York: Pantheon.

Foucault, M. (1973a). *Madness and civilization: A history of insanity in the age of reason*. New York: Vintage.

Foucault, M. (1973b). *The order of things: An archaeology of the human sciences*. New York: Vintage.

Foucault, M. (1979). *Discipline and punish: The birth of the prison*. New York: Vintage Books.

Gergen, K. J. (1991). *The saturated self: Dilemmas of identity in contemporary life*. New York: Basic Books.

Goodall, H. L. (1989). *Casing a promised land*. Carbondale: Southern Illinois University Press.

Hardy, C., & Clegg, S. R. (1996). Some dare call it power. In S. R. Clegg, C. Hardy, & W. R. Nord (Eds.), *Handbook of organization studies* (pp. 622–639). Thousand Oaks, CA: Sage.

Hassard, J. (1993). Postmodernism and organizational analysis: An overview. In J. Hassard & M. Parker (Eds.), *Postmodernism and organizations* (pp. 1–23). Newbury Park, CA: Sage.

Hassard, J., & Parker, M. (Eds.). (1993). *Postmodernism and organizations*. Newbury Park, CA: Sage.

Hatch, M. J. (1997). *Organization theory: Modern, symbolic, and postmodern perspectives*. New York: Oxford University Press.

Hawes, L. C. (1998). Becoming other-wise: Conversational performance and the politics of experience. *Text and Performance Quarterly, 18*, 273–299.

Holmer-Nadesan, M. (1996). Organizational identity and space of action. *Organization Studies, 7*, 49–81.

Holmer-Nadesan, M. (1997). Constructing paper dolls: The discourse of personality testing in organizational practice. *Communication Theory, 7*, 189–218.

Horsfield, B. (2000). Communication and the postmodern organization: A report of qualitative research on the Australian Special Air Service regiment. *Electronic Journal of Communication 10*(1/2). Retrieved May 13, 2003, from www.cios.org/getfile/HORSFIEL_V10N1200

Jablin, F. M., & Putnam, L. L. (Eds.). (2001). *The new handbook of organizational communication* (pp. 3–46). Thousand Oaks, CA: Sage.

Jacques, R. (1996). *Manufacturing the employee: Management knowledge from the 19th to the 21st centuries.* Thousand Oaks, CA: Sage.

Jameson, F. (1983). Postmodernism and consumer society. In H. Foster (Ed.), *The anti-aesthetic: Essays on postmodern culture* (pp. 111–125). Port Townsend, WA: Bay Press.

Jeffcutt, P. (1993). From interpretation to representation. In J. Hassard & M. Parker (Eds.), *Postmodernism and organizations* (pp. 25–48). Newbury Park, CA: Sage.

Kilduff, M. (1993). Deconstructing organizations. *Academy of Management Review, 18,* 13–31.

Laclau, E., & Mouffe, C. (1985). *Hegemony and socialist strategy: Towards a radical democratic politics* (W. Moore & P. Cammack, Trans.). London: Verso.

Lyotard, J. F. (1984). *The postmodern condition: A report on knowledge.* Minneapolis: University of Minnesota Press.

Marsden, R. (1993). The politics of organizational analysis. *Organization Studies, 14,* 93–124.

Martin, J. (1992). *Cultures in organizations: Three perspectives.* New York: Oxford University Press.

Martin, J. (2002). *Organizational culture: Mapping the terrain.* Thousand Oaks, CA: Sage.

Martin, J., & Knopoff, K. (1997). The gendered implications of apparently gender-neutral organizational theory: Re-reading Weber. In A. Larson & E. Freeman (Eds.), *Ruffin lecture series: Vol. 3. Business ethics and women's studies* (pp. 30–49). Oxford, UK: Oxford University Press.

May, S. K. (1993). The modernist monologue in organizational communication research: The text, the subject, and the audience. In G. Barnett & L. Thayer (Eds.), *Communication and organizations: Emerging perspectives* (pp. 1–19). Norwood, NJ: Ablex.

McSwite, O. C. (1997). The perils of nostalgia in the present crisis of modernism. *Human Relations, 50,* 957–966.

Mumby, D. K. (1987). The political function of narrative in organizations. *Communication Monographs, 54,* 113–127.

Mumby, D. K. (1988). *Communication and power in organizations: Discourse, ideology, and domination.* Norwood, NJ: Ablex.

Mumby, D. K. (1996). Feminism, postmodernism, and organizational communication studies. *Management Communication Quarterly, 9,* 259–295.

Mumby, D. K. (1997). Modernism, postmodernism, and communication studies: A rereading of an ongoing debate. *Communication Theory, 7,* 1–28.

Mumby, D. K. (2001). Power and politics. In F. Jablin & L. Putnam (Eds.), *The new handbook of organizational communication* (pp. 585–623). Thousand Oaks, CA: Sage.

Mumby, D., & Putnam, L. L. (1992). The politics of emotion: A feminist reading of bounded rationality. *Academy of Management Review, 17,* 465–486.

Pacanowsky, M. E. (1983). A small-town cop: Communication in, out, and about a crisis. In L. L. Putnam & M. E. Pacanowsky (Eds.), *Communication and organizations: An interpretive approach* (pp. 261–282). Beverly Hills, CA: Sage.

Pacanowsky, M. (1988). Communication in the empowering organization. *Communication Yearbook 11* (pp. 356–379). Newbury Park, CA: Sage.

Parker, M. (1992). Post-modern organizations or postmodern organization theory? *Organization Studies, 13,* 1–17.

Parker, M. (1995). Critique in the name of what? Postmodernism and critical approaches to organization. *Organization Studies, 16,* 553–564.

Putnam, L. L., & Fairhurst, G. T. (2001). Discourse analysis in organizations: Issues and concerns. In F. Jablin & L. Putnam (Eds.), *The new handbook of organizational communication* (pp. 78–136). Thousand Oaks, CA: Sage.

Putnam, L. L., & Pacanowsky, M. E. (Eds.). (1983). *Communication and organizations: An interpretive approach.* Beverly Hills, CA: Sage.

Rorty, R. (1989). *Contingency, irony and solidarity.* New York: Cambridge University Press.

Said, E. W. (1983). *The world, the text, and the critic.* Cambridge, MA: Harvard University Press.

Shorris, E. (1978). *Scenes from corporate life: The politics of middle management.* New York: Penguin.

Smircich. L., & Calas, M. (1987). Organizational culture: A critical assessment. In F. M. Jablin, L. L. Putnam, K. H. Roberts, & L. L. Porter (Eds.), *Handbook of organizational communication: An interdisciplinary perspective* (pp. 228–263). Newbury Park, CA: Sage.

Taylor, B. C. (1990). *Reminiscences of Los Alamos:* Narrative, critical theory and the organizational subject. *Western Journal of Speech Communication, 54,* 395–419.

Taylor, B. C. (1993a). *Fat Man and Little Boy:* The cinematic representation of interests in the nuclear weapons organization. *Critical Studies in Mass Communication, 10,* 367–394.

Taylor, B. C. (1993b). Register of the repressed: Women's voice and body in the nuclear weapons organization. *Quarterly Journal of Speech, 79,* 267–285.

Taylor, B. C. (1996). Make bomb, save world: Reflections on dialogic nuclear ethnography. *Journal of Contemporary Ethnography, 25,* 120–143.

Taylor, B. C. (1997a). Home zero: Images of home and field in nuclear-cultural studies. *Western Journal of Communication, 61,* 209–234.

Taylor, B. C. (1997b). Revis(it)ing nuclear history: Narrative conflict at the Bradbury Science Museum. *Studies in Cultures, Organizations and Societies, 3,* 119–145.

Taylor, B. C. (1997c). Shooting downwind: Depicting the radiated body in epidemiology and documentary photography. In M. Huspek & G. Radford

(Eds.), *Transgressing discourses: Communication and the voice of other* (pp. 289–328). Albany: SUNY Press.

Taylor, B. C. (1999). Browsing the culture: Membership and intertextuality at a Mormon bookstore. *Studies in Cultures, Organizations, and Societies, 5,* 61–95.

Taylor, B. C. (2002). Organizing "the unknown subject": Los Alamos, espionage, and the politics of biography. *Quarterly Journal of Speech, 88,* 33–49.

Taylor, B. C., & Freer, B. (2002). Containing the nuclear past: The politics of history and heritage at the Hanford plutonium works. *Journal of Organizational Change Management, 15,* 563–588.

Taylor, B. C., & Trujillo, N. (2001). Qualitative research methods. In F. Jablin & L. Putnam (Eds.), *The new handbook of organizational communication* (pp. 161–194). Thousand Oaks, CA: Sage.

Trethewey, A. (1997). Resistance, identity, and empowerment: A postmodern feminist analysis of clients in a human service organization. *Communication Monographs, 64,* 281–301.

Trethewey, A. (1999). Isn't it ironic: Using irony to explore the contradictions of organizational life. *Western Journal of Communication, 63,* 140–167.

Van Maanen, J. (Ed.). (1995). *Representation in ethnography.* Thousand Oaks, CA: Sage.

Wendt, R. F. (2001). *The paradox of empowerment: Suspended power and the possibility of resistance.* Westport, CT: Praeger.

Westwood, R., & Linstead, S. (2001). *The language of organization.* Thousand Oaks, CA: Sage.

7

Feminist Organizational Communication Studies

Engaging Gender In Public And Private

Karen Lee Ashcraft

About 10 years ago, this would have been a short chapter—more like a wishful leaflet. A handful of essays, few appearing in our field's major journals, considered the prospect of feminist approaches to organizational communication (e.g., Buzzanell, 1994; Calás & Smircich, 1992; Fine, 1993; Marshall, 1993; Mills & Chiaramonte, 1991). Most of these works hovered at the conceptual level. Little, if any, published work applied feminist perspectives to empirical studies of organizational practice (for some exceptions, see Lont, 1988, and Seccombe-Eastland, 1988). As the mid-1990s drew near, feminist theory lingered on the fringes of the organizational communication literature, while feminist research was scarcely more than a promise.

Unlike most tales of disciplinary history, this one I experienced first-hand. As a graduate student at the University of Colorado at Boulder, I was attempting to craft a research program around the study of gender and organization. My development as a scholar thus coincided with the emergence of feminism in organizational communication; that is, my academic identity and work were taking shape just as feminism was finding a foothold in the field (e.g., Ashcraft, 1998). Later in this chapter, I consider how my own efforts to study gender and organization affirm feminist interest in the political relations between private experience and public knowledge. For now, I'll begin by observing that, from my vantage point, the virtual explosion of feminist organizational communication studies over the last decade appears remarkable. Arguably, feminist scholarship has almost become part of the mainstream of our field, even as it simultaneously clings to a marginal position. It frequently fills our conference programs and graces our "top paper" panels, and it often appears in our major journals. Most textbooks and anthologies that survey organizational communication theory (such as this one) now attend to feminist perspectives. At least in my view, there can be little doubt that feminism is truly "gaining a voice" in our field (Buzzanell, 1994). As I explain in the conclusion of this chapter, I believe that the strength of that voice distinguishes communication from cognate areas of organization theory and research (for example, management and organizational sociology), suggesting unique opportunities for feminist communication scholars.

This chapter considers the development, momentum, and future of feminist voices in organizational communication studies. I am centrally concerned with scholarship that addresses social institutions as gendered formations and, more specifically, that takes communication as a pivotal process that organizes gender and genders organization. I begin by sketching the origins and history of this area of inquiry. Next, I outline key premises that tend to bind feminist organizational communication scholars. By exploring my own ambivalent experience as a scholar in this area, I seek to surface some of the complex tensions entailed in doing feminist theory. I conclude by considering the potential contributions of feminist communication theory to the study of organizing.

Choosing a Backdrop: The Politics of Origins (Or, Why Roots Matter)

The evolution of feminist organizational communication scholarship could be narrated in multiple ways. I might start, for example, with the rise of gender difference research, which arguably introduced gender as a variable relevant to predicting organizational behavior. A different account seems to hold sway among the organizational communication community, where feminist scholarship commonly appears as an offshoot of critical theory (Ashcraft & Mumby, 2004). From this view, critical perspectives secured a place in organizational communication before feminist approaches and thus established a friendly intellectual setting for exploring matters of power, voice, identity, and so forth, as applied to the specific context of gender. Some feminist research implicitly supports this view by invoking critical theoretical constructs, such as ideology or hegemony, to investigate gendered organization (e.g., Clair, 1993). In this light, feminist scholarship looks like a subsidiary branch of critical organization inquiry, narrow in scope compared with the broader emancipatory agenda of the critical project (e.g., Alvesson & Willmott, 1992).

Certainly, both of these accounts—and, no doubt, others—have merit. By telling a different story of origins, I do not mean to deny the influence of such vital movements as gender difference studies or critical organization theory. I grant the partial validity of many historical narratives, including the one I am about to tell. But I also take seriously the claim that how we narrate intellectual history shapes how we envision current relations and future possibilities. For example, to the extent that many organizational communication scholars see feminist approaches as derivative of the critical project, it is likely that feminist scholarship will continue to be cast in dependent relations with critical foundations. This view is consequential, for it preserves the troublesome notion that critical theory can be addressed to a universal (i.e., gender-neutral) human subject, whereas feminist theory is best equipped to inform the special case of gender. As Fine (1993) observed, organizational communication "researchers who espouse the utility of a feminist perspective in communication are frequently asked how their ideas differ from those of critical theorists. (Both feminists and critical theorists should be interested in exploring why the reverse question is never asked)" (p. 143). Mindful of this tendency, I situate feminist organizational communication theory as an extension of the larger feminist movement—an intellectual and activist tradition that can be seen as independent from and, at times, wary of critical theory (Clair, 2002). This alternative, seldom-circulated account of the origins of feminism in our field might enable different possibilities.

I begin with the question of what typically gets obscured when we raise critical theory as the backdrop for feminist theory. First, feminist organization scholars do much more than borrow critical concepts. They draw on another long-standing, independent tradition of accounting for relations of power: feminist theory. This tradition poses a fundamental challenge to any theory of power that claims gender neutrality. Accordingly, feminist organization theorists have demonstrated that critical and mainstream organization studies can function as unwitting allies in constructing men as universal working subjects; they have compellingly argued that refusing the relevance of gender amounts to denying a primary way in which difference, subjectivity, and domination are configured (Acker, 1990). Through this lens, feminist analyses of organization can hardly be seen as a gender-specific subset of critical theory. Rather, they emanate from a distinctive tradition that engages with the critical project around points of alliance *and* tension.

In many ways, feminist ambivalence toward critical organization theory stems from a general history of cautious engagement with academic pursuits. Without abandoning empirical claims altogether (Reinharz, 1992), feminists have usefully exposed the masculinist foundations of science and of varied methodological traditions (e.g., Carter & Spitzack, 1989; Mies, 1983, 1991). Feminist critiques have demonstrated how ostensibly objective procedures for generating knowledge perform and eclipse ideological functions. For example, the variable-analytic approach common to much research on sex differences in organizational communication serves to reify and naturalize a binary model of gender. Here again, feminist organization theory entails ambivalent relations with what some might call its ancestry. Although sex difference studies helped to bring gender to the organizational communication fore, many feminist scholars rightfully question the ideological functions and political consequences of this vast literature (Ashcraft, in press; Buzzanell, 1995; Calás & Smircich, 1993).

Feminist skepticism toward academic endeavors becomes even more apparent if we look beyond the scholarly exercise to organized political activism. This shift in view reveals that feminists were busy experimenting with alternative organizational forms just as critical organization scholars were beginning to envision them. Operating on the premise that bureaucracy is a masculinist form of organizing (Ferguson, 1984), many feminist movement groups developed functional communities that sought to minimize hierarchy and maximize egalitarian relations, to enact group authority via consensual decision making, and to value emotions and other so-called private matters as relevant political and organizational concerns (Ahrens, 1980; Iannello, 1992; Maguire & Mohtar, 1994; Morgen, 1994; Reinelt, 1994; Ristock, 1990; Rodriguez, 1988; V. Taylor, 1995). To be sure, other activist groups also implemented democratic, collectivist, and other participatory alternatives to bureaucracy (Kanter & Zurcher, 1973; Mansbridge, 1973; Newman, 1980; Rothschild-Whitt, 1976, 1979). Arguably, at least in the United States, feminist organizations negotiated greater institutional staying power, for they remain one of the longest-standing social movement forms designed around counterbureaucratic empowerment ideals (Ferree & Martin, 1995; Maguire & Mohtar, 1994; P. Y. Martin, 1990; Reinelt, 1994).

By calling attention to feminist organizational practice, I do not mean to conjure romantic images of triumphant feminist efforts at social transformation. I *do* mean to support my case for the independent heritage of feminist perspectives on organization, as well as to suggest how this tale of origins reframes the dominant understanding of feminist contributions to organizational communication studies. First, feminist organizing reflects an entrenched feminist commitment to do more than talk within the walls of an ivory tower; it embodies the desire for tangible forms of justice that enhance the lives of real people. Although critical organization theorists share this dedication to social change, feminists arguably have done more to implement it. Indeed, that feminist experiments with practice largely preceded feminist theories of organization, while the reverse typifies critical organization studies, signifies an abiding ambivalence among many feminists about the simultaneous importance and impotence of "high theory" and philosophical reflection. Whereas critical organization scholars prioritized emancipation through ideology critique, feminists literally grounded their emancipatory interest in the trenches of practice. The contrast suggests that feminist approaches to organization exemplify a different sort of maturity—one that Fine (1993) calls "revolutionary pragmatism"—that critical organization scholarship has yet to develop and from which it could learn a great deal. The tensions, failures, ironies, and innovations of feminist organizing have produced a legacy of empirical insight about the practical pitfalls and potential of alternative organizational forms. Critical organization scholars, as well as others who study organizing, can learn much from these lived (and still-living) experiments (e.g., Ashcraft, 2001).

In sum, when we situate the larger feminist movement as the backdrop for feminist organizational communication studies, and when we expand the scope of our story of origins beyond traditional academic activities, we can begin to envision different configurations of perspectives or areas of inquiry (Ashcraft & Mumby, 2004). We can imagine less dependent, more reciprocal relations between critical and feminist organizational communication scholarship, wherein the two converge, diverge, and mutually inform. We can see contributions once obscured, such as how feminist studies challenge even critical foundations and model the vital interplay of organization theory and practice. Thus, the brief history I narrate below begins with the broader feminist movements sketched here—with the enduring feminist tradition of theorizing patriarchal power, with feminist critiques of dominant modes of scientific knowing, and with feminist organizational practice. These formations helped to ground the emergence of a coherent feminist theory of organizing in the early 1990s.

The Development of Feminist Organizational Communication Scholarship: A Public Tale

As the 1990s approached, feminist perspectives did not hold much of a place in organizational communication studies. This is not to say that the literature was silent about gender, but that what little it did say reflected significant limitations. The most developed themes concerned the communicative tendencies and struggles of women in (or aspiring to) management. For example, numerous "glass ceiling" studies examined how women's language use, perceptions thereof, and resulting interaction patterns engender barriers to women's professional advancement (e.g., Horgan, 1990; Staley, 1988; Tannen, 1994; Wilkins & Anderson, 1991). A related strand of studies examined gender differences in organizational communication style, with particular attention to leadership communication. This work gradually moved from debating women's leadership capacity to documenting and, sometimes, celebrating or advocating "feminine styles" of leading (Natalle, 1996), which purportedly entail the creation of participative, collaborative, personalized relations that distribute power widely and enhance feelings of self-efficacy, team accomplishment, and community (e.g., Helgesen, 1990; Rosener, 1990).

Despite inconclusive empirical support, gender and leadership studies functioned in tandem with communication-centered glass ceiling studies to yield a crucial insight: Even *perceptions* of gender difference carry profound political consequences, because dominant norms of professional interaction and managerial communication tend to privilege masculinity and devalue habits associated with femininity. To the extent that codes of femininity and professionalism clash, women are more likely to experience the formation and maintenance of work and leadership identities as a tension-filled process (e.g., Jamieson, 1995; Marshall, 1993; B. O. Murphy & Zorn, 1996; Wiley & Eskilson, 1985; Wood & Conrad, 1983).

In this way, early gender and organizational communication research began to merge questions of power with those of difference, yet it did so in limited ways. To begin, it imparted a *binary model of gender difference* in which men and women inhabit distinct speech communities that appear timeless, universal, and static. Such a model obscures historical and cultural variations in the construction of gender difference, as well as the dynamic, interactive processes wherein apparent differences are produced. Second, most of this research depicted *women as different.* Attending to gender meant attending to "women's issues," while men were seldom marked as gendered characters. Third, early scholarship engaged the alleged difference of *only some women* yet treated "women's issues" as a uniform, coherent, and uncontested category of interests. In other words, the research tacitly represented the concerns of certain women—mostly white, middle-class, heterosexual professionals—as the universal concerns of working women. In light of these considerations, efforts to revalue so-called "feminine styles" of organizational communication become profoundly troublesome. Not only can they be invoked to justify a gender-based division and hierarchy of labor, but they also normalize white, middle-class expectations for communication practice (Calás & Smircich, 1993).

Finally, much gender and organizational communication research depicted *difference as an individual and interpersonal matter*. Although it toyed with systemic claims about the masculine bias of managerial and professional communication, this research typically conceived of people as the carriers of prejudice into social systems. This psychologized view of communication treats organization as a neutral setting or container in which humans enact and evaluate gender difference as they go about maintaining work relationships. Consider these common titles: "Gendered Issues in the Workplace" (Natalle, 1996), "Dysfunctional Communication Patterns in the Workplace" (Reardon, 1997), and "Communication in Corporate Settings" (Stewart & Clarke-Kudless, 1993). In each case, the preposition "in" depicts organization as a theater in which gender-related dramas occur, *not* an active player in staging such dramas. Certainly, as some of these citations suggest, this view is alive and well today.

The impetus for challenging the assumption that gender troubles stem from biased people within neutral organizations came from outside the field of communication and, specifically, from feminist interventions in the sociology of management. Acker and Van Houten's (1974) classic review of the renowned Hawthorne studies was one of the first published attempts to analyze the "sex structuring" of organization. The authors argued that organizations deploy gender as a central control mechanism, thereby generating apparent variance in organizational behavior according to sex. Around the same time, Kanter (1975, 1977) also theorized gender difference as a product of structural relations. She argued that women exist at a perpetual disadvantage, concentrated in the invisible and devalued infrastructure of organizations, or sprinkled as tokens near the top. Gender functions as a tool to maintain this hierarchy—chiefly by supplying potent images of how roles should be enacted and by whom. Significantly extending these structural analyses, Ferguson (1984) cast bureaucracy as an organizational form that institutionalizes male domination by binding managers, workers, and clients in dependent, subordinate relations and, in effect, "feminizing" them.

In a particularly influential essay, Acker (1990) argued that organization is not some sort of neutral housing in which gender trouble "happens" to rear its ugly head, nor does gender symbolism simply assist or metaphorically represent organization structure and its consequences. Rather, organizations are fundamentally gendered social formations, and gender is a constitutive principle of organizing. As it integrated and developed previous structural analyses into a radical, coherent theory of "gendered organization," Acker's essay is often hailed as the catalyst for a major shift in scholarly interest—from the study of gendered behavior *in* organizations to the study of organization as a gendered social phenomenon in its own right.

Other scholars also led the shift. For instance, J. Martin's (1990) deconstruction of a narrative about one executive's maternity leave introduced many U.S. management scholars to the claim that gendered tensions are embedded in organization systems. Calás and Smircich (Calás, 1993; Calás & Smircich, 1991, 1993) took a leading role as well, exposing how management and organization theorists actively preserve, promote, and conceal gendered organization with both the form and content of their representational discourse. Also writing to a management audience, communication scholars Mumby and Putnam (1992) analyzed how gendered assumptions are encoded in organization theories, such as that of bounded rationality. Using feminist poststructuralist theory, the authors reconstructed an alternative theory of organizing they dubbed "bounded emotionality." Anthologies based on international collaboration, such as *The Sexuality of Organization* (Hearn, Sheppard, Tancred-Sheriff, & Burrell, 1989), *Gendering Organizational Analysis* (Mills & Tancred, 1992), and *Gender and Bureaucracy* (Savage & Witz, 1992), also began to surface around this time, reflecting and shaping the shift toward studies of gendered organization.

In short order, communication scholars became part of these developments and began to contribute to the growing body of literature on gendered organization. In the *Canadian Journal of Communication,* for example, Mills and Chiaramonte (1991) characterized organization as a "gendered communication act"—as meta-communication, or a running commentary on appropriate interaction and identity formation. In other words, organization provides an abstract "map" of ideal relations among gender, power, and work; members draw on that map as a resource to guide the organizing process. By addressing the evolving relation between organization and everyday interaction, such analyses laid the groundwork for a communicative theory of gender*ing* organization.

Generally speaking, however, the new thread of gender and organizational communication scholarship was not primarily billed as a "communication perspective on gendered organization" but, rather, as "feminist perspectives on organizational communication." Indeed, the early 1990s saw a surge of essays addressed to this topic. Initially cited was Linda Putnam's (1990) conference paper on the utility of feminist perspectives to organizational communication scholarship and, specifically, to dispute process theories. Interested scholars also referred to a 1993 *Communication Yearbook* exchange (which followed an exchange at the 1990 meeting of the International Communication Association) between Judi Marshall, Dennis Mumby, and Connie Bullis. Based on personal experience and her research with women managers, Marshall (1993) began with a portrait of contrast between male and female values. Using this provisional picture as a base, she aligned most organizational cultures with male-dominated communication systems, identified resulting interaction patterns and dilemmas for women, and proposed an "equality for difference" agenda for feminist organizational communication scholars (p. 139). Among other issues of debate that characterized the exchange, Mumby's (1993) response sought to complicate Marshall's dual focus on difference and the experiences of women. Drawing on discomfort as a man attempting to engage feminism, he suggested a feminist perspective that resists the conflation of women and gender by addressing gender relations more broadly. Rather than seeking equality for difference, such a perspective would work to challenge current configurations of difference, undermining and revising the sort of binary, oppositional model (for example, masculine vs. feminine, public vs. private) employed by Marshall.

In some contrast with Mumby's approach, most of the essays emerging at the time linked feminist perspectives with issues pertaining primarily to women. For example, Natalle, Papa, and Graham (1994) opened their chapter in Kovacic's *New Approaches to Organizational Communication* volume, titled "Feminist Philosophy and the Transformation of Organizational Communication," with a section on "the current status of women in organizations" (p. 245). Likewise, in her chapter in Bowen and Wyatt's (1993) *Transforming Visions: Feminist Critiques in Communication Studies*, Fine declared that feminist research begins with "the perspective of women's experience" and aligned feminist projects with "women's problematics" (p. 128) and "women's knowledge" (p. 129). Whereas Natalle et al. (1994) reviewed distinctions among liberal, radical, and materialist feminist theories, explaining the path to organizational justice envisioned by each, Fine's (1993) essay addressed more directly the field of organizational communication. Situating feminism as a distinct, up-and-coming theoretical trajectory in the discipline, she demonstrated how a feminist lens could be used to critique "traditional" research emanating from functional, interpretive, and critical perspectives.

Like Natalle et al.'s (1994) chapter, Buzzanell's (1994) influential synthesis article, titled "Gaining a Voice: Feminist Organizational Communication Theorizing," integrated multiple feminist theories, albeit for a different purpose. Rather than emphasize organizational change, she stressed potential transformations in organizational communication scholarship. Specifically, she considered how the agenda and conduct of research might usefully shift if we challenged pervasive themes—such as competitive individualism, cause-effect/linear thinking, and separation or autonomy—with "feminine/ feminist values" such as cooperative community, connectedness, and integrative thinking.

As this selective review of essays from the early 1990s implies, most of the relevant works that surfaced around this time took the form of synthesis and agenda-setting pieces; that is, they endeavored to pave a path toward new terrain by surveying relevant theory and research, providing some sort of organizing framework, delineating the potential contributions of feminist perspectives, and calling for future research. With rare exceptions (e.g., Buzzanell, 1994), most of these essays appeared at conferences and in anthologies or special issues (addressed to, for example, feminist perspectives in communication studies or emerging perspectives in organizational communication). Themes characteristic of early gender and organizational communication research—such as the tendency to align gender with the concerns of white, professional women and to reify organizations as gender-neutral containers for human interaction—remained latent (and, in a few cases, blatant) in these essays, although some authors noted the need to challenge such assumptions. Fine (1993), for example, critiqued the managerial bias of previous work and directed attention to the gendering of organizational contexts; to the social construction of gender, race, and class; and to the case of multicultural organizations. Finally, and again with rare exception (e.g., Mills & Chiaramonte, 1991), most of the early-1990s essays emphasized the importation of feminist perspectives into organizational communication studies. Few authors explicitly considered what it might look like to develop a communication lens on the feminist claim that organizations are fundamentally gendered.

By the mid-1990s, then, the place of feminism in organizational communication was one of critique, theory, and promise. Feminist scholars had initiated a gendered analysis of "traditional" organization and organization theory; they had begun to conceptualize how feminism might disrupt and enrich the field; and some had even envisioned the kinds of theoretical alternatives feminism could yield. Although there was little published organizational communication research from feminist perspectives at this time, a few noteworthy empirical projects actually preceded the surge of feminist essays in the early 1990s. For example, Bate and Taylor's (1988) anthology, *Women Communicating: Studies of Women's Talk*, included several cases of organizational practice and, specifically, studies of alternative, feminist-inspired communities. Among them, Wyatt's chapter examined leadership patterns in a women's weaving guild; the Lont and Seccombe-Eastland chapters explored dilemmas of feminist ideology and practice at a record company and bookstore, respectively; and Taylor's chapter investigated the merging of feminist principles and bureaucracy in a Canadian government agency. Hence, consistent with my earlier claim about the "revolutionary pragmatism" (Fine, 1993) of feminist approaches, feminist communication scholars were studying alternatives to dominant organizational forms before they had even begun to systematically theorize those forms as gendered.

In the mid-1990s, a few empirical essays began to appear in the mainstream journals of the field. In just the next few years, a critical mass of research emerged that spanned diverse topical, theoretical, and methodological orientations. By the turn of the century, it was no simple matter to summarize the wide range of empirical projects. Here, I can offer only a brief sampling of key research areas. Among other foci, feminist organizational communication scholars have studied (a) how members craft gendered identities, relations, and cultures across varied work contexts (e.g., Ashcraft & Pacanowsky, 1996; Bell & Forbes, 1994; Edley, 2000; Jorgenson, 2002; Pierce, 1995); (b) the discursive dimensions of sexual harassment (Bingham, 1994; Clair, 1993; B. C. Taylor & Conrad, 1992; Townsley & Geist, 2000); (c) other organizational constructions of the public-private divide and, specifically, of relations among work, bodies, sexuality, maternity, and emotionality (Ashcraft, 1999; Gayle, 1994; Spradlin, 1998; Trethewey, 1999a, 2000, 2001); (d) the gendering of dominant and alternative/feminist organizational forms (Ashcraft, 2000, 2001; Buzzanell, Ellingson, et al., 1997; Maguire & Mohtar, 1994); (e) localized struggles and strategies of control and resistance (Holmer Nadesan, 1996; A. G. Murphy, 1998; Sotirin & Gottfried, 1999; Trethewey, 1997, 1999b); (f) the intersection of gender, race, and work (Allen, 1995, 1996, 1998; Ashcraft & Allen, 2003; Grimes, 2001); (g) post-Fordism, globalization, and/or postmodern organization (Gregg, 1993; Holmer Nadesan, 2001); and (h) representations of gender and work in popular culture (Ashcraft & Flores, 2003; Holmer Nadesan & Trethewey, 2000; Shuler, 2000; Triece, 1999). As these and other lines of empirical research crystallized, feminist scholars continued to take theoretical strides. To name just a few developments, they articulated feminist models of conventional conceptual domains, such as negotiation, leadership, socialization, and ethics (Allen, 1996; Fine, 2000). They complicated enduring feminist constructs like "the glass ceiling," and they explored metatheoretical tensions and reached for new alliances, for example, with ecofeminism (Bullis, 1993; Buzzanell, 1995, 2000; Mumby, 1996).

Until rather recently, most feminist research in organizational communication—with its central interests, usual choice of participants, and so forth—arguably supported the impression that feminist perspectives were predominantly about women. Many scholars had challenged this association at a conceptual level, increasingly advocating attention to gender *relations*, or the ways in which women/femininities are constructed in relation to men/ masculinities (e.g., Alvesson & Billing, 1992; Buzzanell, 1994; Mumby, 1993, 1996). But few scholars had yet engaged the study of men *as* men. As part of a larger surge of academic and popular interest in masculinity, gender and organization scholars beyond the field of communication, and particularly from the European organization studies community, began to directly address the intersection of organization and masculinity (e.g., Alvesson, 1998; Cheng, 1996; Collinson, 1992; Collinson & Hearn, 1996a, 1996b). Explicit concern for masculinity took hold in the organizational communication literature toward the late 1990s and remains a growing research interest (e.g., Ashcraft & Flores, 2003; Gibson & Papa, 2000; Huspek & Kendall, 1991; Mumby, 1998).

This historical profile suggests that although feminist communication scholars were not the first to mark organization as fundamentally gendered, they quickly developed a robust and diverse body of theoretical and empirical work addressed to the matter. No longer a new or peripheral interest but still young in its scholarly life, feminist organizational communication scholarship now routinely appears in many of the high-profile journals of our field. In what follows, I suggest what unites the array of works identified by that label.

Shared Premises: What's Communication Got to Do With It?

One of the truisms of feminist scholarship is that feminism is plural. Although the category "feminist" is broadly applied to people and efforts concerned with gender inequality, myriad and competing analyses circulate within that community, generating a multiplicity of perspectives. Like any intellectual tradition, the history of feminist studies is rich with internal struggle—between epistemological and political imperatives, between symbolic and material realities, between deconstructive and reconstructive impulses, between conceptions of power as imposed and self-policed, between stable and fragmented accounts of "woman," and so forth. Over the years, many scholars have organized feminisms into coherent frameworks (e.g., Jaggar, 1983; Tong, 1989), and several authors have applied these frameworks to the specific case of organization studies. Most commonly identified are such schools of thought as liberal, radical, cultural-revisionist, psychoanalytic, Marxist, socialist, poststructuralist, postcolonial, existentialist, and standpoint feminism (Allen, 1998; Buzzanell, 1994; Calás & Smircich, 1996; Mayer, 1995; Meyerson & Kolb, 2000). Although allies in some ways, these perspectives also differ widely in their accounts of gender, power, and knowing, as well as in their visions for social change and associated intervention tactics.

In projects relevant to the aims of this chapter, I have joined others in distinguishing among feminist perspectives somewhat differently—for example, in terms of (a) how they cast the relationship among gender, organization, and discourse and (b) where they sit along a continuum of modernist-postmodernist thought (e.g., Ashcraft, in press; Ashcraft & Mumby, 2004; Mumby, 1996). Consistent with those projects, I am less interested in reproducing typologies shared by the larger feminist and gendered organization studies communities, and more interested in identifying what—across feminist (meta)theoretical orientations—might distinguish feminist *communication* perspectives on organization. It is in that spirit that I identify key theoretical premises below. My sense is that the discussion to follow both reconstructs assumptions loosely shared by feminist organizational communication scholars *and* reflects my own sort of wish list.[1]

1. Gender is a primary way in which social identity and relations of power are configured. Theories that disregard this point—that suggest universal (i.e., gender-free) figures or interests—are neglecting a fundamental condition of contemporary social life and, most likely, obscuring their own gendered subtext.

2. Work is a key site for the organization of gender identity and power relations, and gender is a central mechanism and outcome of organizing work. For example, gender is used as a means to create divisions and hierarchies of labor (mechanism), and certain gendered arrangements become predictable as these divisions and hierarchies become institutionalized (outcome). Hence, organization is fundamentally gendered in process and product. As this premise implies, feminist organizational communication scholars tend to operationalize organization as workplace, even as most remain cognizant that "work" is an ideological construct that can function to erase women's labor (for more on this point, see premise 9).

3. Dominant configurations of gender systematically privilege men/ masculinity relative to women/femininity. Dominant forms of organizing,

ranging from conventional bureaucracy to contemporary technocracy, serve as institutionalized "carriers" of gendered (dis)advantage and, therefore, cannot be presumed neutral.

4. That said, there is no neat picture of domination and subordination to be drawn. For one, feminist organizational communication scholars increasingly recognize that gender cannot be understood adequately apart from other primary ways of articulating identity and power, such as race, sexuality, class, and ability. Furthermore, even "rigid" systems of gender domination are fraught with contradiction and so supply at least some tools that can be used to undermine them. Put simply, relations of power yield loopholes and resources for resistance. As even these two observations suggest, organizational forms, gender identities, and power relations are neither static nor determined; they may reflect a predictable momentum, but they are always also contingent and shifting.

5. Gender, power, and organization are ongoing accomplishments, constantly achieved and destabilized in the mundane activity of everyday life. Thanks to this condition, social and organizational transformation is possible. Given the preceding premises, however, arriving at some utopian state of gendered organizational relations is not possible; and change is far more likely to be gradual, local, and cyclical (or nonprogressive) than revolutionary, universal, and linear.

6. Communication is the process through which gender, power, and organization are accomplished. Accordingly, it is a crucial site of control, resistance, and transformation. By "communication," I believe most feminist organizational scholars in our field mean something along these lines: the dynamic, situated, embodied, and contested process of creating systems of gendered meanings and identities by invoking, articulating, and/or altering available discourses.

7. To mark communication as the central organizing process is *not* to deny material realities beyond communication. Rather, the claim is that communication mediates our knowledge of and relation to material conditions and, thus, merits particular attention. From most feminist perspectives, this is a crucial clarification, for it both avows gender as a social construction and affirms that systems of domination create enduring realities that affect women and men in tangible ways that transcend time and space.

8. Hence, gendered systems of privilege and oppression are not limited to the domain of symbols and discourse; they create institutional, economic, corporeal—in a word, lived—effects. Put simply, they are manifest materially,

that is to say, in the "real world." In light of previous premises (e.g., #5), activism directed toward improving "real-life" conditions for women and men is possible and vital. Consequently, most feminist organizational communication scholars are intensely committed to praxis, or the development of theories that move to reconstruct, not merely deconstruct, alternative ways of gendering organization.

9. Of particular concern is de- and reconstructing the relation between "public" and "private" spheres of human activity. The historical formation of the public-private split has produced enduring material consequences, including the exclusion and control of women in the public sphere; the denial of women's domestic work as legitimate labor; the devaluation of feminized labor in the public sphere; the isolation of women that encourages them to read patriarchal patterns as a private matter of personal experience, thereby minimizing organized resistance and public airing; the illusion of gender-blind bureaucratic objectivity and rationality, which depends on the organizational suppression of emotions, sexuality, and other feminized phenomena; the construction of work-family conflicts as a private responsibility—and the list goes on.

Feminist scholars apply these premises to the conduct of research as well. For example, they take theorizing as a kind of organizational communication practice—a meta-practice, perhaps—that also organizes gender relations but tends to cloak that function in a discourse of scientific objectivity. Accordingly, they tend to hold scholars accountable for practicing reflexivity regarding the relation between knower and known, or exploring relevant connections among one's personal experience, political location, and intellectual activity. In this sense, feminist scholars maintain not only that "the personal is political" but also that matters of ontology and epistemology are profoundly personal *and* political. With that in mind, I suspect my own history of affiliation with feminism and organizational communication could usefully complicate the account provided thus far.

The Development of a Feminist Organizational Communication Scholar: (How) Can Private Tales Inform Public Narratives?

My investment in the tale I have told thus far may already be transparent. As I noted from the outset, to claim feminist (rather than, say, critical) theoretical origins for feminist organizational communication scholarship is to argue for a certain kind of autonomy, legitimacy, and influence. Moreover, a brief glance at a recent book I coauthored with Dennis Mumby (Ashcraft & Mumby, 2004) would reveal that much of the argument and premises outlined above support our vision for the field, as much as I sincerely believe that many feminist communication scholars share these basic commitments. In part, what distinguishes feminist theories is their willingness to acknowledge, without apology, the ideological and political dimensions of their discourse. The underlying rationale, of course, is that all theories harbor these features, though few are prepared to expose them.

Of course, the politics of intellectual pursuits run deeper than my preliminary admissions of personal investment would suggest. My own struggle to engage feminism in our field reflects some of the ways in which gender identities, scholarly selves, and institutional logics intersect, as well as the messy and ironic practices through which "real" people navigate such intersections.

As noted earlier, my development as a feminist scholar coincided with the history traced above. In 1993, I arrived as a PhD student at the University of Colorado, Boulder. When asked to describe my research interests, my catch phrase was something like "the study of gender and conflict in organizational settings." Truthfully, I had little idea what that meant, and even less of a clue that gender was hardly on the register of mainstream organizational communication studies at the time. It didn't take long to figure out the latter. After a bit of nosing around, I got the strong sense that opting to study gender was like signing up to sit on the sidelines. From a management professor, for instance, I heard the sage tidbit, "Study something big and central first, because you can always switch to gender once you're established." I didn't like that sort of advice, but I certainly understood it. After all, why cut myself off needlessly from a chance to play with the big boys (oh, and girls)?

But, for whatever reason, I couldn't shake the interest in gender. While supportive, my professors confessed that they knew little about feminism or gender, much less where to direct me for applications of these issues to organization studies. Although it was tangential to her own research program on computer-mediated communication, Brenda J. Allen graciously agreed to supervise an independent study on the matter. I began to find and read the early-1990s essays reviewed earlier, and thanks to a series of transformative conversations with Brenda J. that semester, I resolved to risk a marginalized academic identity. I chose a different spin from that advised by the management professor. Namely, I maintained that I had fortuitously joined the field just at the time that feminism was "gaining a voice" in organizational communication studies (Buzzanell, 1994), so perhaps I could have a hand in that process, or at least I could cast my work as on the cusp rather than peripheral (a fine line, to be sure). Consciously, I made two related decisions. First, I would try to situate my work as a kind of translation, bringing feminist insights to mainstream organization audiences. Second, in response to the abstract tone of many of the early-1990s critiques, in light of my increasing passion for ethnography, and because of my general inclination toward feasible "solutions" to "real-life" problems, I would try to distinguish my work as providing an empirical base and as emphasizing actual organization practice. In many respects, my work has been shaped by those goals ever since (e.g., Ashcraft, 2000; Ashcraft & Pacanowsky, 1996).

For the most part, I've opted to keep personal struggles with doing feminist research to myself, though I've heard that my ambivalence lurks in my scholarly writing. In a rare confessional moment several years ago, I wrote a piece about the development of my academic identity, which was published as part of a *Management Communication Quarterly* dialogue that grew out of a National Communication Association panel collaboration with Brenda J. (Ashcraft, 1998). There, I described the quandaries of a young woman grappling with the feminist moniker. I must confess that, on the few occasions I've had to re-read that piece, some embarrassment washes over me. Why should anyone care about another well-intentioned, white, middle-class, heterosexual woman's efforts to grapple with her part in privilege and oppression? While a critical process, its public airing can sound more cathartic and self-absorbed than insightful. I guess I'm never quite convinced that my private dilemmas amount to much more than that. What they offer to others or to the knowledge production process, how they inform the politics of public experience, how to articulate them without coming off as a self-indulgent whiner, how to minimize the risks of what feels like exposure—these and related doubts have long impelled me to avoid confessional discourse in favor of a realist representational voice (Van Maanen, 1988). Yet despite several problems I now see in my *MCQ* confessions, I must admit that some of the tensions I expressed there are even more pressing for me today. Upon reflection, I can see how they've shaped everything from the projects I've chosen, to the way I've written, to the professional identity and career path I've pursued ever since.

Take, for instance, my recent turn toward the study of masculinity. Beyond my intellectual interest, it was a sensible move for someone like me, who still feels like an ambivalent feminist and still resists what she sees as naively pro-feminine agendas. I've never been comfortable with what I perceive as the prevalent "feminist scripts" in our field (an insight about my reactions for which I thank Bryan Taylor), particularly when it comes to blanket celebrations or denigrations, respectively, of things associated with women and men, or to the proscribed role of sexuality and playful banter in organizational life. In this sense, my turn toward masculinity blends a healthy skepticism toward common renditions of femininity and feminism with a noxious strain of internalized misogyny, or at minimum, of internalized awe for many things masculine. At least, this is how I explain my internal feeling of pride and external display of disgust when I heard that a university colleague renowned for his sexism had pronounced, upon reading my proposal for a study of masculinity among airline pilots, "Finally, a gender study that's actually *interesting*!"

As that observation hints, I was drawn not merely to masculinity studies but to a project that hits ridiculously close to home: a study of gender, race, and class relations among commercial airline pilots. It's the cherished profession of my father, one of the most precious people in my life. Years of turbulent family relations and moderate health crises nourished between us a bond of rare intensity. Over the years, however, we've parted in politics—a painful split that continues to require periodic healing. In that light, my choice to pursue a project that takes a feminist approach to his profession looks odd indeed, as it requires me to direct a critical gaze at one of the things he holds most dear. From the study's inception, I knew he would be (and, I soon realized, has always been) my most difficult audience, the man about and for whom I write, even though he hasn't read a page of my work.

My father's not the only one in my family to don a pilot's uniform. His father and uncle were airline pilots as well—"pioneers" of flight, in many respects—and other male relatives flew for the military. The short version is that I grew up in the shadow of the pilot profession. As a little girl, I swelled with pride when the boys in my 3rd-grade class fawned over my father on career day. Then there was that smell on his overcoat each time he returned from a trip—an unforgettable potion of jet fuel, cigarette smoke, and what I took as unadulterated adventure. I used to watch my boy cousin don a uniform that hung off his little body, a captain's hat that eclipsed his eyes but not his satisfied smile. I learned to fly when I was 16 and briefly toyed with it as a possible career, until it dawned on me that life offered many important pursuits for a teenage girl, such as cheerleading and a vibrant social life. Maybe "stewardess" was more my style, I began to realize. It wasn't long before a close family friend slapped me on the back and teased, "Remember, kid, there's a reason they call it a cockpit." The joke must have struck a chord with me, for that's exactly what I seem to be studying: how the airline cockpit came to live up to its name.

Obviously, then, I can no longer deny the relevance of my private entanglements with my public scholarship. Perhaps for that reason, I'm growing fairly confident that the airline pilot project will be my undoing (she says, only half facetiously). The men in my family seem to haunt the data—sometimes literally, as when I came across an archived news article in which Captain Ashcraft (my grandfather) explained why women make for shifty airline pilots. More figuratively, I see my father everywhere in the data, including my apparently effective, knee-jerk habit of performing "admiring daughter" when soliciting information from senior, white, male pilots. As the profile of participants continues to expand, so does the repertoire of identity performances. Racial questions, for example, were part of the study's original design. After writing with Brenda J. about racial representations in organizational communication studies (Ashcraft & Allen, 2003), I knew it was high time to take race seriously in my own empirical work. As I've begun to affiliate with minority aviation organizations and to interview African American pilots, I've been overwhelmed with the simultaneous negotiations of race, gender, sexuality, and class in which I've participated. Reflecting anew on my interviews with white pilots, I've begun to see vividly how the relational maneuvering of research yields just as much evidence as the content of conversations (Kauffman, 1991). I can't help but notice how, during interviews and aviation archive visits, I often feel like an interloper, treading carefully and longingly on borrowed space and alternating among girlish sweetness, unabashed flirtation, and playing as "one of the boys." As I continue to gather data and anticipate the analytic process, I am beset by dilemmas of betrayal and loyalty, empathy and critique, compromise and confrontation. How can I weave an honest tale of dominance, entitlement, and exclusion when I also feel wonder, admiration, and envy? And then there's that familiar feeling that my research topic is second rate, or that I'm a wanna-be, a jealous critic—not a doer, not the real thing.

Without a doubt, the airline pilot project shatters all my comfortable notions of what counts as data. I simply can't refute that, as much as anything else, the research process has been about "selling" the worth and legitimacy of the project to diverse, at times competing aviation communities. And it's with some sadness that I realize, each time I make the case, that I'm also still trying to persuade myself. Never have I had my own judgments and projections, my own identity anxieties and ambivalences, my own participation in the power relations I claim to analyze, so clearly thrown in my face. Never have I understood how much these things necessarily infuse research, interpretation, and writing, and I suspect I've only begun to see. What little I've glimpsed thus far is teaching me how scholarly conventions and realist representations, for all their reassuring boundaries between self and study, private and public, obscure not only the politics of knowledge but also powerful evidence about what it means to do gender, race, class, and labor all at once.

The question, then, is not how I, as a white woman intimately tied to the profession I study, can possibly access or comprehend the masculinity and race dynamics at play. Instead, the question becomes, how can anyone? I suppose some feminist standpoint theorists might say that certain subject positions grant access to such knowledge. Or how about this: Maybe it's precisely in paying attention to how people *variously* positioned go about trying—to what that requires of participants and of us, to how we respond to those demands, to how we maneuver selves and affiliations that feel workable, to the ugly moments when it all breaks down—that we can begin to grasp those complex workings. A pithier version might be that we stand to learn a great deal when we take seriously the claim that we're doing what we study as we study it. How to usefully incorporate that awareness into scholarly writing—without, for example, awkward breaks or reckless narcissism—is another matter, one with which I continue to struggle (as you might have detected in reading this section). For that reason, I still sometimes fantasize that I'm the "real doctor" my mother wishes I were, complete with objectivity and detachment, possessed of patent knowledge and essential skills. Confronting the messy contradictions of feminist research is absurdly draining, and occasionally, I have to wonder with what payoff. I suppose time will tell if I'm up to these challenges, but it would be thinly veiled bravado if I claimed to be sure.

At its best, my tale of private struggle could be read to illuminate the complexity of engaging feminist organizational communication scholarship in "real life." The narrative attests to, for example, (a) the contradictory ways in which practicing scholarship can reinscribe gendered organizational patterns; (b) the precarious and often taboo dances of gender, race, sexuality, and class entailed in academic identities, projects, and institutions; (c) the deeply personal agendas and implications of public faces and labor; and (d) the tendency to erase or obscure links between theories of gendered organizing, scholarly practices, and personal experience (e.g., to treat gendered organizing as something that occurs elsewhere and, thus, to let ourselves "off the hook"). Of course, I also realize that readers may form less forgiving interpretations of my tale. Though it certainly was not my intent, some may read my story as a misplaced diary excerpt or, worse yet, as a flailing apology for my own insecurities and failings. Whatever your take (and I hope it leans toward the more generous), let me be clear about my purpose in confessing here: to engage readers in a candid conversation about the ways in which our work identities and activities enact and inform the gendered dynamics we claim to study. At the heart of feminist organizational inquiry is the relationship between public and private spheres, and the mundane, deeply personal politics of research can illuminate the contradictions, ambiguities, and ironies that form the intricate layers of that relationship. For my part, I hope to encourage and enact more reflexive scholarship that embraces, rather than sidesteps or mourns, the practical conflicts amid which most people negotiate working selves. It appears that control and resistance, power and pleasure, innovation and inadequacy often dwell in the same moments, and it is in the face of such paradox that we all struggle to navigate "workable" symbolic and material arrangements. Far from disabling, these kinds of complications indicate promising future directions for feminist theories of organizational communication.

Conclusion

In this chapter, I rendered one possible portrait of the body of scholarship known as feminist organizational communication studies—its relation to other projects in the field, its origins and development, its binding premises, and its latent tensions. As noted along the way, my depiction departs significantly from more typical renditions. I suppose that whether my interpretation resonates with you depends on your response to my central claims: First, in the brief span of a single decade, feminist inquiries in organizational communication have moved from barely peripheral status to occupy a vital, thriving presence in the field. Moreover, it is possible and productive to see feminist theory as independent of and parallel to, rather than derivative of, critical organizational communication studies (Ashcraft & Mumby, 2004). For instance, given its capacity to balance tricky theoretical tensions with steadfast commitment to praxis, feminism can serve as a model or guide for other critical projects. In addition, feminist voices arguably carry greater weight (or speak with more legitimacy, enjoy louder volume—proportionately, anyway) in organizational communication studies than they do in cognate areas of organization theory and research, such as management studies or organizational sociology. I believe that this particular strength suggests a timely opportunity for feminist organizational communication scholars to articulate their unique contribution to wider audiences.

Indeed, I sought to stimulate the development of that potential with this chapter. My attempt, in the third section of the essay, to distinguish assumptions shared by many communication scholars implied a related suggestion: the need for increased attention to communication as subject rather than merely object of study. In other words, I encourage the development of feminist *communication* theories of gendered organization, in addition to the more common emphasis on feminist perspectives *in* or *on* organizational communication.

Using my own experience as a source of illustration, I also suggested a need to address latent tensions haunting the relation between public and private domains, especially those surrounding the emotionality and sexuality of labor and research relations. The development of theories that respond to conflicted pressures endemic to everyday life may begin with candid assessment of our own working selves and communities. Clearly, we perform gendered organizing even as we investigate it. It becomes crucial, then, that we apply theoretical accounts of fragile identities and power relations, as well as the ongoing hegemonic processes that seem to secure them, to unravel our own tendencies toward binary and essentializing logics. In my view, it makes little sense to speak of who can legitimately do what sort of feminist scholarship and much more sense to examine how people, variously positioned, take on the dilemmas that beset most of us, albeit differently. In what ways, for example, might our own logics and practices of studying organization resist *and* reproduce gendered identities and institutions? Hence, I cautiously proposed that feminist organizational communication theory begin to include more systematically the sort of work experiences usually presumed private and reserved for personal sensemaking. Public reflection (not self-absorption, although a fine line may divide them) on the situated politics of doing scholarship can do more than disrupt safe yet tired professional scripts, stimulating complex, realistic responses to our own and other organizational communities. It can also yield a rich source of data that, as yet, remains largely untapped and underdeveloped in our analyses of gendered organizing.

Now, let's suppose that you resist some or all of these claims—that you find the portrait sketched here less than compelling. Very well, then, but do tell me more, for if it accomplishes nothing else, I hope this chapter will prompt you to engage feminist organizational communication theory and enliven the conversation.

Note

1. The reader may notice that I have omitted citations from this section, although varied inspirations for the premises identified may well be evident. However, by suspending the academic habit of assigning credit and aligning with some works while inevitably neglecting others, I hope to momentarily free the premises from entrenched theoretical "camps" and encourage readers to consider them at face value.

References

Acker, J. (1990). Hierarchies, jobs, bodies: A theory of gendered organizations. *Gender and Society, 4,* 139–158.

Acker, J., & Van Houten, D. R. (1974). Differential recruitment and control: The sex structuring of organizations. *Administrative Science Quarterly, 19,* 152–163.

Ahrens, L. (1980). Battered women's refuges: Feminist cooperatives vs. social service institutions. *Radical America, 14,* 41–47.

Allen, B. J. (1995). "Diversity" in organizations. *Journal of Applied Communication Research, 23,* 143–155.

Allen, B. J. (1996). Feminist standpoint theory: A black woman's (re)view of organizational socialization. *Communication Studies, 47,* 257–271.

Allen, B. J. (1998). Black womanhood and feminist standpoints. *Management Communication Quarterly, 11,* 575–586.

Alvesson, M. (1998). Gender relations and identity at work: A case study of masculinities and femininities in an advertising agency. *Human Relations, 51,* 969–1005.

Alvesson, M., & Billing, Y. D. (1992). Gender and organization: Toward a differentiated understanding. *Organization Studies, 13,* 73–102.

Alvesson, M., & Willmott, H. (Eds.). (1992). *Critical management studies.* Newbury Park, CA: Sage.

Ashcraft, K. L. (1998). "I wouldn't say I'm a feminist, but . . .": Organizational micropractice and gender identity. *Management Communication Quarterly, 11,* 587–597.

Ashcraft, K. L. (1999). Managing maternity leave: A qualitative analysis of temporary executive succession. *Administrative Science Quarterly, 44,* 240–280.

Ashcraft, K. L. (2000). Empowering "professional" relationships: Organizational communication meets feminist practice. *Management Communication Quarterly, 13,* 347–392.

Ashcraft, K. L. (2001). Organized dissonance: Feminist bureaucracy as hybrid form. *Academy of Management Journal, 44,* 1301–1322.

Ashcraft, K. L. (in press). Gender, discourse, and organizations: Framing a shifting relationship. In D. Grant, C. Hardy, C. Oswick, N. Phillips, & L. L. Putnam (Eds.), *Handbook of organizational discourse.* Thousand Oaks, CA: Sage.

Ashcraft, K. L., & Allen, B. J. (2003). The racial foundation of organizational communication. *Communication Theory, 13,* 5–38.

Ashcraft, K. L., & Flores, L. A. (2003). "Slaves with white collars": Decoding a contemporary crisis of masculinity. *Text and Performance Quarterly, 23,* 1–29.

Ashcraft, K. L., & Mumby, D. K. (2004). *Reworking gender: A feminist communicology of organization.* Thousand Oaks, CA: Sage.

Ashcraft, K. L., & Pacanowsky, M. E. (1996). "A woman's worst enemy": Reflections on a narrative of organizational life and female identity. *Journal of Applied Communication Research, 24,* 217–239.

Bate, B., & Taylor, A. (Eds.). (1988). *Women communicating: Studies of women's talk*. Norwood, NJ: Ablex.

Bell, E. L., & Forbes, L. C. (1994). Office folklore in the academic paperwork empire: The interstitial space of gendered (con)texts. *Text and Performance Quarterly, 14*, 181–196.

Bingham, S. G. (Ed.). (1994). *Conceptualizing sexual harassment as discursive practice*. Westport, CT: Praeger.

Bowen, S., & Wyatt, N. (Eds.). (1993). *Transforming visions: Feminist critiques in communication studies*. Cresskill, NJ: Hampton.

Brewis, J., & Linstead, S. (2000). *Sex, work and sex at work: Eroticizing the organization*. London: Routledge.

Bullis, C. (1993). At least it is a start. In S. A. Deetz (Ed.), *Communication Yearbook 16* (pp. 144–154). Newbury Park, CA: Sage.

Buzzanell, P. M. (1994). Gaining a voice: Feminist organizational communication theorizing. *Management Communication Quarterly, 7*, 339–383.

Buzzanell, P. M. (1995). Reframing the glass ceiling as a socially constructed process: Implications for understanding and change. *Communication Monographs, 62*, 327–354.

Buzzanell, P. M. (Ed.). (2000). *Rethinking organizational and managerial communication from feminist perspectives*. Thousand Oaks, CA: Sage.

Buzzanell, P. M., Ellingson, L., Silvio, C., Pasch, V., Dale, B., Mauro, G., et al. (1997). Leadership processes in alternative organizations: Invitational and dramaturgical leadership. *Communication Studies, 48*, 285–310.

Calás, M. B. (1993). Deconstructing charismatic leadership: Re-reading Weber from the darker side. *Leadership Quarterly, 4*, 305–328.

Calás, M. B., & Smircich, L. (1991). Voicing seduction to silence leadership. *Organization Studies, 12*, 567–602.

Calás, M. B., & Smircich, L. (1992). Re-writing gender into organizational theorizing: Directions from feminist perspectives. In M. Reed & M. Hughes (Eds.), *Rethinking organization: New directions in organization theory and analysis* (pp. 227–253). Newbury Park, CA: Sage.

Calás, M. B., & Smircich, L. (1993, March/April). Dangerous liaisons: The "feminine-in-management" meets "globalization." *Business Horizons*, 71–81.

Calás, M. B., & Smircich, L. (1996). From "the woman's point of view": Feminist approaches to organization studies. In S. R. Clegg, C. Hardy, & W. R. Nord (Eds.), *Handbook of organization studies* (pp. 218–257). Thousand Oaks, CA: Sage.

Carter, K., & Spitzack, C. (Eds.). (1989). *Doing research on women's communication: Perspectives on theory and method*. Norwood, NJ: Ablex.

Cheng, C. (Ed.). (1996). *Masculinities in organizations*. Thousand Oaks, CA: Sage.

Clair, R. P. (1993). The use of framing devices to sequester organizational narratives: Hegemony and harassment. *Communication Monographs, 60*, 113–136.

Clair, R. P. (2002). Book review. *Management Communication Quarterly, 16*, 118–122.

Collinson, D. (1992). *Managing the shop floor: Subjectivity, masculinity, and workplace culture*. New York: De Gruyter.

Collinson, D., & Hearn, J. (Eds.). (1996a). *Men as managers, managers as men: Critical perspectives on men, masculinities and managements*. London: Sage.

Collinson, D., & Hearn, J. (1996b). "Men" at "work": Multiple masculinities/ multiple workplaces. In M. Mac an Ghaill (Ed.), *Understanding masculinities: Social relations and cultural arenas* (pp. 61–76). Buckingham, UK: Open University Press.

Edley, P. P. (2000). Discursive essentializing in a woman-owned business: Gendered stereotypes and strategic subordination. *Management Communication Quarterly, 14*, 271–306.

Ferguson, K. (1984). *The feminist case against bureaucracy*. Philadelphia: Temple University Press.

Ferree, M. M., & Martin, P. (Eds.). (1995). *Feminist organizations: Harvest of the new women's movement*. Philadelphia: Temple University Press.

Fine, M. (1993). New voices in organizational communication: A feminist commentary and critique. In S. Bowen & N. Wyatt (Eds.), *Transforming visions: Feminist critiques in communication studies* (pp. 125–166). Cresskill, NJ: Hampton.

Fine, M. (2000). Walking the high wire: Leadership theorizing, daily acts, and tensions. In P. M. Buzzanell (Ed.), *Rethinking organizational and managerial communication from feminist perspectives* (pp. 128–156). Thousand Oaks, CA: Sage.

Gayle, B. M. (1994). Bounded emotionality in two all-female organizations: A feminist analysis. *Women's Studies in Communication, 17*(2), 1–19.

Gibson, M. K., & Papa, M. J. (2000). The mud, the blood, and the beer guys: Organizational osmosis in blue-collar work groups. *Journal of Applied Communication Research, 28*, 68–88.

Gregg, N. (1993). Politics of identity/politics of location: Women workers organizing in a postmodern world. *Women's Studies in Communication, 16*(1), 1–33.

Grimes, D. S. (2001). Putting our own house in order: Whiteness, change and organization studies. *Journal of Organizational Change Management, 14*, 132–149.

Hearn, J., Sheppard, D., Tancred-Sheriff, P., & Burrell, G. (Eds.). (1989). *The sexuality of organization*. London: Sage.

Helgesen, S. (1990). *The female advantage: Women's ways of leadership*. New York: Doubleday.

Holmer Nadesan, M. (1996). Organizational identity and space of action. *Organization Studies, 17*, 49–81.

Holmer Nadesan, M. (2001). Post-Fordism, political economy, and critical organizational communication studies. *Management Communication Quarterly, 15*, 259–267.

Holmer Nadesan, M., & Trethewey, A. (2000). Performing the enterprising subject: Gendered strategies for success (?). *Text and Performance Quarterly, 20*, 223–250.

Horgan, D. (1990, November-December). Why women sometimes talk themselves out of success and how managers can help. *Performance & Instruction,* 20–22.

Huspek, M., & Kendall, K. (1991). On withholding political voice: An analysis of the political vocabulary of a "nonpolitical" speech community. *The Quarterly Journal of Speech,* 77, 1–19.

Iannello, K. P. (1992). *Decisions without hierarchy: Feminist interventions in organizational theory and practice.* London: Routledge.

Jaggar, A. M. (1983). Political philosophies of women's liberation. In L. Richardson & V. Taylor (Eds.), *Feminist frontiers: Rethinking sex, gender, and society* (pp. 322–329). New York: Random House.

Jamieson, K. H. (1995). *Beyond the double bind: Women and leadership.* New York: Oxford University Press.

Jorgenson, J. (2002). Engineering selves: Negotiating gender and identity in technical work. *Management Communication Quarterly,* 15, 350–380.

Kanter, R. M. (1975). Women and the structure of organizations: Explorations in theory and behavior. In M. Millman & R. M. Kanter (Eds.), *Another voice: Feminist perspectives on social life and social science* (pp. 34–74). Garden City, NY: Anchor Books.

Kanter, R. M. (1977). *Men and women of the corporation.* New York: Basic Books.

Kanter, R. M., & Zurcher, L. A. (1973). Concluding statement: Evaluating alternatives and alternative valuing. *Journal of Applied Behavioral Science,* 9, 381–397.

Kauffman, B. J. (1991). Feminist facts: Interview strategies and political subjects in ethnography. *Communication Theory,* 2, 187–206.

Lont, C. M. (1988). Redwood Records: Principles and profit in women's music. In B. Bate & A. Taylor (Eds.), *Women communicating: Studies of women's talk* (pp. 233–250). Norwood, NJ: Ablex.

Maguire, M., & Mohtar, L. F. (1994). Performance and the celebration of a subaltern counterpublic. *Text and Performance Quarterly,* 14, 238–252.

Mansbridge, J. J. (1973). Time, emotion, and inequality: Three problems of participatory groups. *Journal of Applied Behavioral Science,* 9, 351–367.

Marshall, J. (1993). Viewing organizational communication from a feminist perspective: A critique and some offerings. In S. A. Deetz (Ed.), *Communication Yearbook 16* (pp. 122–141). Newbury Park, CA: Sage.

Martin, J. (1990). Deconstructing organizational taboos: The suppression of gender conflict in organizations. *Organization Science,* 1, 339–359.

Martin, P. Y. (1990). Rethinking feminist organizations. *Gender and Society,* 4, 182–206.

Mayer, A. M. (1995, May). *Feminism-in-practice: Implications for feminist theory.* Paper presented at the annual conference of the International Communication Association, Chicago, IL.

Meyerson, D. E., & Kolb, D. M. (2000). Moving out of the "armchair": Developing a framework to bridge the gap between feminist theory and practice. *Organization,* 7, 553–571.

Mies, M. (1983). Towards a methodology for feminist research. In G. Bowles & R. D. Klein (Eds.), *Theories of women's studies* (pp. 117–139). London: Routledge & Kegan Paul.

Mies, M. (1991). Women's research or feminist research? The debate surrounding feminist science and methodology. In M. M. Fonow & J. A. Cook (Eds.), *Beyond methodology: Feminist scholarship as lived research* (pp. 60–84). Bloomington: Indiana University Press.

Mills, A. J., & Chiaramonte, P. (1991). Organization as gendered communication act. *Canadian Journal of Communication, 16,* 381–398.

Mills, A. J., & Tancred, P. (Eds.). (1992). *Gendering organizational analysis.* Newbury Park, CA: Sage.

Morgen, S. (1994). Personalizing personnel decisions in feminist organizational theory and practice. *Human Relations, 47,* 665–684.

Mumby, D. K. (1993). Feminism and the critique of organizational communication studies. In S. Deetz (Ed.), *Communication Yearbook 16* (pp. 155–166). Newbury Park, CA: Sage.

Mumby, D. K. (1996). Feminism, postmodernism, and organizational communication: A critical reading. *Management Communication Quarterly, 9,* 259–295.

Mumby, D. K. (1998). Organizing men: Power, discourse, and the social construction of masculinity(s) in the workplace. *Communication Theory, 8,* 164–183.

Mumby, D. K., & Putnam, L. L. (1992). The politics of emotion: A feminist reading of bounded rationality. *Academy of Management Review, 17,* 465–486.

Murphy, A. G. (1998). Hidden transcripts of flight attendant resistance. *Management Communication Quarterly, 11,* 499–535.

Murphy, B. O., & Zorn, T. (1996). Gendered interaction in professional relationships. In J. T. Wood (Ed.), *Gendered relationships* (pp. 213–232). Mountain View, CA: Mayfield.

Natalle, E. J. (1996). Gendered issues in the workplace. In J. T. Wood (Ed.), *Gendered relationships* (pp. 253–274). Mountain View, CA: Mayfield.

Natalle, E. J., Papa, M. J., & Graham, E. E. (1994). Feminist philosophy and the transformation of organizational communication. In B. Kovacic (Ed.), *New approaches to organizational communication* (pp. 245–270). Albany: SUNY Press.

Newman, K. (1980). Incipient bureaucracy: The development of hierarchies in egalitarian organizations. In G. M. Britan & R. Cohen (Eds.), *Hierarchy and society* (pp. 143–163). Philadelphia: Institute for the Study of Human Issues.

Pierce, J. L. (1995). *Gender trials: Emotional lives in contemporary law firms.* Berkeley: University of California Press.

Putnam, L. L. (1990). *Feminist theories, dispute processes, and organizational communication.* Paper presented at the Arizona State University Conference on Organizational Communication, Tempe, AZ.

Reardon, K. (1997). Dysfunctional communication patterns in the workplace: Closing the gap between men and women. In D. Dunn (Ed.), *Workplace/ women's place: An anthology* (pp. 165–180). Los Angeles: Roxbury.

Reinelt, C. (1994). Fostering empowerment, building community: The challenge for state-funded feminist organizations. *Human Relations, 47*, 685–705.

Reinharz, S. (1992). *Feminist methods in social research*. New York: Oxford University Press.

Ristock, J. L. (1990). Canadian feminist social service collectives: Caring and contradictions. In L. Albrecht & R. M. Brewer (Eds.), *Bridges of power: Women's multicultural alliances* (pp. 172–181). Philadelphia: New Society Publishers.

Rodriguez, N. M. (1988). Transcending bureaucracy: Feminist politics at a shelter for battered women. *Gender and Society, 2*, 214–227.

Rosener, J. B. (1990). Ways women lead. *Harvard Business Review, 68*, 119–125.

Rothschild-Whitt, J. (1976). Conditions for facilitating participatory-democratic organizations. *Sociological Inquiry, 46*, 75–86.

Rothschild-Whitt, J. (1979). The collectivist organization: An alternative to rational bureaucratic models. *American Sociological Review, 44*, 509–527.

Savage, M., & Witz, A. (Eds.). (1992). *Gender and bureaucracy* (Vol. 39). Oxford, UK: Blackwell/The Sociological Review.

Seccombe-Eastland, L. (1988). Ideology, contradiction, and change in a feminist bookstore. In B. Bate & A. Taylor (Eds.), *Women communicating: Studies of women's talk* (pp. 251–276). Norwood, NJ: Ablex.

Shuler, S. (2000, November). *Breaking through the glass ceiling without breaking a nail: Portrayal of women executives in the popular business press*. Paper presented at the annual conference of the National Communication Association, Seattle, WA.

Sotirin, P., & Gottfried, H. (1999). The ambivalent dynamics of secretarial "bitching": Control, resistance, and the construction of identity. *Organization, 6*, 57–80.

Spradlin, A. (1998). The price of "passing": A lesbian perspective on authenticity in organizations. *Management Communication Quarterly, 11*, 598–605.

Staley, C. C. (1988). The communicative power of women managers: Doubts, dilemmas, and management development programs. In C. A. Valentine & N. Hoar (Eds.), *Women and communicative power: Theory, research, and practice* (pp. 36–48). Annandale, VA: Speech Communication Association.

Stewart, L. P., & Clarke-Kudless, D. (1993). Communication in corporate settings. In L. P. Arliss & D. J. Borisoff (Eds.), *Women and men communicating* (pp. 142–152). Fort Worth, TX: Harcourt Brace Jovanovich.

Tannen, D. (1994). *Talking from 9 to 5: Women and men in the workplace: Language, sex, and power*. New York: Avon Books.

Taylor, A. (1988). Implementing feminist principles in a bureaucracy: Studio D The National Film Board of Canada. In B. Bate & A. Taylor (Eds.), *Women communicating: Studies of women's talk* (pp. 277–302). Norwood, NJ: Ablex.

Taylor, B. C., & Conrad, C. (1992). Narratives of sexual harassment: Organizational dimensions. *Journal of Applied Communication Research, 20*, 401–418.

Taylor, V. (1995). Watching for vibes: Bringing emotions into the study of feminist organizations. In M. M. Ferree & P. Y. Martin (Eds.), *Feminist organizations: Harvest of the new women's movement* (pp. 223–233). Philadelphia: Temple University Press.

Tong, R. (1989). *Feminist thought: A comprehensive introduction.* Boulder, CO: Westview.

Townsley, N. C., & Geist, P. (2000). The discursive enactment of hegemony: Sexual harassment and academic organizing. *Western Journal of Communication, 64,* 190–217.

Trethewey, A. (1997). Resistance, identity, and empowerment: A postmodern feminist analysis of clients in a human service organization. *Communication Monographs, 64,* 281–301.

Trethewey, A. (1999a). Disciplined bodies. *Organization Studies, 20,* 423–450.

Trethewey, A. (1999b). Isn't it ironic: Using irony to explore the contradictions of organizational life. *Western Journal of Communication, 63,* 140–167.

Trethewey, A. (2000). Revisioning control: A feminist critique of disciplined bodies. In P. M. Buzzanell (Ed.), *Rethinking organizational and managerial communication from feminist perspectives* (pp. 107–127). Thousand Oaks, CA: Sage.

Trethewey, A. (2001). Reproducing and resisting the master narrative of decline: Midlife professional women's experiences of aging. *Management Communication Quarterly, 15,* 183–226.

Triece, M. E. (1999). The practical true woman: Reconciling women and work in popular mail-order magazines, 1900–1920. *Critical Studies in Mass Communication, 16,* 42–62.

Van Maanen, J. (1988). *Tales of the field: On writing ethnography.* Chicago: University of Chicago Press.

Wiley, M. G., & Eskilson, A. (1985). Speech style, gender stereotypes, and corporate success: What if women talk more like men? *Sex Roles, 12,* 993–1007.

Wilkins, B. M., & Anderson, P. A. (1991). Gender differences and similarities in management communication. *Management Communication Quarterly, 5,* 6–35.

Wood, J. T., & Conrad, C. (1983). Paradox in the experience of professional women. *Western Journal of Speech Communication, 47,* 305–322.

Wyatt, N. (1988). Shared leadership in the weavers guild. In B. Bate & A. Taylor (Eds.), *Women communicating: Studies of women's talk* (pp. 147–176). Norwood, NJ: Ablex.

8

Structuration Theory

Marshall Scott Poole

Robert D. McPhee

Some ideas and events can be attributed to the zeitgeist, the spirit of the times, rather than to any single scholar or group. Structuration is one such idea.

Starting in the early 1960s, there was a debate in many disciplines on the relationship of human behavior and communication to social structures. The most prominent line of social scientific communication scholarship at this time was based on social psychology and searched for causes of behavior such as underlying dispositions and attitudes, external cues such as messages, and contextual factors such as interpersonal relationships and status. This research searched for general relationships using experimental and survey methods and emphasized statistical analysis. One problem with this school of thought was that it tended to downplay the role of social structure. For instance, in organizational communication it led to a focus on manager-subordinate relationships, groups, and communication networks, and directed attention away from social institutions or large-scale structures such as inter-organizational networks. Communication network analysis, the one type of research that had the potential to illuminate larger structures, did not help much: at the time theories of networks tended to be grounded in individual level processes such as balance, rather than structural principles. When they were attended to, the properties of systems were most often cast as constraints on behavior that acted from outside the individuals involved.

An alternative view was advanced by scholars who argued that human action and interaction generated social reality. Roots of this tradition in the United States extend to the pragmatists John Dewey and William James and the symbolic interactionist thought of George Herbert Mead and J. H. Cooley. Two particularly influential books were Peter Berger and Thomas Luckmann's phenomenological *The Social Construction of Reality* (1966) and analytic philosopher Ludwig Wittgenstein's *Philosophical Investigations* (1958). In the 1960s and early 1970s, the action view was strongly expressed by the ethnomethodologist Herbert Garfinkel (1967), who focused on the methods people use to construct everyday life, and the dramaturgical analysis of Erving Goffman (1959), who emphasized the social construction of roles and situations. Many in the communication field were attracted to this emphasis on the role of action. It fit with the common assumption that communication was a process.

We were exposed to both of these traditions as graduate students. We were drawn into communication studies as college debaters under Donald Cushman at Michigan State University. Cushman was a founder of communication rules theory, and he exposed us to the literature of symbolic interactionism, analytic philosophy, and even a little critical theory, along with rhetorical theory. But Michigan State was also a hotbed of behavioral communication studies, and much of our research as graduate students reflected that paradigm. Poole went on to doctoral studies at the University of Wisconsin under eclectic behavioral scientists Joseph Cappella and Dean Hewes; McPhee earned his doctorate under Cushman at MSU. In short, we both did lots of reading in the action tradition, but we still were strongly influenced by behavioral and empiricist methods and theories.

Both of us were hired as assistant professors at the University of Illinois. At Illinois, action approaches were booming, with scholars such as Jesse Delia, Ruth Anne Clark, Larry Grossberg, Cheris Kramarae, and later Barbara and Daniel O'Keefe teaching constructivism, phenomenology, conversational analysis, Marxism, and the early literature of poststructuralism. This was a great time for learning but also a frustrating encounter, because the action approaches were developed in a highly individualistic way that was compatible with cognitive social psychology. There seemed to be no room for organizations and no clear connection between powerful organizational ideas and a conception of human action.

In 1979, we found Anthony Giddens's *Central Problems in Social Theory* (1979) in Chicago's famous Seminary Cooperative Bookstore. It was a revelation. Giddens developed action theory in a way that recognized and corrected its weakness in dealing with institutions. Giddens used his new position, called structuration theory, to articulate important and highly insightful critiques of major interpretive and poststructuralist positions, as well as of the functionalist systems theory. Better still, structuration theory avoided the typical knee-jerk rejection of quantitative methods and empirical propositions that characterized much interpretive and critical theorizing (and continues to do so today). His critiques were accompanied by reformulations of empirical ideas that were compatible with interpretive and critical studies. Best of all, Giddens's theory was rigorous and internally coherent.

The theory of structuration enabled communication scholars to "have their cake and eat it too." It encompassed both social structure and human action in a common framework that could explain individual behavior and the development and effects of social institutions such as the economy, religion, and government. Structuration theory emphasized the role of processes in the constitution of society and, thus, fit well with conceptions of communication as a process. It encompassed stability and change as well, enabling communication scholars to study and understand both in terms of the same theory. It also offered an understanding of how different levels of analysis— individual, group, organization, society—related to one another, and it allowed powerful communication theorizing at a truly organizational level of analysis.

We began to write articles proposing structuration theory as a general metatheory for communication studies (McPhee & Poole, 1980) and, in collaboration with David Seibold, as a foundation for group communication theory (Poole, Seibold, & McPhee, 1985). Our first application in organizational communication was to the study of organizational climate (Poole & McPhee, 1983). Other organizational communication scholars who worked with structuration theory early on included Patty Riley (1983; cf. Banks & Riley, 1993) and Charles Conrad (1983). Interest in the perspective spread fast, in part because of the rise of interpretive and cultural views of organizations.

In the next section, we discuss the main principles of Giddens's structuration theory. Following this, we will explore several examples of organizational communication research employing structuration theory. We will conclude by considering debates and controversies in structuration theory, strengths and weaknesses in the theory, and future directions.

Main Concepts of Structuration Theory

Suppose you are a member of a team that has to produce a report about some department or unit in your university and you choose the library. Like all large units in any organization, the library can be seen as an organization in its own right, with employees, administrators, customers, suppliers, and so on. Your report might stress structural aspects of the library such as its departments (reference, circulation, etc.), the number of books it owns, and its number and types of employees. However, if the theory of structuration guided your research, your viewpoint on many of these topics would be quite different than if you used more traditional theories.

System/Practice/Structure

Structuration theory (ST) would focus your attention on the library as a *system* comprising departments (circulation, lost and found, new acquisitions, etc.) that are interrelated by their place in the organizational structure of the library and by various procedures. But for ST, the system is not a system of objects (like parts of an auto engine)—it is a system of *human practices*. Practices are patterns of activity that are meaningful to those engaged in them, such as ordering new books or attending a meeting to plan a library orientation. Practices organize human activities in relation to one another; for instance, in the new acquisitions process, assistants might first compile lists of desirable books, with the manager deciding what to order based on the unit's budget. In this case, the practice prescribes the sequence of actions and the budget as the final criterion for what can be ordered. Practices involve improvisation, because there are always differences in how they are carried out, depending on the context. For example, an overworked manager of the acquisitions department might decide to change the acquisition process to give her assistants more influence. If this worked out, she might make it part of formal procedures. Practices can be very small in scale— answering a question is a practice, as is grabbing a book off the shelf. But practices can be on a large scale, too—library management is a practice, as is the 2-month process of auditing the library's expenditures.

In traditional systems theory, the structure of the library system refers to the relations among its operations and divisions. However, in ST those relations are regarded as part of the system itself, and *structure* has a more specialized meaning. ST defines systems as observable patterns of relationships in practices, which include relations among operations and divisions. For ST, *structure* is the rules and resources drawn on by actors in taking part in system practices. A *rule* is any principle or routine that guides people's actions. For instance, the library's shelving area might be called "the dungeon"; that label is a rule telling people what to call the area and conveying its dank isolation. A *resource* is anything people are able to use in action, whether material (money, tools) or nonmaterial (knowledge, skill). In the library, budgets are one important resource, as is a degree in library science that gives librarians special knowledge.

Production and Reproduction—The Duality of Structure

We now come to a central idea of structuration theory. Structuration theory holds that when we draw on structural rules and resources to act within a social system of practices, we also keep that system going—in the technical terminology of ST and other social theories, we *reproduce* the system and its structure. When we use the library electronic catalog to find a book, we find out the book's location on the shelves, but we simultaneously keep the catalog "alive" as a useful resource. That is reproduction, and it happens in a number of ways: We maintain our skills in using the catalog, we avoid asking staff to find the book and motivating them to develop another process for finding books, and we add one to the count of customers of the catalog kept in the computer. On the other hand, if we encounter a problem, we might complain to the library staff and urge them to change the catalog's interface. This negative outcome contributes to reproduction, too, although this type of reproduction also involves *transformation* of the system. "Reproduction" doesn't imply that the system endures without change; instead, a transformation is reproduction of the system in a new direction. Most libraries have electronic catalog software that programmers could easily adapt to allow low-resolution pictures of book authors to show up as part of every catalog entry, and we're thankful they don't transform things that way because it would really slow down using electronic catalogs.

The key idea in ST is that every action, every episode of interaction, has two aspects: It "produces" the practices of which it is part (e.g., finding books), and it "reproduces" the system and its structure, usually in a small way, as changed or stable. Structuration theory thus explains the system itself as the product of human actions operating through a duality in which structures are both the medium and the outcome of actions. The library is not a giant institution that exists independent of its customers and employees; as an organization, it is produced and reproduced in human interaction. Interaction, including communication, is thus amazingly powerful (although ST does recognize that the amount of transformation possible through the actions of a single group of employees or customers is usually very small). Later in this chapter, we discuss research that has shown how people both produce and reproduce the structural resources of organizations.

Agency

Some communication theorists today try to argue that the "age of the human" is past and that we should explain communication phenomena using only regularities inside communication itself. Structuration theorists are opponents of that move. They argue that several facts about human beings are always assumed whenever people explain communication.

First, people have three levels of consciousness. The first is *discursive consciousness*, which refers to things we can put into words; we are aware of some rules and resources in such a way that we can express and explain them to others and use them to give an account of our actions. The second is *practical consciousness*, the knowledge and skills that we can't put into words but use in action—for instance, riding a bicycle or reading someone's personality. Librarians and most other workers can tell what the atmosphere in their office is as soon as they step in the door—conflictful, hurried—just by looking at other people's faces, but it would be difficult for them to explain this in any detail.

The third level of consciousness is *the unconscious*—experiences that we cannot easily call to any level of awareness. This level is important because it is the repository of many childhood insecurities about life that are excluded from our awareness by our sense that everyday life is meaningful and routine. If something odd or threatening happens, we work to find meaning for it; otherwise, we work to keep everyday routines going (even if the routine is "going out every night and searching for excitement"). This work is what Giddens calls our "ontological security system," and its tendency toward routine helps explain the routines people accept in organizations.

Another important fact about human agents is that they are *knowledgeable*. Organization members know a lot about their usual surroundings—where the returned books go, where the soda machine is, what carrels are available for quiet study. They depend on this knowledge for their everyday routines, but in a practical way: They may not know how to program the library computers, but if they've used the catalog enough they know shortcuts and glitches.

Finally, human agents have the ability to *reflexively monitor* their conduct. Library workers, for instance, can think about what they are doing, map out a schedule, and decide what tasks they want to avoid or tasks that really have to be done to avoid crisis. Giddens does not think groups can be agents, but he allows that groups, and even organizations and societies, can engage in this kind of reflexive monitoring, too, in a process he calls *institutional reflexivity*. Organizations can do this by gathering information about their operations—including the surveillance of workers and their productivity—and using the information to change to become more efficient.

Three Dimensions or Modalities of Action

Structuration theory also tells us to watch for three aspects in any social system or social interaction episode: meaning, power, and norms. These are a part of every interaction. If a library manager asks a librarian, "Could you stay a little late to help shelve books?" the librarian can interpret the message as not a simple request but an order—that is its meaning. The librarian knows whether the manager has the power to give that order and make it stick—it might be against union rules to demand overtime work without pay, for instance. Finally, the librarian knows whether it is legitimate for the manager to ask. There might be lots of books needing shelving, or other librarians may have stayed late other days, so by the norms of fair exchange it is this one's turn. Structuration theory notes that these three aspects of action can be distinguished but are interwoven. Most important, the system of meanings and communication practices in the library may be constructed or used in a way that gives unequal power to some employees (generally the managers) and makes their power seem legitimate. In the example we have been discussing, the manager makes his order sound like a request—much more humane than a demand. And the words "a little" have an ambiguity that the manager can exploit, because it seems like not much to ask, but once the employee starts shelving, "a little" may stretch into several hours.

Because power is involved in all aspects of life as one of the modalities of structuration, a central focus of ST is on how power can be used to dominate social systems. This critical focus on understanding how some agents can use resources to control aspects of a system for their own interests is a central aspect of ST. Typically, though not always, the operation of power is hidden in complexities of the system, so it is often necessary for scholars to carefully delve into deeper layers of the structurational process to grasp the locations of power. For example, the library manager is likely to have a degree in library science that certifies her as qualified to manage employees, who generally have less formal backgrounds. The schools of library science, which carefully control who is allowed to study and how degrees are given, thus become part of a circuit of resources that underlie the manager's authority. The privileging of credentials helps the manager to control employees because the manager and employees are playing on an uneven field. In this case, the domination of employees by managers is fairly innocuous, but it may also lead to concrete harm to the employee. Kirby and Krone (2002), for example, used ST to analyze cases in which employees were prevented from taking maternity leave to care for their newborn infants; the means of control were pressure and negative interpretations of taking leave that were structured in their organizations.

Institutions and Action

Where do structures come from? In some cases, they are created by agents, as when a librarian invents a new type of classification system. Most of the time, however, they are borrowed or appropriated from existing bodies of rules and resources. Throughout our lives, we are taught structures and how to use them in our families, schools, workplaces, and places of worship, as well as by the media. Organizations present us with a ready-made stock of structures and other employees who are willing to show us how they figure in organizational practices. When structures are in discursive consciousness, they can be explicitly explained to us; student workers in the library, for instance, may be given a procedures manual. Many structural features, however, are in practical consciousness—we use them, but we cannot explain how, and sometimes we are not aware of them—and in these cases, we "learn by doing" as we engage in various organizational practices. The structures scattered throughout society are inevitably adapted to specific contexts in which they are produced and reproduced, but there are also more general patterns of structures. For example, we know what the characteristics of a generic library are—it has books and librarians, you can check out books, it is publicly funded, and it is a "common good," open for all to use. This generic notion of library is a *social institution* that provides a model for setting up libraries and for using them.

Social institutions are those parts of a society that are regarded as important by its members and are taken for granted. Examples of institutions in U.S. society include the library, the school, the larger educational system of which these are a part, the Super Bowl, the U.S. government, synagogues, and the capitalist economic system. As these examples indicate, institutions can exist at various levels, from a specific entity like the Super Bowl, to fairly standard organizations like libraries, all the way up to diffuse and complex entities like the capitalist economic system. Institutions usually transcend particular cases, and they are built up and last over very long periods of time. Major resources in the society are devoted to supporting and sustaining institutions. They provide stability to the systems and structures in a society because members of the society draw structures from them and use them to understand the structuring processes they encounter in day-to-day life. You can walk into a library in Percy, Illinois, or in San Francisco and pretty much know how your transactions are going to work because the institution of the library has been nurtured over the years. It provides a model for the design of libraries (the modalities of meaning and norms), attracts social resources for libraries (the power modality) because libraries are valued in our society, and provides a pattern for us to engage in library practices.

The idea of duality of structure also implies that institutions are built up through continuous practices. In a real sense, every time we engage in a practice, we are helping to produce and reproduce the institutions that undergird it—the library, language, and so on. This implies that institutions can be changed through structuration and that our activities can, in tiny ways, contribute to their survival or demise. Institutions seem so stable that this may seem to be stretching a point, but remember that in 1900 there were people who claimed that the automobile was a fad and that we'd never give up horses as a primary transportation mode. Decades of changes in practice, as people one by one bought cars and developed an economy and infrastructure built around automobiles, ultimately led to the exile of horses to the recreational realm.

Giddens regards the modalities of structuration discussed in the previous section as the link between action and institutions. To put it in the terminology of ST, as agents engage in practices, they draw on structures grounded in the institutional realm and produce and reproduce them in the structuring of meaning, norms, and power. This contextualizes the structures to a particular practice and has the potential to change the institution, if particular modes of action that change the structure become widely established in the society.

Time and Space

Structuration theory emphasizes the role of time and especially space in human affairs, including organizational communication. The library is divided into different *locales*, within which very different patterns of communication and different patterns of structuration take place. The areas for library patrons are separated from staff areas by walls, desks, and counters, and much library work takes place outside the presence of customers. Communication routines are very different in the lobby, at the circulation desk, at billing, and back in cataloging. There are special desks for checking out books and face-to-face help, but in many cases customers' deepest access into library processes is via the Internet.

This fact brings us to a key insight Giddens stressed about organizations: They are *power containers*. They can exercise, and supply to users, tremendous power because of several features. First, they bring together workers, resources (the books), administrators, and records of performance in a concentrated arena where work can be organized and controlled. Library customers can come in and consult a wealth of books easily. Indeed, libraries are set up alike to allow customers brand-new to a region to use them, a phenomenon that Giddens calls the *disembedding* of organizations (and other relationships, too, in more modern times) from particular times and places. Second, there is a specific schedule for work, allowing for surveillance of workers' efficiency and for control of worker and organizational performance. Third, since earliest history, technologies have allowed organizations to extend their control from these power centers to outlying regions. At first, writing served this purpose; now, a variety of communication and transportation media—telephones, the Internet, mobile libraries—"bind" space and time in new patterns with significance different from the old barriers of separation. Giddens calls the construction of new spatio-temporal arrangements *distanciation.*

Reflections

Structuration theory is a useful theory for communication because it focuses squarely on interaction as the arena in which structuring occurs. It is also useful for understanding communication because it is a process-based theory. It explains how social systems such as organizations are produced and reproduced through ongoing structuration processes. Rather than regarding them as static, "solid" entities, ST shows how organizations are created and sustained by human action and how, potentially, they can be changed. Structuration theory also has the potential to bring a critical edge to the analysis of organizational systems because it charges scholars to look for the role of power and domination in structuring processes that underlie organizations. Because it is closely tied to the understanding of practices, ST has the potential to yield knowledge that is eminently practical: As we come to understand structuring processes, we give people insights into how systems can be changed or designed differently.

Applications of Structuration Theory in Organizational Communication

More than 50 studies in the organizational communication field and several hundred on topics related to organizational communication have been informed by structuration theory. It is not possible to cover them all, but we can detail some applications of the theory that exemplify how it has been used by different scholars.

At the Individual Level

One main focus of research in organizational communication has been the *identification* individuals develop with organizations; structuration theory has proven valuable in making our views of it richer. Organizational identification is linked not only to commitment to an organization but also to personal identity, because our relationships to organizations and social groups—workplaces, religious institutions, clubs, neighborhoods—are often important parts of our identities. Scott, Corman, and Cheney (1998) developed a structurational model of organizational identification in which identity is viewed as "a set of rules and resources that function as an anchor for who we are" and identification as "interaction or other behaviors illustrating one's attachment" (p. 303). In this model, identification is system and identity is structure. There is a duality of identity and identification in which identity figures both in the process of forming and maintaining attachment to the organization and as the product of this process.

Identity is often viewed as a person's "essence" or "core," implying that it is relatively stable and unchangeable. Scott et al. note problems with this view, however, including the fact that identities may change over time and that people may also emphasize different aspects of their identity in different situations. For example, the authors of this chapter emphasize our "professorial" identities while working at our universities but readily switch to our "father" identities when talking to our sons. Moreover, our professorial identities—our view of what being a professor entails and the personal meaning of being a professor to each of us—are different now from what they were when we had just finished graduate school and taken our first jobs.

Scott et al. (1998) replace the essentialist view with a view of identity as a structure of resources (our beliefs, attitudes, and knowledge; our work experience; our knowledge about ourselves) and rules (norms, routines, and habits that characterize us) that people can draw on when they interact in social situations. For instance, when we teach our classes, we draw on rules and resources including accumulated knowledge, norms about appropriate "professorial" behavior, and particular standards such as the importance of rigor and of discussing challenging current issues in class. As we enact the role of professors, we think of ourselves as professors—we draw on the resources of professorial identity and use them to achieve identification with our professorial status. The act of teaching also reproduces the very rules and resources on which we have drawn. An enthusiastic discussion that students are clearly learning from tends to reinforce the standard about class discussions, reproducing it as part of "what professors do," whereas persistent problems with getting students to engage in class discussions would weaken the standard as part of our identities.

Appropriation of identities that fit a particular situation is also influenced by institutions such as the organizations we belong to. Hence, we identify with our occupation partly out of individual choice and partly because of our structural positions and titles in our universities.

Scott et al. argue that distanciation helps to create separate subidentities in a process they term "regionalization." Regional identities develop because we enact particular identities fairly consistently in the various activities we engage in (and these activities generally occur in different times and places). For instance, the authors of this chapter are "fathers" when they are with their families at home, and this creates a particular region of our identities that is somewhat independent of other subidentities such as professor. Scott et al. propose that the various rules and resources involved in identification are grouped into specific identities associated with particular activities and that these activities are connected with the regional identities. They also suggest that four particularly important regions of our identities that pertain to organizations are group, organizational, personal, and occupational. For us, membership in work groups—our Communication Departments—helps to define our identity, and we frequently express our identification by praising our departments. In the same vein, people may identify with their occupational group—baker, professor, physician—or with their organization—Arizona State University, Bank of America, Jack's Body Shop. People also develop personal identities comprising their unique interests, skills, and talents. Depending on the situation, any one of these or some combination of them may be called upon as a relevant identity.

"Front" and "back" regions of the specific identities also can be distinguished, along the lines of Goffman (1959). Front regions are associated with what is approved and official in a culture. These aspects of the identity are used to maintain face in an organizational or other situation. By contrast, back regions are those aspects of the identity that are kept from public display, for example, complaining about the organization or acting "unprofessorial" by playing cards in our office. The back region often involves defining identities by what they are not. Although it may seem that the back regions of identities are undesirable, they also serve the useful function of letting individuals release tensions and react to uncomfortable aspects of their current "front region" identities. People often are ambivalent about their identities, appreciating some aspects and regretting others, and back regions of identity, which may be revealed only to close friends or confidants, offer an opportunity to cope with this ambivalence.

Scott et al. (1998) argue that their model of identity-identification structuring can account for multiple identities and for the multiple identifications common in organizational life. It also can shed light on changes in identities over time and across situations. There is a balance of action and structure in that the model incorporates the active role of people in creating and maintaining their identities but also acknowledges the role of social structures in shaping identity.

At the Group Level

Poole and DeSanctis (1990, 1992; DeSanctis & Poole, 1994) developed *adaptive structuration theory* (AST) to explain the use of information technologies in task-oriented groups. We applied it mainly to the study of groups using computerized group decision support systems, but it has been used by other scholars to understand implementation of information technology in work units (Majchrzak, Rice, Malhotra, King, & Ba, 2000) and organizational standards (Browning & Beyer, 1998, discussed below), among other things.

Before discussing adaptive structuration theory, we will describe group support systems (GSSs) in order to put our examples into context. Group support systems combine communication, computer, and decision technologies to support meetings, decision-making, and related group activities. In a typical GSS, members are provided with a networked PC that allows them to enter data and control the operation of the system. The GSS offers a range of procedures, such as agenda setting, idea recording, and voting routines. Specialized decision modeling or structured group methods such as multi-criteria solution evaluation and brainstorming usually are available. Often there is also a large display screen for common group information, such as lists of ideas or tabulations of votes. In face-to-face meetings, members use the computer system and also talk directly to one another. In dispersed settings, groups may also use a text messaging, voice, or video communication channel. GSSs have been used in strategic planning meetings, for scientific research collaboration, for product design development, and for the management of quality teams.

In their studies of GSSs, DeSanctis and Poole investigated structuration at two levels. First, they studied structuration at the microlevel by tracking interaction moves that appropriate, produce, and reproduce structures (see, e.g., Poole & DeSanctis, 1992). Second, they identified global patterns of structuration that characterize the process across an entire decision or series of decisions, focusing on phases or general patterns of structuration (e.g., Poole, DeSanctis, Kirsch, & Jackson, 1995). Poole, DeSanctis, and their colleagues have employed a mixture of qualitative and quantitative methods in research.

A key concept in adaptive structuration theory is *appropriation* (DeSanctis, Poole, & Dickson, 2000), the ways in which groups take structural features built into a technology, such as a voting feature in a GSS, and use them in interaction. For example, members of a group may use a voting system to promote democratic deliberation, or some members may use voting results to pressure members of the minority into going along with the "will" of the group (i.e., the majority position). Studies have indicated that different groups appropriated a group decision support system in diverse ways and that mode of appropriation affected group outcomes. Another study found that communication variables mediated the impact of technology on three outcome variables: consensus change, perceived solution quality, and member satisfaction with decision procedures.

Poole and DeSanctis (1990, 1992; DeSanctis & Poole, 1994) distinguished two aspects of technological structures: their *spirit* (the general values, goals, and attitudes the technology promotes, such as democratic decision making), and the specific *structural* features built into the system (such as anonymous input of ideas or a voting procedure). A structural feature is a specific rule or resource that operates in a group, whereas spirit is the principle of coherence that holds a set of rules and resources together. Usually, the features of an information technology like a group support system are designed to promote its spirit, although some features may be inconsistent as a result of sloppy design. Members can appropriate technology features in ways consistent with the spirit (a faithful appropriation) or in ways inconsistent with the spirit (an ironic appropriation). Using a GSS voting procedure to promote democratic participation in a group is an example of a faithful appropriation (why else would one bother to build in a voting procedure except to promote participation?), whereas using the vote to pressure minorities into conformity would be an ironic appropriation, one that went against the principles behind the system. Poole and DeSanctis argued that faithful appropriations were more likely to result in effective uses of an information technology that realized its intended purpose.

Adaptive structuration theory depicts structuring interaction as a series of *structuring moves*, microlevel actions that appropriate and may adapt structural features. Drawing on theories of rhetorical tropes, Poole and DeSanctis (1992; DeSanctis & Poole, 1994) developed a typology of 37 appropriation moves, organized into nine general categories. These categories are based on the following distinctions: (a) Does the move involve a single structure or more than one structure? and (b) does the move consist of an active use of the structure, an attempt to understand or clarify the structure, or a response to another member's appropriation move?

Two categories code moves that involve a single structure: *Direct appropriation* represents active use of the structure, whereas *constraint* represents an attempt to interpret and understand the structure. For example, a direct appropriation of a GSS involves simply using some feature of the GSS, whereas explaining how to use the GSS would be a constraint move because the explanation would focus members' attention on a particular interpretation of what the feature means and how it should be used. Four categories code moves involving more than one structure; two main examples are *combination* moves and *enlargement* moves. In a combination move, two structures are melded in various ways, as when a group decides to use parliamentary procedure to run meetings in which it uses the GSS; in this case, the rules of parliamentary procedure are combined with those for using the GSS. The *enlargement* category is used to code moves in which two structures are likened to each other. In one study, members of quality teams likened the GSS they were using to a "secretary" and "coach," which added to the meaning of the GSS and probably created expectations in members' minds about what the GSS could do for them.

Each of these appropriation moves must be accepted by other members to influence structuration of the GSS, so responses to the moves are also coded. *Affirmation* and *negation* represent the positive and negative modes of response to others' appropriations, whereas *ambiguity* represents uncertainty and confusion in response to some structure. *Ironic* appropriations can occur in constraint, enlargement, or contrast moves that impose definitions on the structure that are inconsistent with its features (e.g., "the voting procedure in this GSS can be used to determine who agrees with the leader"), or in substitution or combination moves that put structures inconsistent with the spirit together (e.g., the secretary metaphor created false expectations that the GSS had artificial intelligence, leading some members to reject the system when it did not make active suggestions to them).

Poole and DeSanctis used this scheme to identify (a) profiles of the general types of appropriations made by groups as well as which members made and controlled them, (b) the phases of appropriation that occurred in the groups, (c) critical junctures at which appropriation of the GSS changed, (d) conflicts in the structuring process, and (e) ironic uses of the GSS. In several studies, they found that groups that made ironic appropriations were less effective at managing conflicts, were less satisfied with their decisions, and had lower levels of consensus on their decisions than those with faithful appropriations. They also found that having a process facilitator or leader led to more faithful appropriations and more favorable outcomes. Majchrzak et al. (2000) found that appropriations consistent with the spirit of the GSS were more effective; they also found that the spirit of an information technology could change as members adapted it to different tasks.

A number of other scholars have applied structuration theory to groups (as reviewed by Poole, Seibold, & McPhee, 1996). David Seibold, Renee Meyers, Dale Brashers, and Sunwolf have used ST to explore how argumentation works in groups (Canary, Brossman, & Seibold, 1987; Meyers & Brashers, 1998; Meyers & Seibold, 1990; Seibold, Meyers, & Sunwolf, 1996; Sunwolf & Seibold, 1998). Keough and Lake (1993) studied the use of values as a structuring resource in negotiation teams. Witmer (1997) studied the structuration of group culture in an addiction recovery group, illuminating how the larger social institution, the national organization, shaped the structuration of the local chapter.

At the Organizational Level

One of the most important aspects of any organization is its formal structure, and communication researchers have explored communication "inside" formal channels for decades (McPhee & Poole, 2001). Setting up an effective structure, and using it well, has long been a tool recommended by business scholars. But explorations of formal structure have long been plagued by a paradox: On one hand, formal structuring creates efficiency and is an easy road to coordination; on the other hand, formal structure inexorably becomes oppressive, inflexible, and stifling. One current of structuration research attempts to explain this paradox.

After reviewing earlier literature about formal structure, McPhee (1985; also see McPhee and Poole, 2001) identified two main themes. First, formal structure substitutes for (and rules out) other communication; if someone is designated as manager, the group doesn't have to argue or vote on who should be the leader. Second, formal structures are an authoritative (and often constraining) meta-communication system for the organization— official acronyms may be mocked, but they are used, and the "vertical chain" of communication may be resented or circumvented, but all members are aware of it and use it as well as they can. McPhee (1985) used the structurational concept of *distanciation* to explain these attributes of formal structure: Sites of power in the organization are separated by the fact that formal structure is wielded as a tool in powerful sites, is simply the focus of work in others (such as human resources departments), and is a contextual constraint in the least powerful sites.

One type of formal structure that illustrates this pattern is the vertical hierarchy. It is often conceived of as a "chain of command" or "chain of communication," yet research repeatedly has found that almost no communication flows for any distance through this chain. So how does the chain work? In a study of several different organizations, McPhee (1988, 2001) found that the chain of command was produced and reproduced on three different, sometimes overlapping, levels. At the top was an executive level that was the nexus of a large number of individual chains of command. At this level, broad, organization-wide responsibilities limited managers' oversight and participation in any single chain of command, so formal mechanisms substituted for direct involvement with lower levels. Below this top level was a managerial level where managers were directly involved both in communicating with and in designing structure for the unit under them. These managers were separated from their subordinate unit in two respects: They saw the organization in very different terms from the members of the lower level unit, and they were literally limited in the amount of communicating they could do with the lower level by their great workload. The lowest level was a technical level where the formal structure was taken as a given, but supervisors and workers at this level frequently felt misunderstood and resisted the programs of the managers. Within each level, there was a highly interconnected communication network, quite a bit of consensus about important problems, and similar senses of organizational position. Between levels, there were gaps in communication and perspective, sometimes handled well but often handled badly by parties on both sides of the gap. These studies showed that the character of a hierarchy varies at and between the different levels and that the production and reproduction of the hierarchy maintains these variations, but also that action at all three of these distanciated levels is involved in keeping the hierarchy of even moderate-sized organizations going.

Fordham-Hernandez and McPhee (1999) found a similar pattern in a midwestern foods company. A consultant had persuaded the president of the company to institute a more participatory structural arrangement. The story of the change and how the new arrangement worked varied from the top levels (the president and consultant), to the managerial level (a vice president who was mainly responsible for the change), to the lower levels. The president and consultant saw themselves as the architects and implementers of change, whereas people toward the bottom saw them as irrelevant to and uninvolved in the change, and described the change in very different ways. Once again, the hierarchy is not the same system of rules and resources for people throughout the organization; it varies in a complex way and creates different milieus at different levels. Structuration theory thus leads us to think of formal structure in a new way, as the product of divergent perspectives relating differently to the abstract organizational schema. The structure is not a conduit for messages, but instead a tool or constraint that is often misunderstood on all sides.

Another traditional organizational communication construct that has been transformed by structuration researchers is organizational climate. Traditionally, organizational climate has been thought of as a general property ("This company is supportive") measured by giving employees standardized questionnaires and looking for patterns of agreement. Structuration researchers in communication (Poole & McPhee, 1983) argued that climate should be regarded instead as a structure of rules and resources present at a deep level underlying organizational interactions. Thus, the supportiveness of the organization can be an item of knowledge contextualized differently by different people—some see it as true everywhere, others see it as true for only a select group of employees, others see it as true for innovation activity but not in other spheres, and still others see it as a myth preached by the powerful. This notion allows for a number of insights, developed systematically by Poole (1994). First, a core consisting of basal constructs and kernel climate tenets can be identified ("This company is supportive"), and this core is then interpreted in different ways by different situated groups. Second, the important issue of agreement about climate is broadened to include level of understanding of agreement (these two ideas together are called "consensus"). Third, climate can relate narrowly to specific practices in the company (innovation) as well as to the whole. Fourth, climate consensus can be explained by the pattern of practices it describes as well as by various macro variables such as organizational structure, official employee communication channels (termed "climate apparati"), and the overall communication network.

A study by Bastien, McPhee, and Bolton (1995) showed that climate structures can result directly from discourse themes extracted from interviews or recorded discourse. In a study of a large municipal bureaucracy, the researchers identified kernel themes such as "secrecy," reflected in surface themes such as "intended secrecy." For instance, when a planning director was fired, the grapevine spread the news but the planning director kept denying it, then told his subordinates and asked them to "keep the secret." Important findings in the study were the varied ways climate themes like this spread and became so consensual in the organization that they became kernel themes. One key process of theme was spread through inversion: After management initiated the secrecy policy, employees started using the theme to describe their communication with managers. Another process was sedimentation, as the climate theme was built into and assumed by other organizational practices—for instance, a planning office operated in a way that kept it isolated and its findings secret from the rest of the organization. The structurational approach thus implies new ways to think about and detect organizational climates, and it gives new insights into how they develop.

Other structurational research at the organizational level includes Corman and Scott's (1994; McPhee & Corman, 1995) reticulation theory of the structuration of communication networks; studies of communicative genres such as memos, by Yates and Orlikowski (1992); and Riley's (1983) classic study of the structuration of organizational cultures. Mumby's (1988) study of the structuring of organizational power relations through narrative presents important insights about structuration. Kirby and Krone (2002) present an intriguing study of how structuration processes prevent fair application of family leave policies in organizations.

At the Interorganizational Level

Larry Browning and colleagues (Browning & Beyer, 1998; Browning, Beyer & Shetler, 1995; Browning & Shetler, 2000) have applied structurational concepts to the study of SEMATECH, an interorganizational consortium of information technology companies formed to improve competitiveness in the semiconductor industry. Their application of structuration theory is somewhat looser than those discussed earlier and uses structuration theory as a source of concepts for a grounded theory of interorganizational cooperation and standards setting. Browning and colleagues place particular emphasis on the interplay between power and meaning. In their study of standard setting, Browning and Beyer (1998) show how the willingness of two rather powerful members of SEMATECH, Intel Corporation and Motorola, to share information about their products and how they worked with suppliers set up a norm of cooperation that other firms felt obligated to follow in exchange for the valuable information they had received from Intel and Motorola. This opening up of communication among firms highlighted the fact that the information they had been hoarding because they believed it to be proprietary was actually fairly commonly known by all firms.

Once the illusion of special standards and knowledge had dissipated, the companies realized that by developing voluntary standards for parts and quality control they could greatly reduce costs, increase quality, and innovate more rapidly. This, in turn, promoted the emergence of standards bodies and quality training across the industry, which became institutionalized quite rapidly. This fundamental change in the structures was initiated by the voluntary actions of Intel and Motorola, which fostered reciprocity and the formation of norms, which were then projected into the organizational structures of SEMATECH and the quality training organizations it gave rise to.

Browning and Beyer note that the structuration processes they observed, unlike many reviewed in this chapter, were spread out over considerable time periods and that sometimes structures produced in one set of actions were not reactivated until months later by actors different from those originally involved in producing them. They also observed that structures were transmitted to distant locations through being "re-embedded" in symbols or sets of procedures, such as quality programs, and symbols, such as awards for excelling in quality improvement.

Critiques, Currents, and Directions

Probably the most common critique of ST in communication research is that Giddens has not developed a balanced duality of action and structure, but instead overemphasizes action. To those versed in traditional notions of structure—for example, dominance of economic processes by giant corporations, or the distribution of wealth across social classes, or inequalities and domination between genders—Giddens's novel conception of structure as rules and resources drawn on in action can seem to give too much power to individual agents. It seems to imply that if we wanted to change certain structures to create a perfect society with no inequalities, we could just get together and start doing it—no problem. Some scholars who lodge this criticism are influenced by the work of Michel Foucault, who aimed to give social-structural accounts of both social interaction patterns and agency, arguing that individuals had little or no agency.

However, ST gives considerable emphasis to social institutions as a basic part of explanations of society and communication. ST attempts to cover the whole continuum from micro interaction to macro institutions, thereby according influence to both agents and structural tendencies. Giddens discusses three types of constraints on action: material constraint, constraint through threats of punishment, and structural constraint of actions we can perform by the available structural possibilities. As noted above, these vary by personal place in the social system, by context, and by history. The power of agency is also limited by sedimentation, in which structures and practices are built on a web of other structures and practices. As this accumulates, the whole web becomes harder to transform, as is the case with language and other less material structures. In ST, action and structure are always engaged in a dialectic in which, depending on the nature of the structuring process and the context in which it occurs, sometimes agency is a stronger influence and sometimes institutions, but most often both figure in important ways.

In communication research, there are several ways in which action and structure are balanced. In Poole and DeSanctis's AST, "features" are direct structural and material constraints on a group's action, while the "spirit" of the technology is a sedimented structural element that constrains (and enables) action. As the climate themes discussed by Bastien et al. (1995) are used and reused, their sedimentation makes it harder for the organization to change its climate, but changing conditions may open the door for human action to refashion the themes. Finally, McPhee's (1985) analysis shows how the production and reproduction of a formal organizational structure takes place on multiple different sites, which makes it difficult for any single set of actors to control the structuring process.

In a related critique, Conrad (1993) charged that structurational rules of communication are often conceived on the model of linguistics, as simple, relatively flexible formulas, rather than on the model of social pragmatics, which views rules as partially embedded in contexts and, therefore, not wholly under the control of actors. However, Giddens (1979, 1984) uses a definition that is quite close to Conrad's description of pragmatics: He defines rules as "whatever guides interactive practice," and he does not stipulate any abstract form rules must take, as the communication rules theorists did. For instance, he says that to understand the rule of castling in chess, we should not look at a chess rule book; instead, we need to study either the (strategic, interactive, and contextual) way castling works in a game or the (strategic, interactive, and contextual) way it developed during the history of chess. Conrad's and Giddens's positions on rules are useful reminders that the structurational concept of rules is quite different from those of Cushman and other rules theorists.

Seyfarth (1998) argues that ST should be grounded in individual cognitions and that intersubjective structures are reifications that cannot account for how structures are created and sustained in interaction. However, although structures are carried in part by memory traces of individual actors, structuration is sustained by social interaction and therefore cannot be encapsulated in any individual cognition. Research on transactive memory, for example, shows how individual cognitions maintain coherency at the group level only through systemic relationships with other individuals' memories. Seyfarth's argument makes a good point concerning the importance of individuals in structuration, but it does not supplant the system as the primary locus of structuration.

Another critique of ST is that it does not adequately conceptualize social or organizational change. Archer (1982, 1995) argued that structuration theory conflates routine social practices that are largely bounded and determined by social-structural constraints with cases in which agents take control of a system to initiate and implement change programs that transform the structures of their social systems. She calls her perspective the "morphogenetic" approach to emphasize the divergence needed between standard social analysis and the analysis of social change. In communication, Taylor and Van Every (2000) have made a somewhat similar charge that "macro agents" are able to articulate the essence of cumulated organizational sensemaking in a way that can guide or transform organizations. A related stance is Contractor and Seibold's (1993) proposal that self-organizing systems theory is a superior alternative to structuration theory because it emphasizes complex system dynamics that can lead to change (or stability) involving processes that structuration theory ignores.

However, ST can be used to develop accounts and explanations of both organizational change and stability. Giddens (1984) discussed change resulting from a slow accumulation of small structural changes and also as driven by basic structural contradictions that spread in complex ways through social systems. The research of Poole and DeSanctis on group technology, of Bastien and colleagues on climate, and of Browning on interorganizational networks all focus on change processes, as does quite a bit of other structurational research. These researchers argue that stable systems, like changing ones, require reference to agency to "keep things going," and that changing systems, like stable ones, involve action that is constrained and enabled by lots of structural constraints that remain relatively constant. An important advantage of ST is that it accounts for stability and change within the same theoretical framework.

ST also has been criticized for lacking a critical edge. Giddens is sometimes portrayed as a politically moderate theorist who does not recognize adequately the power imbalances and domination that characterize today's world. Critics charge that Giddens's theory does not center on (although it clearly believes in) critique of capitalist domination and exploitation, nor does it focus on inequity and structural domination along gendered, racial, or other lines (although Giddens recognizes and expresses strong concern about these problems). Giddens's account of globalization also is seen by some as giving short shrift to continuing impacts and processes of colonialism. Instead, it focuses on the ways the structural resources of modernity have empowered people and given them vastly different ranges of choices (and accompanying risks) than people of earlier epochs have faced. Giddens argues that a politics of lifestyle choice will slowly replace the politics of emancipation of the past, as more and more people are escaping conditions of servitude and misery.

Although we agree that more recent developments in Giddens's ST pay too little attention to inequities and dominance, the original foundations of ST provide a good framework for critical inquiry. Many structurational studies have dealt with issues of power and domination (see, e.g., Kirby & Krone, 2002). The studies reviewed above have clear implications for critical analysis of organizational communication, though they have not pursued them as strongly as many in critical studies would advocate (Mumby, 1993). We hope future researchers take a more critical stance in developing the future of the structurational perspective.

References

Archer, M. (1982). Morphogenesis versus structuration: On combining structure and action. *British Journal of Sociology, 33,* 455–483.

Archer, M. (1995). *Realist social theory: The morphogenetic approach*. Cambridge, UK: Cambridge University Press.

Banks, S. P., & Riley, P. (1993). Structuration theory as an ontology for communication research. In S. Deetz (Ed.) *Communication yearbook 16* (pp. 167–196). Newbury Park, CA: Sage.

Bastien, D. T., McPhee, R. D., & Bolton, K. A. (1995). A study and extended theory of the structuration of climate. *Communication Monographs, 62,* 87–109.

Berger, P. L., & Luckmann, T. (1966). *The social construction of reality*. Garden City, NJ: Doubleday.

Browning, L. D., & Beyer, J. M. (1998). The structuring of shared voluntary standards in the U.S. semiconductor industry: Communicating to reach agreement. *Communication Monographs, 65,* 220–243.

Browning, L. D., Beyer, J. M., & Shetler, J. C. (1995). Building cooperation in a competitive industry: SEMATECH and the semiconductor industry. *Academy of Management Journal, 38,* 113–151.

Browning, L. D., & Shetler, J. C. (2000). *Sematech: Saving the U.S. semiconductor industry*. College Station: Texas A&M University Press.

Canary, D. J., Brossman, B. G., & Seibold, D. R. (1987). Argument structures in decision-making groups. *Southern States Speech Journal, 53,* 18–37.

Conrad, C. (1983). Organizational power: Faces and symbolic forms. In L. Putnam & M. Pacanowsky (Eds.), *Communication and organizations: An interpretive approach* (pp. 173–193). Beverly Hills, CA: Sage.

Conrad, C. (1993). Rhetorical/communication theory as an ontology for structuration research. In S. Deetz (Ed.), *Communication yearbook 16* (pp. 197–208). Newbury Park, CA: Sage.

Contractor, N. S., & Seibold, D. R. (1993). Theoretical frameworks for the study of structuring processes in group decision support systems: Adaptive structuration theory and self-organizing systems theory. *Human Communication Research, 19,* 528–563.

Corman, S. R., & Scott, C. R. (1994). Perceived networks, activity foci, and observable communication in social collectives. *Communication Theory, 4,* 171–190.

DeSanctis, G., & Poole, M. S. (1994). Capturing the complexity in advanced technology use: Adaptive structuration theory. *Organization Science, 5,* 121–147.

DeSanctis, G., Poole, M. S., & Dickson, G. W. (2000). Teams and technology: Interactions over time. In M. A. Neale, E. A. Mannix, & T. L. Griffith (Eds.), *Research on managing groups and teams: Technology* (Vol. 3). Stamford, CT: JAI.

Fordham-Hernandez, T., & McPhee, R. (1999, May). *Cognitive maps of organizational narratives and processes: Differences across levels of an organizational hierarchy*. Presented at the Organizational Communication Division, International Communication Association, San Francisco.

Garfinkel, H. (1967). *Studies in ethnomethodology*. Englewood Cliffs, NJ: Prentice-Hall.

Giddens, A. (1979). *Central problems in social theory: Action, structure, and contradiction in social analysis*. Berkeley: University of California Press.

Giddens, A. (1984). *The constitution of society: Outline of the theory of structuration.* Cambridge, MA: Polity.

Goffman, E. (1959). *The presentation of self in everyday life.* New York: Anchor.

Keough, C., & Lake, R. (1991). Values as structuring properties of contract negotiations. In C. Conrad (Ed.), *The ethical nexus: Values, communication and organizational decisions* (pp. 171–189). Norwood, NJ: Ablex.

Kirby, E. L., & Krone, K. J. (2002). "The policy exists but you can't really use it": Communication and the structuration of work-family leave. *Journal of Applied Communication Research, 30,* 50–77.

Majchrzak, A., Rice, R., Malhotra, A., King, N., & Ba, S. (2000). Technology adaptation: The case of a computer-supported inter-organizational virtual team. *MIS Quarterly, 24,* 569–601.

McPhee, R. (1985). Formal structure and organizational communication. In R. McPhee & P. Tompkins (Eds.), *Organizational communication: Traditional themes and new directions* (pp. 149–177). Beverly Hills, CA: Sage

McPhee, R. (1988). Vertical communication chains: Toward an integrated approach. *Management Communication Quarterly, 1,* 455–493.

McPhee, R. D. (2001, March). *Discursive positioning in organizational hierarchies: Four cases.* Paper presented to the Organizational Communication Division, Western States Communication Association Annual Conference, Coeur D'Alene, ID.

McPhee, R. D., & Corman, S. R. (1995). An activity-based theory of communication networks in organizations, applied to the case of a local church. *Communication Monograph, 62,* 132–151.

McPhee, R. D., & Poole, M. S. (1980). *A theory of structuration: The perspective of Anthony Giddens and its relevance for contemporary communication research.* Paper presented at the annual convention of the Speech Communication Association, New York.

McPhee, R. D., & Poole, M. S. (2001). Communication and organizational structure. In F. Jablin & L. Putnam (Eds.), *Handbook of organizational communication* (pp. 503–543). Thousand Oaks, CA: Sage.

Meyers, R. A., & Brashers, D. E. (1998). Argument and group decision-making: Explicating a process model and investigating the argument-outcome link. *Communication Monographs, 65,* 261–281.

Meyers, R., & Seibold, D. R. (1990). Perspectives on group argument: A critical review of persuasive arguments theory and an alternative structurational view. In J. Anderson (Ed.) *Communication yearbook 13* (pp. 268–302). Newbury Park, CA: Sage.

Mumby, D. (1988). *Communication and power in organizations.* Norwood, NJ: Ablex.

Mumby, D. (1993). Critical organizational communication studies: The next ten years. *Communication Monographs, 60,* 18–26.

Poole, M. S. (1994). The structuring of organizational climates. In L. Thayer & G. Barnett (Eds.), *Organization-communication IV* (pp. 74–113). Norwood, NJ: Ablex.

Poole, M. S., & DeSanctis, G. (1990). Understanding the use of group decision support systems: The theory of adaptive structuration. In J. Fulk & C. Steinfield (Eds.), *Organizations and communication technology* (pp. 175–195). Newbury Park, CA: Sage.

Poole, M. S., & DeSanctis, G. (1992). Microlevel structuration in computer-supported group decision-making. *Human Communication Research, 19,* 5–49.

Poole, M. S., DeSanctis, G., Kirsch, L., & Jackson, M. (1995). Group decision support systems as facilitators of quality team efforts. In L. R. Frey (Ed.), *Innovations in group facilitation techniques: Case studies of applications in naturalistic settings* (pp. 299–322). Cresskill, NJ: Hampton.

Poole, M. S., & McPhee, R. D. (1983). A structurational analysis of organizational climate. In L. Putnam & M. Pacanowsky (Eds.), *Communication and organizations: An interpretive approach* (pp. 195–220). Beverly Hills, CA: Sage.

Poole, M. S., Seibold, D. R., & McPhee, R. D. (1985). Group decision-making as a structurational process. *Quarterly Journal of Speech, 71,* 74–102.

Poole, M. S., Seibold, D. R., & McPhee, R. D. (1996). The structuration of group decisions. In R. Y. Hirokawa & M. S. Poole (Eds.), *Communication and group decision-making* (2nd ed., pp. 114–146). Thousand Oaks, CA: Sage.

Riley, P. A. (1983). A structurationist account of political culture. *Administrative Science Quarterly, 28,* 414–437.

Scott, C. R., Corman, S. R., & Cheney, G. (1998). Development of a structurational model of identification in the organization. *Communication Theory, 8,* 298–335.

Seibold, D. R., Meyers, R. A., & Sunwolf. (1996). Communication and influence in group decision making. In R. Y. Hirokawa & M. S. Poole (Eds.), *Communication and group decision-making* (2nd ed., pp. 242–268). Thousand Oaks, CA: Sage.

Seyfarth, B. (1998). *Are reasons structures?: A cognitive structurational approach toward explaining small group processes.* Unpublished doctoral dissertation, University of Minnesota–Minneapolis.

Sunwolf & Seibold, D. R. (1998). Jurors' intuitive rules for deliberation: A structurational approach to communication in jury decision making. *Communication Monographs, 65,* 282–307.

Taylor, J., & Van Every, E. (2000). *The emergent organization: Communication as its site and surface.* Mahwah, NJ: Erlbaum.

Witmer, D. (1997). Communication and recovery: Structuration as an ontological approach to organizational culture. *Communication Monographs, 64,* 324–349.

Wittgenstein, L. (1958). *Philosophical investigations* (3rd ed., G.E.M. Anscomb, Trans.). New York: Macmillan.

Yates, J., & Orlikowski, W. J. (1992). Genres of organizational communication: A structurational approach to studying communication and media. *Academy of Management Review, 17,* 299–326.

9

Engaging Organization
Through Worldview

James R. Taylor

Thisis a chapter about the quest for a theory. It is not an account of the empirical research I have engaged in. Instead, it is the story of a personal odyssey that I undertook beginning in graduate school, without any clear idea of where my voyage eventually would take me. My motivation was a question that I could not answer but could not quite put out of my mind: "What is an organization?" The chronicle that follows is a cleaned-up version of that quest. I have omitted the many false starts I made, and the many dead ends I found myself in, along the way. But in its essentials, the chronicle is as true to my experience as I can make it, in retrospect.

Introduction

Ideas are strange things. Like maple leaves leisurely helicoptering their way down to earth in the autumn, they mostly fall close to the tree on which they

AUTHOR'S NOTE: I would like to pay homage to Professor Klaus Krippendorff of the University of Pennsylvania, who has exerted a powerful influence on my theorizing throughout my academic career. It was from him that I learned the pleasure of abstract speculation, on one hand, and a concern for the practical implications of ideas, on the other.

grew, but now and then they are carried over some considerable distance by the wind, or by birds. They may lie dormant in the new location, only to take root many years later. For me, the concept of worldview was like that. I sat in on a course in computer simulation at the University of Pennsylvania in 1968–1969 in which worldview figured as a central principle, but I began to see its potential for answering a different kind of question only much later. Now I recognize it as the core concept of my whole theory of communication and its role in the construction of organization.

I soon found out, however, that the word "worldview" mostly generated the wrong kind of response from my listeners. My concept is dualistic: In my version there are two, and *only* two, worldviews. People usually objected that there are many worldviews, and of course there are, for them. Not for me, though—but then I don't hold a copyright on the term. So I decided some time ago to put the notion of worldview in cold storage, until it was time to try it out again. This seems to be that time.

I said that it had occurred to me that worldview might be a clue to the answer to a question, one that had in fact preoccupied me from the beginning. The question sounds trivial enough: *What is an organization?* You might think the answer should be self-evident: Hundreds, even thousands, of definitions of organization have been offered at one time or another. Here is an example:

> Organizations are social units (or human groupings) deliberately constructed and reconstructed to seek specific goals. . . . Organizations are characterized by: (1) divisions of labor, power, and communication responsibilities, divisions which are not random or traditionally patterned, but deliberately planned to enhance the realization of specific goals; (2) the presence of one or more power centers which control the concerted efforts of the organization and direct them toward its goal; these power centers also must review continuously the organization's performance and re-pattern its structure, where necessary, to increase its efficiency; (3) substitution of personnel, i.e., unsatisfactory persons can be removed and others assigned their tasks. (Etzioni, 1964, p. 3)

For me, there were two problems with this way of thinking about organization. First, I had worked for 10 years for a large corporation, and the functionalistic characterization I have just cited matched up rather badly against my personal experience of what it was like to work for an organization and, even more, what it was like to be a manager in one. Second, I was a student of communication. Communication is about process, and there isn't much process of any sort that figures in definitions such as this, much less communication process. Such characterizations dichotomize the organizational world into macro and micro domains: systems and institutions, on one hand, and individuals, on the other. There is no middle world where communication is happening, in such a way of thinking—no "meso" level.

Definitions such as this, in other words, take organization as a given, not something to be accomplished. They are all about what happens *after* the organization has formed, and not at all about how it got to *be* an organization in the first place and how it *continues to remain so*. So the question, as I saw it, was: How does organization get constituted? Even more specifically, I considered: How is it constituted in the process of communicating? In other words, what is there about communication that makes it an agent of *organizing*, as Weick (1969, 1979) was by then calling the process perspective on organization.

The Basic Idea of Worldview

In system design, doing a computer simulation of some set of activities calls on a random number generator to fix the time of occurrence of each "event" (a customer arriving at a checkout counter of a supermarket, a plane pulling up to an airport gate). The time of the event must be assigned as a characteristic to either a customer ready to check out at a now available counter, or the clerk who is there, or, alternatively, a plane arriving at a gate that has just become free, or the ground crew who do the unloading. The logic of worldview is clear enough: If we were to assign the time of the event to *both* customer *and* clerk, or plane *and* gate, the same event would be occurring at two different times, which is absurd; if to *neither*, there would be no event.

Software applications designed to support this type of simulation must assume one of two "worldviews," depending on whether they assign the time of the event to the customer or to the checkout clerk, to the plane crew or to the gate crew. The worldview of simulation languages accordingly was classified as either "event-oriented" (time of occurrence is taken to be a characteristic of the service facility) or "particle-oriented" (time of occurrence is taken to be a characteristic of the client). It's a difference of perspective corresponding to the doctor's or the patient's, to take a different example (Taylor, 1993; Taylor, Gurd, & Bardini, 1997).

Think of organizational activities then as a matrix, where the set of customers define the abscissa and the group of clerks the ordinate (Figure 9.1). Any given "event" (for example, $EP_{t=i}$) is thus defined as the intersection of a P row (a client activity) and an E column (a server activity) at time t. For the supermarket customer, checking out is only one in a string of associated actions, including (but not limited to) entering the store, choosing what to buy, checking out, paying, and putting the purchases in the car to drive home.

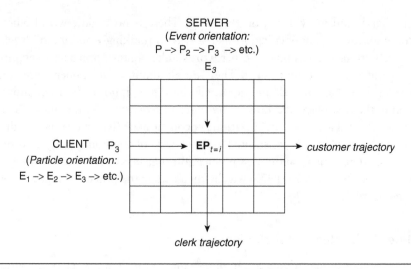

CLIENT P_3
(Particle orientation:
$E_1 \rightarrow E_2 \rightarrow E_3 \rightarrow$ etc.)

Figure 9.1   A Matrix of Activities Illustrating the Principle of Worldview

That is one activity trajectory. The clerk's, by contrast, is defined as dealing with one customer after the other, following more or less the same routine with each. It is a different activity trajectory. The intersection of the two—an event with a time coordinate—defines the modal activity of any store: without customers, no buying; without checkout clerks and other employees, no selling. We could thus think of this two-dimensional matrix as a representation of the core activity of an organization. By doing so, we would establish a rock-bottom basis for what is meant by the term "organization."

Underpinning the 2 × 2 matrix of individual cells that define this matrix representation of organization, of course, is a transaction involving a *corporate* actor (the store, on the row axis) and a *collective* actor (the public, on the column axis).

Notice that this representation defines two levels: a *macro* (the matrix that represents the activity system as a whole) and a *micro* (the activities occurring in a single cell, independent of their placement in the matrix). Thus, the simulation perspective perpetuates the taken-for-granted macro-micro division that characterizes views of organization such as the one I cited earlier. That this should be the case is not too surprising because simulation technologies both reflect and perpetuate the ways of seeing the world typical of management practice and theory. The lack of a "meso" dimension would, however, come back to preoccupy my thinking later, as we shall see.

At the time, though, I was saying to myself, why not apply the same logic I have described, linking servers to clients, to what occurs *within* an organization? I recalled my own experience in the Canadian Broadcasting Corporation (Taylor, 1982).[1] Broadcasting is about making and airing programs that will, one hopes, draw an audience, attract sponsors (private or public), and thus justify the existence of the network. Let us call this link with the audience the *essential* transaction: the one that defines the mission of the entire enterprise. The responsibility for assembling the elements that go to make up a program was assigned, in the CBC, to a producer. To put together the parts of a program, the producer had to call on the services of many kinds of specialists: writers, researchers, film editors, sound and lighting technicians, set designers, production assistants, publicity people (all the functions that scroll past as credits at the end of the show, in other words). Each of the steps in assembling a program thus boils down to a transaction where the producer is in the position of an in-house customer, and the various specialists play a role analogous to that of the clerk, in that they "serve" the customer. Because there are many producers they have many "customers."

Put all the producers and all the specialists together, I reasoned, and the result is a broadcasting organization such as the CBC. It is an oversimplified picture, I agree, because it leaves out so many other actors in the organizational sphere—people like accountants and supervisors. Including them, however, seemed to present no particular conceptual barrier, because the matrix would simply be complicated a bit to become a matrix of matrices: n-dimensional rather than two-dimensional.

On reflection, I believe that this is how any organization must be constructed. Webster's dictionary defines organization as an "organizing," or a "being organized": an arranging of activities, in effect, to make them more systematic. When all the responses collectively manifest a systematic pattern, I reasoned, it will have become an "organization."

Many people's energies and skills are mobilized in accomplishing the mission of a complex organization such as broadcasting, merchandizing, or running an airline. The beauty of the worldview concept is that each of those contributing activities is itself embedded within an activity chain that has its own finality. Collectively, they are all in the process of becoming "organized."

The Counterintuitive Connotations of Worldview

The terms "particle orientation" and "event orientation" I had borrowed from simulation science are, however, I soon realized, singularly uninformative in conceptualizing worldview. Anyone who had not sat through a course in simulation found the terms hard to comprehend; they didn't match up with people's intuitions, including, as it turns out, my own.

Consider my broadcasting example again. When a producer turns to a film editor for assistance, both are linked to each other by their joint preoccupation with a "particle," P, namely the film. Furthermore, the editing of the film is an "event," E. Neither E nor P expresses the idea of an encounter of agents, and thus the cell that is shown in Figure 9.1 as $EP_{t=i}$ is a misnomer. P is ambiguous because it refers both to the object being treated (a film to be edited) and the beneficiary of the event (the producer who needs the editing done). E is ambiguous because it refers both to the event and the agent (the film editor). To capture the intuitive sense of worldview, I realized, the term should be rewritten to include not just two but *three* nodes, let us say A and B (film editor and producer, i.e., *two* agents), linked by their respective orientations to one object-particle, X (the film). The resulting triadic event is $ABX_{t=i}$ (where, as before, the "t" stands for the time of the event and X is the object that A and B are jointly oriented to, i.e., the film).

The difference is that for one agent, the producer, the operation is a means to an end; for the film editor, it *is* the end: Film editing is a vocation. The editor is preoccupied with the means to accomplish an operation that the producer delegates to him or her. The two actors are linked by a common orientation to the "particle," the film, and their co-orienting to a common object defines a communicational event, but their contextual embedding in their organization is different. The producer is acting as an agent for the network; his or her object is the program in which the film appears. The editor is acting as an agent for the producer, and his or her object is the film itself. They may relate to each other through their common preoccupation with the film-particle, but the object has a different status for each. The film is what Star and Griesemer (1989) call a "boundary object" because it links two distinct communities of practice and two worldviews.

Problems With the Initial
Worldview Conceptualization of Organization

The concept of an activity matrix, modified as I have just explained, suggested a first tentative answer to my question, "What is an organization?" The organization, I was tempted to think, is defined by the matrices of activities needed to carry out certain tasks, performed by actors whose activities intersect (within the broadcasting corporation, for example), for beneficiaries (the audience).

There are some problems, however, with defining the organization this way. One shortcoming is that it does not specify the boundaries of the organization: who is inside, who outside. Suppose, for example, that one of the producers wants a special effect requiring technical skills that are not to be found within the organization. Why not farm out the job? No reason not to at all, of course; it happens all the time. Or indeed, why not outsource the production process as well? Again, perfectly possible. However, if *all* the activities are outsourced, then, following my definition, there is no organization left! Or perhaps we would want to say we were dealing with a *virtual* rather than a *real* organization. But this tells us that there is something missing in my initial definition—it can't just be a question of structuring of activities. The matrix defines a structure but not its rationale or its origin.

One clue as to what is missing in the matrix that describes the activities of agents in the organization is that we have left out of account the *finality* of the activity—its basic rationale, in other words. The activity of the producer manifests more directly the finality of the broadcasting organization than that of the editor because the program is the means by which the corporation relates one-to-one to its audience. The broadcaster's relation to the audience is what I call an "essential transaction" (Taylor, 2002). The producer is delegated by the organization to carry out the task of producing a program and, in this sense, expresses more or less directly its finality, while the work of the film editor is, in this perspective, a contributing activity. But then the producer, in turn, makes a contribution to an even more essential task: that of devising and outputting a complete program schedule for the network. There is thus a hierarchy of means–end relationships (a phenomenon I have called "imbrication;" Taylor, 2001b, 2002).

The organization, in other words, cannot be simply reduced to an account of its activities because the organization as such *does not even directly figure as an actor* in the activity matrix shown in Figure 9.1. Yet it is the organization that ultimately is responsible to its clients, not delegated agents: You blame the company.[2] It is the organization that enters into the essential transaction with a collective client community and thus provides the rationale for all its accessory activities, whether performed by actors recognizable as attached to it (employees) or not (contractees). The structuring of activities is a manifestation of organization, but it does not resolve the issue of existence. My question "What is an organization;" had not yet been answered.

A Digression: The Practical Consequences of Worldview

The practical utility of conceiving of organization as a worldview matrix, even in the limited way I initially formulated the idea, would shortly be brought home to me. In 1981, I was persuaded to take leave from my academic work to become planning advisor to the administrative head of the Department of Communication, an agency of the federal government of Canada. One of my responsibilities there was to develop and supervise a study of the implementation of information-based technologies into four government departments, including the host department. As one component of this work, we incorporated a study of the internal activities of a department that was inspired by the worldview perspective (a more detailed description of this research appears as Chapter 2 of my 1993 book *Rethinking the Theory of Organizational Communication*). The "particles" we chose to focus on were letters addressed to the Minister of Communication by citizens. These were then referred to specialized services within the department for preparation of a draft answer.

Here, what I have called the "essential transaction" dictated that the Minister provide a prompt and responsive letter to the citizen. But somehow the essentiality got lost from view in the day-to-day realities of departmental work, with the result that the letter-drafting became an activity driven by its own internal logic. What should have been a contributive activity—writing a draft—soon became seen as what was essential. The hierarchy had taken over: not just a hierarchy of processes, but also a hierarchy of offices—a bureaucratic "ladder of authority."

The implicit assumption, I suppose, was that if all the individuals did their job correctly, the process would look after itself. It didn't. Some letters were taking up to a year to answer. Yet, so firmly engrained in the managerial philosophy of the department was the event-oriented view of organization that the fate of the particle, in its trajectory through the various stages of drafting a letter, was simply not taken into consideration. (Incidentally, this study was initially published in 1983, a decade before the 1993 Hammer and Champy book on re-engineering, in which they make similar observations as to the domination of an event-oriented perspective in contemporary organizations, although they do not use that term.)

I had seen much the same thing happen to the CBC while I was there: a progressive shift away from concentrating on the process of producing a program to an emphasis on managing the people who produced it. We have all heard evidence of the same phenomenon in the post-9/11 world when security agencies such as the Federal Bureau of Investigation (FBI) and the Central Intelligence Agency (CIA) were forced to concede that they had also become, in effect, the victim of the dominance of an event orientation—a tendency that we often think of as "bureaucratic" because it focuses on the offices (Weber's "bureaux"), not on the process. In the intelligence community, it appears, the particles also got "stuck": Vital information never got passed on to complete what should have been, in principle, a coherent trajectory of intelligence sharing.

Because the organization arises in an intersection of agencies, connected to common objects but from a different worldview, there is always a choice of vantage point in conceptualizing its activities, for the researcher as well as for the people there. Not only are the event-oriented and the particle-oriented points of view incommensurable, *neither is logically superior to the other*. It is as important to do the work well by concentrating on the event (quality control) as it is to manage the particle trajectory (re-engineering).

The difference of perspective I am describing is, it occurred to me, psychologically as well as theoretically grounded in reality. Program producers, I knew from my experience in broadcasting, simply do not conceive of their organization in the same way as the specialist services that provide the elements of the program: the editing of a film, for example. The two communities, producers and editors, do not experience the same organizational world: They are divided by worldview. Because these worldviews are embedded in communities of practice, each characterized by its own cognitive rules and procedures for making sense, they are exceptionally resistant to influence.

[End of digression]

Worldview and the Constitution of Organization

It was a promising start on the question of the genesis of organization (the question I raised before my "digression"), but I still had not come to grips with the issues of how the organization *comes to be constituted in the first place* and *how it gets reproduced*. It is to these questions that I turned.

Consider Figure 9.1 again. The events that constitute the *cells* of the matrix refer to encounters between two agents (who may be individuals, or small teams, or even organizational units that outsource to other organizational units): All involve microdynamics. But the *matrix* describes an essential transaction linking an organization to its constituency: the macro perspective. Each side is distinguished by its particular practices. Only the pattern of an intersection of means and ends is the same: individual customers versus clerks, producers versus film editors, patients versus health providers (a micro perspective), corporation versus public (a macro perspective).

The matrix thus encapsulates two versions of agency: individual versus collective. The producer and the editor are both agents (responsible for their performance to someone), but as individuals. The organization is a corporate actor that relates to a collective set of beneficiaries, by delivering products and services to them. If I was to account for the *emergence* of organization in communication, I needed to explain the shift from individual to collective: a bottom-up rather than the more conventional top-down matrix-to-cell perspective. The concept of agency was going to have to be rethought.

Practically and theoretically speaking, I asked myself, how do entities such as organizations "scale up" from encounters between individual actors to the collective intra-organizational departments they represent, who then scale up to the even larger collective center of agency that the organization represents? I decided I would have to use the same logic—the identical theory of communication—to explain the embedding of collective agencies in even more encompassing entities as I would use in explaining interpersonal interaction. Otherwise, I would have had to resort to explanations that were not grounded in communication theory, and that, I was resolved not to do. With these considerations in mind, I turned to the issue of how to "scale up."

Scaling Up: The Origin of Co-orientation Theory

Consider any one of the cells illustrated in Figure 9.1. In every case, there are two agents, each characterized by his or her (or their) own means-end preoccupation. They are linked to each other by a common orientation to an object on which their attention is jointly focused, although from different perspectives. There is a theory that very nicely expresses this relationship. It is called *co-orientation theory*, and it was originally outlined by Theodore Newcomb, in an article published in 1953 (for a critique of his formulation, see Taylor, 2001b).

Briefly, the theory says this. The welding together of the activities that give reality to an organization necessitates communication. Communication is dialogic in its form. Someone has to generate a text, spoken or written, and someone has to interpret it. The text is consequently a co-constructed making of sense, focused on a common object, although perhaps from contrasting worldviews, reflecting different expertise, ideologies, and involvements. The agents that relate to the object are embedded in divergent commitments: to the performance of the essential activity (satisfying some beneficiary, such as a client or a customer) and to the performance of the contributive activity (based in expertise or technical skill of some kind). Borrowing from Newcomb, I think of this elementary unit of organizational communication as an A – B – X relationship.

This may initially appear to be no more than a reformulation of classic information theory: Source A addresses a message to destination B about X. But there is a radical shift of perspective involved, and it is explained by the factor of agency. A and B are not just "messaging"—they are caught up in activity, and their interaction is both grounded in an already ongoing arena of action and also directed to proactively having an effect on that environment. Nor is X merely a message. It is a preoccupation: a focus for both their actions and the target of their interpretive making of sense, always, bear in mind, from the perspective of their respective involvements. X is their connection to a mixed material-social world that has to be attended to, and dealt with, or enacted (Weick, 1979).

The texts they generate in interacting with each other (speech included) are not just about "transmitting information." Speech-in-context is itself, as Austin (1962) decisively showed, a form of action, and it needs to be understood in that way. Similarly, as the many analyses performed by researchers in the tradition of conversation analysis (CA) have amply demonstrated, communication is not a case of one person sending a message to another, who "decodes" or interprets it. The A – B – X relationship is intensely interactive. Meaning is not transmitted; it is negotiated, jointly established in conversation.

In any interaction where there are different finalities in play, although the means of one may logically *appear* to the outsider to complement the ends of the other, practically speaking, a relationship still has to be established. The terms of the relationship have to be negotiated. Communication is the means by which the mutual understanding gets to be established (or fails to do so).

Establishing a relationship has three components. First, the two agents who are co-oriented to what is for them a common object, however different their perspectives on it, need to come to an understanding of the reality that confronts them: the facts of the situation. Second, the two co-orienting agents need to agree on what has to be done and who is to do it. Third, how you deal with each other, and how you establish your respective roles and privileges in any single encounter, will always reflect previous—and set the framework for subsequent—interaction. Negotiating relationship, in the context of organization, is, after all, usually not just a one-off affair. This is why I underline the role of relationship.

The mechanism in language that produces co-oriented interaction is modality. Modality gets expressed in speech by modes of address by formulating what you say as a firm opinion, for example, or conveying to other people what you want by making a request. Establishing mutual statuses and conveying more emotionally charged attitudes of affiliation and power is indexed by features of talks such as politeness versus bluntness, directness versus indirectness, and other more or less subtle signals that tell the person you are interacting with how you see their (and your own) respective social positions (Goffman, 1959).

If all goes well, you end up forming a unified agent whose component individual agencies have constituted a co-oriented relationship. This, in its simplest manifestation, is the basic unit of organizing: getting co-oriented using language.

Scaling Up From the Single Encounter to More Complex Forms of Interaction

The real problem with the simulation model I began with was that it shared the same bias as the definition of organization I cited at the beginning: It took the existence of organization (the matrix) as already given. Let us now, as communication theorists, reverse the perspective by starting with co-orientation, and then use that as a platform to build up to organization. Rather than first define the matrix and then identify the values of the cells, an analytic-deductive approach, we begin with the cells and synthetically-inductively scale up to a matrix of whatever complexity is needed.

First, we have to take into account that there is no guarantee that A, B, and X will be positively co-oriented. Newcomb (1953) saw co-orientation as characterized by polarity, positive or negative, where negative co-orientation means something like conflict. But suppose our members have succeeded in co-orienting positively. Now they act as if they were a single agent. The respective actions of the agents involved are coordinated; they constitute a team. Although they began as an "I" and a "you" (related to an "it" or "they"), they have now become, for others as well as themselves, a "we (it)."

"We's" are, of course, entitled to then enter into relationships with other "you's," whether individual or collective. What started as an interpersonal relationship is now mushrooming into a more complex web or network of embedded relationships. In each of those composite "we's," there had to have been a developing understanding of who was responsible for which kind of performance. Roles, in other words, are emerging. A × B × X is turning into A/B/X.

Once A × B × X is transformed into A/B/X, something very important happens. Now what began as individual agencies (one per actor) have been incorporated into a collective entity, A/B/X. As actors in the context of the unit, each member has now become an agent in the full sense of that term (according to Webster's dictionary): not only acting, but also acting *for* or *representing* their organization. Now when each enters into some activity, they do so as individual agents who represent a collective organization of which they are a member. Producers and editors work for their broadcaster and enjoy both the advantages and inconveniences that come from doing so: restrictions on their freedom of action, on one hand, but on the other, access to the considerable resources, both "allocative" and "authoritative" (Giddens, 1984), that the larger agency possesses. They have been empowered to do things they would otherwise never have been able to envisage (Cooren & Taylor, 2000; Taylor & Cooren, 1997). Scaling up to organization from communication now appears a natural phenomenon, not an aberration. The matrix shown as Figure 9.1 incorporates this syncretism, provided we read it synthetically, rather than analytically.

The 17th-century philosopher Thomas Hobbes, in his famous work *The Leviathan*, wondered how the self-aggrandizing individuals we humans are (as he saw it) could ever form a stable society. Why was it not inevitably a "war of all against all"? Co-orientation theory, I suggest, shows why the emergence of organization is inevitable. The authority of both A and B has been enhanced by their being entitled to speak in the name, and with the authority of, their organizational unit (Taylor & Cooren, 1997). People thus have a selfish reason to be co-oriented, if no other.

Objects, however, define a shared preoccupation: farmers who all farm, fisherfolk who all fish, miners who all mine, philosophers who all philosophize, lawyers who all litigate, physicians who all practice medicine, and so on. The people who play a similar role in co-orientational relationships begin to recognize their own identity as a community of practice that is distinct from other communities with different preoccupations. They have a new reason to be co-oriented: They share a common interest. Collectively, they define one of the axes of the *n*-dimensional set of activities that constitutes the organization as a locus of activity.

I have explained how I believe organization emerges out of interaction, as a constructive dynamic resulting in the consolidation of collective actors. Organizations, however, once formed, perpetuate themselves. That ability to reproduce themselves as universes of patterned transactions involving a complex network of interconnected agents needs to be explained. People join and leave organizations all the time, but the organization is relatively self-perpetuating in spite of the transience. To complete my theory, I realized, I needed to take account of the role of language in organizing, because it is the structuring role of language, I believed, that accounts for the constancy (Taylor & Giroux, 2004; Taylor & Robichaud, 2004).

Language and the Reproduction of Organization

Communication, as Newcomb understood in formulating his theory of co-orientation, is channeled through dialogue. Conversation is a bilateral phenomenon: It links at a minimum one person who assumes the responsibility of initiating an interaction, and at least one other who accepts the position of respondent or co-initiator. The mutual dependency on text-making and interpreting imposes the discipline of a bilateral performance, whether mediated or face-to-face. Short of this, there can be no conversation.

Language is, however, social in origin. It is not the property of an individual, but a collective resource on which he or she is allowed to—indeed must—draw. Furthermore, language is not just a collection of words that take on meaning because they refer to things and events—the "correspondence" view on language. On the contrary, language is a system that conforms to an internal logic, in which words take on meaning because of the way they relate to and interact with other words: not a collection, but a system. When you formulate an utterance in language—a text—you are using a tool that comes with its own built-in properties that you do not control any more than you do the inner workings of the computer you work on every day, or the car you drive to work. You use language, but beware: It is using you as well!

Could language be the carrier of organizational patterning? Does it incorporate the programs or "scripts" of organizing? Do people consciously or unconsciously act out elements of the scripts in their conversations with each other? Would this explain the capacity of organization to reproduce itself in communication? I wondered. Perhaps, I thought, organizations are immanent in the texts that people generate in constructing a conversation and in making sense of their own constructive activity (Taylor & Giroux, 2004).

I developed this idea to illustrate the concept of worldview in a talk I gave at the University of Colorado in 1996 (Taylor, 2000a). It was a way of explaining why I made the kind of distinction I did between text and conversation. Again it illustrates worldview. Let me quote from the Colorado talk (slightly revised and updated here): "Given an imaginary sequence involving two people in communication, **A** and **B**, and their "messages," T_1, T_2, T_3, etc., communication might appear as in Figure 9.2:

"Suppose, however, that we bracket the sequence differently, no longer on the model of [A–T_i–B, etc.], but instead using the alternative bracketing, that of [T_i–A–T_j–B–T_k, etc.].

"Now rather than people interacting via the mediation of "messages," we have "messages" interacting via the mediation of speakers. The perspective has gone from *intersubjective* to what Cooren calls *interobjective* (Cooren, 1995, 1996, 2000) (See Figure 9.3).

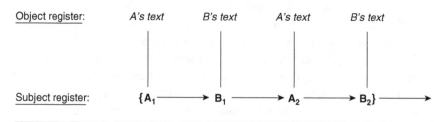

Object register: A's text   B's text   A's text   B's text

Subject register: {A₁ ——→ B₁ ——→ A₂ ——→ B₂} ——→

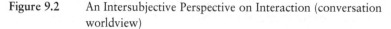

Figure 9.2   An Intersubjective Perspective on Interaction (conversation worldview)

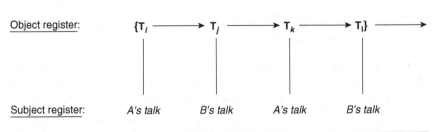

Figure 9.3   An Interobjective Perspective on Interaction (text worldview)

"Think of communication as an encounter of interacting subjects and language objects. From a *subjective* point of view, the speakers/hearers are agents, and language is merely a resource on which they draw to produce and interpret a text, in the business of communicating. The resource of language makes symbol-based communication possible. It enables conversation. When, however, we privilege the point of view of the object (i.e., the text), we reverse our communicational worldview: It is now two objects (i.e., elements of text) that, *through their being used in conversation*, take on an existence as a more complex structure than that of a message. The text thus brought into existence now has the potential to live an autonomous life of its own (it can be recorded), separated (or 'distanciated;' Ricoeur 1981, 1986/1991; Taylor, Cooren, Giroux, & Robichaud, 1996) from its origin."

I went on in that Colorado talk to situate the two perspectives, historically. The text-in-conversation worldview is one that focuses on the dynamic of the interactive process. It draws on the rich tradition of ethnography, ethnomethodology, conversation analysis, speech act theory, and authors such as Erving Goffman, William Labov, Edward Hall, Emanuel Scheflen, Harvey Sacks, Albert Scheglof, Paul Watzlawick, Janet Beavin, and Don Jackson. The conversation-in-text worldview, on the other hand, traces its roots to a different source: structuralism and semiology, rhetoric, narrative, and discourse analysis. Its most influential voices have been those of Kenneth Burke, Michel Foucault, Jacques Derrida, Roland Barthes, Jean Baudrillard, Paul Ricoeur, and Algirdas Greimas.

Alvesson and Kärreman (2000) have recently baptized the two perspectives as, respectively, conversational *discourse* (with a lowercase "d") and textual *Discourses* (with an uppercase "d"). The significance of this inversion of perspective, another illustration of worldview, is this: There is no one privileged way to conceptualize a communication theory of organization. The challenge is not to choose which interpretation to adopt, but to understand the consequences of looking at organization through the alternative lenses of text-in-conversation (or "discourse") and conversation-in-text or "Discourse").

Conceptualizing Organization
as a Phenomenon of Text-in-Conversation

Consider organization from the perspective of text-in-conversation first. People employ strings of language—they make spoken texts—to construct a conversation. Language supplies the tools for both transforming the material-social object to which people are jointly oriented into a topic, or theme, of conversation (an extraconversational dimension) and for expressing an attitude to it, and thus laying the basis for a relationship of commonality of attitude (an intraconversational dimension). They go from $A \times B \times X$ to $A/B/X$, using conversation to do so. We have already explored this dimension.

From the perspective of conversation, organization thus appears to be a synthetic construction. The conversation is, as Sigman (1995) puts it, "consequential": What occurs there matters because it is there that the fate of the organization is settled. Why can't we have peace in the Middle East? Because the two sides are unable to establish the right kind of dialogue. Why did the management-union negotiation break down? Because they couldn't agree on an agenda. And so on.

The current vogue in studies of dialogue is frequently animated by the perception that if people could establish a productive way of dealing with each other in their interactions, many organizational problems would be dissolved. Habermas's (1976/1979, 1998) concept of communicative competence is predicated on the primacy of interaction. Boden's (1994) study of conversation encourages the belief that organization is generated in the conversations of members, as they negotiate the meaning of the events in which they are caught up.

Conceptualizing Organization
as a Phenomenon of Conversation-in-Text

Now, let us consider the notion of organization from a different perspective, that of conversation-in-text. Language is not uniquely a tool for constructing conversation; it is also a medium of sensemaking (Weick, 1995). It is in language that we interpret the experiences we have, including the conversations we engage in. Language explains what Weick (1995) calls the "retrospective," and Giddens (1984) calls the "reflexive," interpretation of the unending flow of experience. Language holds up a mirror in which we can see ourselves and the involvements to which we are committed. Our current sensemaking becomes, reflexively and retrospectively, the context and frame of every future interaction. Every human interaction is understood in context: that of what people understand to be the organizational context where they locate themselves.

Meaning is born in the interaction of sensemaking and context: what is going on now, conversationally, projected onto the screen of our prior experience and expectations, which now become an interpretive lens to read the meaning of our current experience. This is the dynamic that Weick (1979) called "enactment." Every conversational exchange around some object is open to more than one interpretation; it is always, to again use Weick's term, "equivocal." We select from the gamut of possible readings of what is being said and done the particular interpretation that best fits our expectations. It is in this sense that language-as-text constitutes organization. We enact organization in such a way that its situated interaction conforms, as far as possible, to our expectations.

This, of course, raises the question of what is the property of language that enables us to inscribe our ideas about organization in language? How are expectations constructed? The answer is to be found in a dimension of language that is now receiving increasing attention among organizational scholars: narrative.

The Role of Narrative in Constituting Organization

Communication scholars increasingly accept that the principal resource language affords to describe human action and motive is narrative (Boje, 1991, 1995, 2001; Boje, Alvarez, & Schooling, 2001; Czarniawska, 1997, 1998, 1999). It is the natural medium of sensemaking, the device we typically use to describe strings of activity, and interactions with others (Bruner, 1991).[3]

Stories give a composite picture of several actors caught up in a narrative of actions and reactions out of which a web of relationships is constructed. Stories create protagonists and oppose them to antagonists: the "white hats" and the "black hats." They establish a framework of enablers (allies, patrons, instruments, opportunities) and barriers (opponents, complications, evil forces). They create a schedule of phases of action to be realized, from recognition of a challenge, to the recruitment and motivation of key actors, to the qualification of protagonists, to the evaluation or "sanction" of the ending. They structure the conversational world by interpreting it and, in the process, shape the meaning we give to events. They polarize the web of relationships in which we find ourselves by making some out to be our friends, and others our opponents, and perhaps even hostile opponents: enemies. They attribute intentions to actors' acts—*reasons* why they behave the way they do, Bruner observes, rather than *causes* of behaviors. They thus construct a map on which are inscribed the agencies that I have argued are the binding force of the organization. They color interaction, even moralize it. Greimas (1993) writes, "human action does not seem to have meaning unless it is rooted in the universe of values that frames it" (p. 22, my translation).[4]

It is true that the story may typically be told as a sequence of interactive exchanges, involving specific actors, specific events, and specific circumstances. Nevertheless, as Bruner (1991) observes, the story is in its essence "generic." Particular happenings are what he calls a "vehicle," not a "destination," because the particulars of a story are "tokens of broader types" (p. 6). Beneath the "figural" (the specific), in other words, lies the "structural" (the generic) (Greimas, 1987). We may think of ourselves as unique, but in the domain of narrative we are exemplars, and our experience has meaning because it exemplifies and may over time modify the deeper categories of narrative. If this were not so, experience would *have* no meaning; it would amount to no more than sensation. Only by observing and interpreting ourselves as actors do we *become* actors in the full sense of the word. Organization is constructed out of people's experience, but it also enfolds and makes sense of it.

Every action, if it is to have an organizational character, must be set within two kinds of tacit contractual framework: that which motivates and justifies the action, and that which judges its eventual performance. In my example, then, the CBC was both mandated and judged by society, although the respective modalities of mandating and evaluating were different, institutionally: in one case Parliament, in the other the audience and its interpreters (see note 2). But all organizations are ultimately legitimated and judged by Society. As Giddens (1984) has observed, power and legitimacy are intimately tied to, and both are contingent on, and motivate, meaning.

Conclusion

I have now traced the path I followed in developing an answer to the question I started with: "What is an organization?" It is time to review the steps of my inquiry and draw some conclusions.

First, I argued that the structural basis of an organization corresponds to a network of interlocking activities. One convenient way to represent the network is as a matrix of transactions involving individual actors who co-orient to each other because of their common interest in some object. They do so, however, from different perspectives, because for one the object is a means to an end, while for the other it is the end, or main focus, of their work. Following the lead of system analysts, I called this difference of perspective their respective *worldviews*. Normally, we think of this basic structure of intersecting activities as an effect of planning on the part of management. However, all the empirical research I have done, as well as my personal experience of complex organization, led me to a different view, namely that however planned the structure had been initially, it continually evolved in practice to transactional patterns that deviated significantly from the original design. Organizations *self*-organize, and they do so as a result of the dynamic of local interaction. The self-organization is a communication phenomenon, and in this sense communication is a meso-level that needs to be theorized if we are to understand the relation of macro (structure) to micro (practice), and vice versa.

I then came to believe that communication is not best described as messaging, or knowledge transmission, but as a practical activity in its own right that has as its outcome the formation of relationships. The communication activity does indeed generate shared knowledge as people talk their way to a common view, but it also sets the stage for acting as a unit on the outside world, while it simultaneously instantiates relationships of authority, trust, and identity. The construction of relationships is not limited to interpersonal interaction; more complex interagent transactions result in the formation of collective, as well as individual identities and associational patterns.

All this occurs in language. Language, however, is both a medium of interaction (a conversational dimension) and a medium of sensemaking (a textual dimension). I tried to show the richness of the *worldview* concept, because although we use language to negotiate relationships, language simultaneously "uses" us in the sense that it informs our understanding of what is occurring, and it supplies the program or script that enables us to construct an organization. Not only do we self-organize in communication; the facility of language also both enables and constrains us to *re*-produce organizational form over time.

The co-orientational dynamic links more than individuals, of course; it connects classes of individuals such as producers versus editors, doctors versus administrators, and clerks versus supervisors. What distinguishes each category of organizational member is its sharing of a common worldview. The individuals collectively constitute a community of practice. On the other hand, the communities are also divided from each other by worldview. It follows that because an organization is a complex mix of differentiated communities of practice, it is also a mosaic of worldviews. That diversity poses a challenge of integration. The kind of unitary model of organization that is sometimes portrayed in the management literature is a fantasy. An organization of any considerable size and complexity is a *multiverse* of different rationalities, each grounded in a practice (Taylor, 2001a). The implication is clear: The human actors who people different communities of practice in an organization speak a different language. To understand what others in the "same" organization are saying, they must literally translate. A degree of distortion is inevitable (Brown & Duguid, 2000).

What we call an "organization" is, in fact, a congeries of communities of practice, each characterized by its particular cognitive domain (Maturana, 1988), and simultaneously linked to, and alienated from, other communities within the organizational ambit with which they nevertheless share a common fate. Organization is, consequently, a restless ongoing search for closure: for the resolution of irresolvable contradictions, for a solution to the dilemma of means that fit badly with ends, and for identities that in the act of self-affirmation may be denials of others. If there is a "system," then, it is unlike the one our predecessors conceived of.

So where does organization come from?

Jacques Derrida (1971, 1986) has illuminated the mechanism by which an organization takes on an existence (Charland, 1998; Taylor, 2000b). His example of the genesis of organization is the United States itself. For Derrida, the American *Declaration of Independence* illustrates a curious logic. The gentlemen who signed it did so in the name of a non-existent nation that came into existence in the act of their signing, and, in doing so, gave them the authority to be signers in its name. The authority to speak, and to sign, is vested in them at the moment, and by the fact, of their signing. As Derrida (1986, p. 10) explained this odd circularity, "The signature invents the signer." (Think worldview, and what he is saying seems less bizarre: a singular merging of text and conversation.[5])

Obviously, the action of the delegates assembled in Philadelphia in 1776 would have been an empty gesture in the absence of a system of activities that concretely manifested the reality of a new country. On the other hand, the system of activities would have remained a collection of colonies in the absence of the declaration. The United States is thus both an ideological and a real entity. By analogy, an organization is not just a creation of language; in the absence of a real activity matrix (people, technologies, material resources, plant, etc.) it remains a "dummy" company, not a real organization. By the same token, in the absence of an act of self-constitution through the medium of language it does not exist either.

The same principle holds for all organization of the kind that is capable of acting as a collective entity. It is from the organization that the authority emanates which in turn justifies the actions of those who identify with it and who speak in its name, as its representatives (Taylor & Cooren, 1997). But it is vice versa their activities that legitimate and support the organization.

So my image of organization is this. On one hand, it is a web of interlocking co-orientational relationships, more or less stable, and more or less amicable/competitive. On the other hand, it is an endless search to give meaning to organization by grounding it in a persuasive story of challenge and response, in which some individuals find an identity as heroes and others are identified as treasured allies or treacherous adversaries. The story is never completely shared nor finished, so the intention it expresses must be re-established repeatedly.

Organizations, in my experience, are restless sites of human activity and ongoing struggles to reconcile ideology and practice. The process of reconciling the contradictions of collective action is inherently self-organizing. Organization is, I think, best thought of as a form of life and, like other forms of life, always evolving.

A Brief Postscript

The story of my quest for of a theory of communication sufficiently rich and complex to explain the genesis of organization is not ended. What I have been describing is where I have been, not where I am going. My current research is carrying me into a new area—that of complexity theory—which I see as being the logical next step in continuing my odyssey. After all, the development of a scientific theory has no endpoint. Each step we take merely opens up a new vista that invites us to go further on the next mile.

Notes

1. The Canadian Broadcasting Corporation was originally conceived on the model of the British BBC, as a monopoly state broadcasting network (affiliated in Canada, however, with numerous privately owned and operated local stations). Radio continues to this day to adhere to this pattern. The Corporation reports to Parliament and not to the government of the day, an important distinction because this reporting relationship was intended to ensure a measure of independence (the post-Iraq controversy pitting Tony Blair against the BBC sheds an interesting light on the tension this independence may produce). With the arrival of television, however, the preferred model for emulation was CBS and, secondarily, NBC (ABC was not a major player at that time). The monopoly situation that had previously existed was abandoned with the election of a conservative government in the late 1950s, when competing networks were born. Thus the CBC was, and is, a hybrid, when compared with its American equivalents: It combines some of the functions of PBS as a public broadcaster with many of the characteristics of any other large network in North America, including the corporate sponsorship of many programs (news continues, however, to be nonsponsored). I worked for the CBC at the time that it was striving to adapt to its new niche as one of several engaged in a competitive search for audience. There was, in other words, a need to establish a new identity.

2. At the time I left the CBC to return to graduate school, the corporation was embroiled in a bitter battle pitting Public Affairs producers against their own management. The ostensible issue at stake was the future of a Public Affairs program titled *This Hour Has Seven Days*. The program had achieved in its 2-year existence an extraordinary audience, rivaling that of *Saturday Night NHL Hockey* (the runaway winner of the audience race at the time). *Seven Days* was a blend of irreverent humor, cutting-edge journalism, and ombudsmanship, with an exceptional track record of unearthing the peccadilloes of public figures. It gloried in stirring the pot, and it developed a loyal following at a time when the media were considerably more discreet than they now are. But it upset senior management, who thought many of its elements were in "bad taste"—not in the tradition of the CBC. There may well have been political pressure in the background as well, although that was never established. The dispute finally made its way to a committee of Parliament, and it was very evident from the testimony that the issue indeed was precisely the responsibility of the CBC to its public. The producers argued, unsuccessfully, that the success of their show demonstrated public acceptance of and support for the program. Management argued that it alone was uniquely mandated to interpret the responsibility of the agency to its public. *Seven Days* producers saw themselves as forerunners of a new CBC style; management, located in Ottawa, away from the principal production centers of Toronto and Montreal, did not. Management being, in the end, management, won, and the show was cancelled. Not too long after, in fact, the department itself was dissolved, and its components were integrated into News. All of this occurred at the time I mentioned before, when the CBC was adjusting from being a monopoly to a time of heightened competition. There were, of course, parallels to the declining independence of public affairs programming in the major American networks as well, in the post-Murrow, post-Friendly era of broadcasting (Auletta, 1991). This incident left a deep imprint on my consciousness, and it undoubtedly has influenced my views on organization in general ever since.

3. Bruner's article is a lucid and perceptive overview of narrative theory that takes account of the cognitive as well as the structural dimension of narrative. It is the best introduction to narrative theory that I have yet found.

4. Greimas is one of the greatest analysts of narrative in the literature, although his work is not well known in North America.

5. Searle (1989, p. 541) describes this as a performative speech act, or "declaration," in that its point "is to change the world in such a way that the propositional content matches the world, because the world has been changed to match the propositional content. . . . Declarations thus have simultaneously both the word-to-world and the world-to-word directions of fit."

References

Alvesson, M., & Kärreman, D. (2000). Taking the linguistic turn in organizational research: Challenges, responses, and consequences. *Journal of Applied Behavioral Science, 36,* 136–158.

Auletta, K. (1991). *Three blind mice: How the TV networks lost their way.* New York: Random House.

Austin, J. L. (1962). *How to do things with words.* Oxford, UK: Oxford University Press.

Boden, D. (1994). *The business of talk: Organizations in action.* Cambridge, MA: Polity.

Boje, D. M. (1991). The storytelling organization: A study of story performance in an office-supply firm. *Administrative Science Quarterly, 36,* 106–126.

Boje, D. M. (1995). Stories of the storytelling organization: A postmodern analysis of Disney as "Tamara-land." *Academy of Management Journal, 38,* 997–1035.

Boje, D. M. (2001). *Narrative methods for organizational and communication research.* Thousand Oaks, CA: Sage.

Boje, D. M., Alvarez, R. C., & Schooling, B. (2001). Reclaiming stories in organization: Narratologies and action sciences. In S. Linstead & R. Westwood (Eds.), *The language of organization* (pp. 132–175). London: Sage.

Brown, J. S., & Duguid, P. (2000). *The social life of information.* Boston: Harvard Business School Press.

Bruner, J. (1991, Autumn). The narrative construction of reality. *Critical Inquiry,* 1–21.

Charland, M. (1998, November). *The rhetoric of the people in non-sovereign democracies: The constitutions of British North America.* Paper presented at the National Communication Association, New York.

Cooren, F. (1995). *Énonciation, médiation et organisation: Proposition d'un modèle transformationnel des actes de langage.* Doctoral dissertation, Département de Communication, Université de Montréal.

Cooren, F. (1996, May). *The communication-organization link revisited: The organizing property of interobjectivity.* Paper presented to the 46th International Communication Association Annual Conference, Chicago.

Cooren, F. (2000). *The organizing property of communication.* Amsterdam: John Benjamins.

Cooren, F., & Taylor, J. R. (2000). Association and dissociation in an ecological controversy: The great whale case. In N. W. Coppola & B. Karis (Eds.), *Technical communication, deliberative rhetoric, and environmental discourse: Connections and directions* (pp. 171–190). Stamford, CT: Ablex.

Czarniawska, B. (1997). *Narrating the organization: Dramas of institutional identity.* Chicago: University of Chicago Press.

Czarniawska, B. (1998). *A narrative approach in organization studies.* Thousand Oaks, CA: Sage.

Czarniawska, B. (1999). *Writing management: Organization theory as a literary genre.* Oxford, UK: Oxford University Press.

Derrida, J. (1971). Signature Évènement Contexte. *Actes du XV° Congrès de l'Association des Sociétés de Philosophie de Langue Française, Université de Montréal.* Montréal: Éditions Montmoorency. (Also published as the introductory chapter to *Limited Inc.*, 1988)

Derrida, J. (1986). Declarations of independence. *New Political Science, 15,* 7–15.

Etzioni, A. (1964). *Modern organizations.* Englewood Cliffs, NJ: Prentice-Hall.

Giddens, A. (1984). *The constitution of society: Outline of the theory of structuration.* Cambridge, MA: Polity.

Goffman, E. (1959). *The presentation of self in everyday life.* New York: Doubleday Anchor.

Greimas, A. (1987). *On meaning: Selected writings in semiotic theory* (P. J. Perron & F. H. Collins, Trans.). Minneapolis: University of Minnesota Press.

Greimas, A. (1993). Preface. In J. Courtès (Ed.), *Sémiotique narrative et discursive* [The semiotics of narrative and discourse] (pp. 5–25). Paris: Hachette.

Habermas, J. (1979). *Communication and the evolution of society* (T. McCarthy, Trans.). Boston: Beacon. (Original work published 1976)

Habermas, J. (1998). *On the pragmatics of communication.* Cambridge, MA: MIT Press.

Hammer, M., & Champy, J. (1993). *Reengineering the corporation: A manifesto for business revolution.* New York: HarperBusiness.

Hobbes, T. (1947). *Leviathan, or the matter, forme and power of a commonwealth ecclesiastical and civil.* London: J. M. Dent. (Original work published 1914)

Maturana, H. (1988, October). *Ontology of observing: The biological foundations of self-consciousness and the physical domain of existence.* Retrieved June 25, 2004, from www.inteco.cl/biology/ontology/

Newcomb, T. (1953). An approach to the study of communicative acts. *Psychological Review, 60,* 393–404.

Ricoeur, P. (1981). *Hermeneutics and the human sciences* (J. B. Thompson, Trans.). Cambridge, UK: Cambridge University Press.

Ricoeur, P. (1991). *From text to action* (K. Blamey & J. B. Thompson, Trans.). Evanston, IL: Northwestern University Press. (Original work published 1986)

Searle, J. R. (1989). How performatives work. *Linguistics and Philosophy, 12,* 535–558.

Sigman, S. J. (1995). *The consequentiality of communication.* Hillsdale, NJ: Lawrence Erlbaum.

Star, S. L., & Griesemer, J. R. (1989). Institutional ecology, "translations," and boundary objects: Amateurs and professionals in Berkeley's Museum of Vertebrate Zoology, 1907–1939. *Social Studies of Science, 19,* 387–420.

Taylor, J. R. (1982). Computer-aided message systems: An organizational perspective. In N. Naffah (Ed.), *Office information systems* (pp. 631–651). Paris: INRIA/ North Holland.

Taylor, J. R. (1983). Conceptual barriers to productivity and les obstacles conceptuels à la productivité. *Optimum: The Forum of Management, 14*(1, 2), 19–42, 56–84.

Taylor, J. R. (1993). *Rethinking the theory of organizational communication: How to read an organization.* Norwood, NJ: Ablex.

Taylor, J. R. (2000a). Apples and orangutans: The worldviews of organizational communication. *Saison Mauve, 3*(1), 45–64.

Taylor, J. R. (2000b). Is there a "Canadian" approach to the study of organizational communication? *Canadian Journal of Communication, 25*(1), 145–174.

Taylor, J. R. (2001a). The rational organization re-evaluated. *Communication Theory, 11*(2), 137–177.

Taylor, J. R. (2001b). Toward a theory of imbrication and organizational communication. *American Journal of Semiotics, 17*(2), 1–29.

Taylor, J. R. (2002). Imbrication and organization. In J. Barjis, J. L. G. Dietz, & G. Godlkuhl (Eds.), *Proceedings of the Seventh International Workshop on the Language-Action Perspective on Communication Modeling (LAP 2002)*. Delft, The Netherlands: Delft University of Technology.

Taylor, J. R., & Cooren, F. (1997). What makes communication "organizational?" How the many voices of the organization become the *one* voice of *an* organization. *Journal of Pragmatics, 27,* 409–438.

Taylor, J. R., Cooren, F., Giroux, N., & Robichaud, D. (1996). The communicational basis of organization: Between the conversation and the text. *Communication Theory, 6*(1), 1–39.

Taylor, J. R., & Giroux, H. (2004). The role of language in self-organizing systems. In G. Barnett & R. Houston (Eds.), *Self-organizing systems* (pp. 127–163). New York: Hampton.

Taylor, J. R., Gurd, G., & Bardini, T. (1997). The worldviews of cooperative work. In G. Bowker, L. Gasser, S. L. Star, & W. Turner (Eds.), *Social science research, technical systems, and cooperative work* (pp. 379–413). Mahwah, NJ: Lawrence Erlbaum Associates.

Taylor, J. R., & Robichaud, D. (2004). Finding the organization in the communication: Discourse as action and sensemaking [Special issue on textuality and agency: Constitutive elements of organization]. *Organization, 11*(3), 395–413.

Weick, K. E. (1969). *The social psychology of organizing*. Reading, MA: Addison-Wesley.

Weick, K. (1979). *The social psychology of organizing* (2nd ed.). Reading, MA: Addison-Wesley.

Weick, K. E. (1995). *Sensemaking in organizations*. Thousand Oaks, CA: Sage.

10

Globalization Theory

Cynthia Stohl

Experiencing Globalization

> *The concept of globalization implies, first and foremost, a stretching of social, political and economic activities across frontiers such that events, decisions and activities in one region of the world can come to have significance for individuals and communities in distant regions of the globe.*
>
> —(Held, McGrew, Goldblatt, & Perraton, 1999, p. 15)

On a beautiful New Zealand spring day in November, 1983, I was rushing to the office of the plant manager of a multinational company to submit my final research report on communication and quality circles. As I entered the factory, I found myself face-to-face with the union secretary. "This is great," I said. "I was told you weren't going to be here today. I was just on my way to give X [the American plant manager] his report and then was going to put your copy in the mail. But since you're here, take the report now—it will save me a trip to the post office." He thanked me and accepted the report (the same one I had prepared for management as per my agreement with both management and the union before starting the research project), and I continued to the head office. Once there, the plant manager and I went over the results and conclusions contained in the report. We discussed some very positive findings as well as a few issues of contention that were apparent in my analyses of worker and managerial communication patterns. After an hour, I gave my final thank yous and good-byes, then went home. My family and I left for a month holiday in Australia before our return to the United States to usher in 1984.

I was feeling really good. After completing my dissertation in 1982 on the relationship between social networks and development of children's communication competence, I had just finished my first international study, building upon my dissertation findings and my interest in organizational participatory groups and networks. While my husband was on a Fulbright appointment in New Zealand, I had spent 6 months in Christchurch working in an American-owned tire manufacturing plant collecting qualitative and quantitative data from 258 union members, 25 supervisors, and 10 managers. I was a participant observer in at least 50 quality circle meetings and spent more than 75 hours on the production line with the union workers making tires. I had found that workers involved in quality circles were more knowledgeable about key organizational issues and procedures; had developed richer, more diverse, and more multiplex communication networks; and had more positive attitudes than workers who were not part of the quality circle program. However, I also found that the most dissatisfied workers in the factory were former circle workers who expressed frustration about particular issues based on their knowledge, networks, and experiences within the participation program. The paradoxical effects of participatory programs and the changing patterns of communication were theoretically and pragmatically interesting, and they extended my earlier work into a new domain.

One month later, when I returned home to the United States, three telegrams (no e-mail in those days) from the U.S.-based international division head were waiting for me. With increasing urgency, each message demanded that I call him immediately. I didn't. Instead, I first called colleagues in New Zealand and discovered that 3 weeks after I left there was an unanticipated work stoppage (for the first time in 3 years). Several phone calls later, I was able to piece together what had happened. Directly after the union secretary received the report, he shared it with the line workers. In contrast, it took the plant manager much longer to get the report "down" to the supervisory level. He had first sent it to the United States, where executives evaluated what should be done with it. By that time, the workers were demanding some sort of reaction to some of the issues raised in the report as well as other concerns they had voiced. The supervisors (who hadn't seen the report and therefore didn't actually know what was contained in it except through rumors) were increasingly frustrated. When the work stoppage occurred, the U.S.-based American management blamed not only me for writing the report but also the plant manager for letting me give the report to the union. The union workers were furious with the American management and New Zealand supervisors. The supervisors were angry with everyone, and the finger pointing continued for weeks. Within a year, the plant manager was replaced. Soon thereafter, the quality circle program was replaced with a new form of workplace participation, the relationship between union workers and the management changed, and within a few years a Japanese company bought out the multinational corporation.

How and why such serious consequences followed the dissemination of information that was relatively positive and already known by many was both upsetting and fascinating to me. There were many causal possibilities, but equally possible was that there were no links and the later events were completely unrelated. Certainly the last of the changes was completely independent of my study results. As a new communication PhD, I understood the importance of emergent networks and the significance of the patterns of communication for message production and reception. I knew the intercultural theories that would help explain the differences in the behavior, attitudes, and interpretations of the American and Kiwi management and the New Zealand and Polynesian union workers, and I also recognized that subcultural difference existed between labor and management, and between salaried and hourly workers. All of these clearly were important pieces in filling in parts of the puzzle of the times. But these micro and macro theories did not provide a very satisfying or full explanation of the events that were unfolding. I needed to find a theory that encompassed the complexity and volatility of what was happening in the organizational world. And perhaps, as I honestly look back after all these years, I was also searching for a perspective that would strengthen my resolve that my role as a participant observer did not make me responsible for what was rapidly unfolding. A theory of globalization would help systematically contextualize these events.

In this essay, I will explore the evolution of globalization theory, focusing on the work most relevant for organizational communication. The first section, "Globalizing Organizations," summarizes some of the earliest communication and management theories that addressed issues related to organizational communication in an increasingly interconnected world. These early theories were designed to (a) understand how organizational survival and efficacy in contemporary society is built upon the ability to understand and address cultural differences within the workplace and across markets (theories of divergence), or (b) identify the environmental, technological, and organizational mechanisms that result in the similar structuring and organizing of experience throughout the world (theories of convergence). The next section, "Organizing Globalization," addresses more recent conceptualizations of globalization and organizational processes that holistically incorporate the historical, political, economic, social, and cultural tensions and transformations that were and still are taking place. An explication of the various debates and approaches to globalization within and across these academic disciplines is presented. Significantly, a commonality across perspectives is the critical role organizations play in the development, maintenance, and transformation of the global system. The third section, "Theorizing Globalization," clarifies the ways in which globalization is approached in contemporary literature through a brief survey of the metaphors and definitions found in globalization theories. The final section, "Communicating and Globalizing," explicates the organizational communication implications of six dynamic and interdependent processes found within most theories of globalization.

Globalizing Organizations

> In the last hundred years, the political interstate system came to provide the dominant organizational forms for cross-border flows, with national states as its key actors. It is this condition that has changed dramatically since the 1980's as a result of privatization, deregulation, the opening up of national economies to foreign firms, and the growing participation of national economic actors in global markets. . . . Increasingly NGOs, government regulators, mayors, professional associations, and others operate transnationally and thereby constitute a variety of cross-border networks. (Sassen, 2002, pp. 1, 2)

The 1980s were a time of great upheaval in the world of organizations. What was happening in the American company I had studied in a very distant part of the world was related to the economic, political, social, and technological context that was facing all organizations across the globe. The world was changing—new communication technologies such as fax machines and portable computers were easing the flow and speed of communications across time and space (Rice & Associates, 1984); some organizations were becoming more powerful than nation-states and had larger GNPs (Feld & Jordan, 1988); partnerships between national governments, multinational organizations, and local communities were becoming commonplace (Perrucci & Stohl, 1998); and problems of the environment, human rights, and disease were increasingly seen as global and not national issues

(Simmons & Oudraat, 2001). In short, economic integration was just one form of global exchange that was increasing exponentially; there were also escalations in political, cultural, and personal global interconnections. In other words, the boundaries between domestic and international organizing of all kinds, whether by nongovernmental advocacy organizations, corporate organizations, or nonprofit or volunteer organizations, were progressively more blurred. To understand any organizational communication phenomena, it was critical to understand how organizations were positioned in relation to the larger communicative, economic, political, cultural, and social forces of the times.

And so I began to search for theories of organizing and communication that would capture both the macro and the micro aspects of collective action in an increasingly interconnected world. I sought to find a theory that would provide constructs that would help me explore the significance of these permeable boundaries and interconnected networks through which interpersonal communication was framed and through which organizational decisions, reactions, and relations emerged. I needed a theory grounded in the fundamental principle that micro agents and macro structures interactively shape each other, but although many communication theories created space for the study of multiple levels of collective action, the ones I was familiar with did not embody or specify the historical, political, economic, technological, and cultural aspects that were needed. Nor did they capture the degree and intensity of increasing linkages between domestic and global organizing. I was in search of theory to help me understand this complex and rapidly changing organizational landscape.

It is important to note that "globalization" wasn't a popular term at that time. The word "globalization" first appeared in Webster's dictionary in 1961, but virtually no academic or journalistic articles or books published before 1975 included the words globalism, globalizing, or globalization (Scholte, 2000). In interpersonal and organizational communication, cross-cultural and intercultural communication were well established (e.g., the first *Handbook of Organizational Communication* published in 1987 had a chapter titled "Cross Cultural Perspectives," Triandis and Albert). In mass communication, influenced heavily by the prescient work of Marshall McLuhan and his notion of the global village, there was a focus on media and international telecommunications issues.

It wasn't until the mid-1990s that the terms "globalizing" and "globalization" were found in the organizational communication literature. Even as late as 1993, I published an article in *The Journal of Applied Communication Research* titled "International Organizing and Organizational

Communication" (Stohl, 1993b), although I recognize, in retrospect, that I was really writing about the globalization of organizational processes. In 1994, when researchers in other fields had turned their attention to the importance of macro-cultural issues in organizational studies (as evidenced, for example, by special issues focusing on globalization in many of the major organizational journals[1]), communication scholars were still lamenting the lack of attention to communication issues in the multinational organization (see Wiseman & Shuter, 1994, p. 7).

Therefore, it is not surprising that my early search for a comprehensive theory was unsuccessful. I was able to find *theories of divergence and convergence*. Theories of divergence (e.g., Hall, 1981; Hofstede, 1984; Triandis, 1983) focus on issues of cultural variability and how those differences make a difference in how people enact, organize, and make sense of their organizational experience. An underlying premise of these theories is that in contemporary organizations, traditional national boundaries mean less and intercultural communication becomes more central and important. Metaphors associated with divergence theories often emphasize the energy/synergy, excitement, beauty, creativity, and options enabled by allowing differences to flourish in a global workplace; for example, the global marketplace, kaleidoscope, bazaar, or garden (Contractor, 2002; Gannon, 2001; Mitroff, 1987).

Divergence theories, grounded in issues of practical rationality (Habermas, 1984), focus on human interpretation and experience of the world as meaningful and intersubjectively constructed. Communication is the essence of culture, and organizational effectiveness is rooted in the ability of people from different cultures to work together. Divergence theories identify key dimensions of cultural variability (e.g., power distance, monochronic/polychronic approaches to time, high context/low context). Each dimension is then associated with particular practices or interpretations (Stohl, 1993a). Many researchers in organizational behavior, management, and communication rely heavily on these theories to explain how managers can create cultural synergy, improve workplace satisfaction, facilitate team effectiveness, and manage differences (e.g., Bantz, 1993; Harris & Moran, 1999; Krone, Garrett, & Chen, 1992; Stage, 1999) in workplaces that are increasingly multicultural and dispersed across time and space.

In contrast, theories of convergence focus on how and why organizations are becoming similar worldwide (e.g., Bartlett & Ghoshal, 1989; Hickson, Hinings, MacMillan, & Schwitter, 1974). The convergence literature refers to a set of imperatives embedded in the global economy that result in similar organizational structuring across nations. Even when cultural differences are recognized, the theories minimize these differences and emphasize the similarity of structural adaptation.

The changing patterns and structures of communication typically related to the demands of globalization require flexibility, responsiveness, speed, and efficient knowledge production, generation, and dissemination. These organizing features are most likely to be found in nonhierarchical, emergent, interorganizational and intraorganizational networks (Ghoshal & Bartlett, 1990; Miles & Snow, 1995; Monge & Fulk 1999; Nohria & Berkley, 1994). A great deal of empirical work addressing convergence processes has been conducted by administrative science and strategic management scholars who have been concerned with the macro restructuring of global industrial and service sectors and transborder organizational alliances (e.g., Astley, 1985; Burger, 2002).

Convergence metaphors may be optimistic (e.g., a melting pot, the end of history [Fukuyama, 1992]), neutral (e.g., networks [Lipnack & Stamps, 1986; Powell, 1990]) or negative (e.g., cultural imperialism [Tomlinson, 1999]). In recent years, one of the most popular convergence metaphors was developed by the sociologist George Ritzer (1993) in *The McDonaldization of Society*. McDonaldization is "the process by which the principles of the fast-food restaurant are coming to dominate more and more sectors of American society as well as the rest of the world" (Ritzer, 1993, p. 4). Ritzer powerfully demonstrates how across the globe, the four fundamental values of McDonald's production—efficiency, calculability, predictability, and control through nonhuman technology—are being imported into many aspects of our lives, from childbirth to death, from sports and sex to education, economics, and entertainment. Basing his work on the classic sociological and organizational theorist Max Weber, Ritzer explores how rational organizational systems that seem to facilitate organizational survival turn in on themselves, leading to irrational and undesirable global outcomes.

Most convergence theories operate within a framework of technical/instrumental rationality concerned predominantly with issues of organizational survival and effectiveness. The theories posit mechanisms that increase the likelihood of organizational isomorphism (e.g., DiMaggio & Powell, 1991); that is, the tendency for organizations to become increasingly similar. These mechanisms are rooted in the increased competitiveness of the global market and the institutional mechanisms related to legitimacy (coercive mechanisms), modeling behavior (mimetic mechanisms), and the increasing professionalism and standardization of professional norms (normative mechanisms). I refer the reader to Stohl (2001) for a detailed review of divergence and convergence perspectives.

As fascinating and useful as these metaphors and theories were to me, however, they did not focus specifically on the mutually dependent micro and macro trends and meanings embedded in the increasing interconnectedness of contemporary societies. Neither perspective alone or even both together adequately accounted for the complex organizational processes that I watched unfold throughout the 1980s. The environmental and technological pressures for the organization I studied to become more and more similar to other large global manufacturing organizations was obvious in its choice to implement a Japanese-based participation program of quality circles (the convergence perspective). That decision clearly clashed with the proprietary pull of cultural identifications, traditional values, and conventional practices of social life in the various ethnic groups that constituted the New Zealand workforce (divergence perspectives). However, there was little place in any of these theories to explore the theoretical and methodological issues and tensions associated with identity, technology adoption and adaptation, informational dynamics, economics, the role of nation-states, interconnectedness, and global regulatory organizations that clearly were critical features of the organizational landscape.

The insufficiency of these theories also became obvious at the 1992 conference at Arizona State University on new directions for organizational communication. I gave an address (Stohl, 1992) titled "Exploring the New Organizational Horizon: IGOS [international governmental organizations], INGOs [international nongovernmental organizations], and BINGOs [business international nongovernmental organizations]." In the paper, I claimed that our field needed to develop a global perspective, to study all forms of international organizing, and to rethink how we situated and understood the internal/external linkages of organizational communication. I even developed a preliminary agenda for organizational communication. I was, however, unable to provide a satisfactory response to a fundamental question posed by a respected senior scholar in the audience. "What," he asked, "are the theoretical constructs of this new global system that would help us understand what is going on in organizations today?"

A final concern regarding both the divergence and convergence perspectives was that most of the theories treated the increasing intensification of economic, political, cultural, and social interconnectedness as neutral phenomena. Yet these processes and effects clearly have significant and long-term consequences for individuals, organizations, communities, nation-states, and society. Life in the New Zealand community changed in both large and small ways as a result of the increasing proportion of exchanges across borders that were taking place. Integration may promote prosperous stability as well as sow the seeds of discordant stratification. Theories of globalization need to provide constructs and theoretical propositions that capture the mutual oppositions, disjunctures, paradoxes, differentiation, and unity that are embodied in the process.

Organizing Globalization

> Not another book on globalization! No doubt many a prospective reader will at first despair that a further title has squeezed onto already overcrowded shelves. Has this hype-propelled bandwagon not already slaughtered too many trees? (Scholte, 2000, p. xiii)

How the academic world has changed since 1984! Not only is global-ization at the forefront of most discussions about contemporary society, it is "an idea whose time has come" (Held et al., 1999, p. 1). People every-where are talking and writing about it. A plethora of new theories abound. Social scientists, philosophers, humanists, economists, journalists, public intellectuals, and others across the globe have written treatises addressing globalization.

Most generally globalization is seen as "the widening, deepening, and speeding up of worldwide interconnectedness in all aspects of contemporary social life" (Held et al., 1999, p. 5), but it also is conceived more narrowly. When globalization is viewed as an economic phenomenon, the means of production, exchange, distribution, and consumption are highlighted, neo-liberalism ideology is seen to permeate society, the world market dominates, and transnational links often transcend and supplant nation-states. When globalization is viewed as a political phenomenon, the exercise of power, coercion, surveillance, and control over people and territories is paramount. When it is conceived as a cultural phenomenon, symbolic exchange through rituals, everyday practices, mass media, face-to-face communication, and cultural performances are central. The intensification of global conscious-ness, reflexivity, perceptions of risk, the struggle for identity, and community are overriding features of this approach. Table 10.1 presents a selected list of globalization theorists and the relevant definitions, concepts, and con-structs associated with each.

It is important to note that diverse approaches can be found within as well as across disciplines and that different aspects of, and positions regard-ing, globalization are highlighted and challenged. In political science, debates rage over whether globalization means the end of sovereignty, the demise of national political autonomy, the end of history, the closing stages of the social democratic era, and, most generally, where the real locus of power is in the global system (Fukuyama, 1992; Krieger, 1999; Ohmae, 1995; Waters, 1995). Globalization is variously framed as a unified process that is accelerating beyond the control of single nation-states, a process that is contingent upon governmental policies "making and unmaking globalization" (Holm, 2003), or business as usual where the power of the

(Text continued on page 241)

Table 10.1 Selected List of Globalization Theorists

Theorist	Definition	Primary Areas of Focus	Arguments	Constructs
Arjun Appadurai (1997)	Globalization is characterized by two forces, mass migration and electronic mediation	Cultural globalization Migration Urbanization Identity	The complexity of the global economy has to do with certain fundamental disjunctures among economy, culture, and politics that we can understand through cultural flows Deterritorialization is one of the central forces of modern society The imagination works as a social force, producing new resources for identity and energies for creating alternative ways of organizing society Everyday experiences of inequalities can be countered with the creation of social networks that often transcend traditional boundaries Images of lifestyle, popular culture, and self-representation circulate internationally through the media and are often borrowed in unanticipated ways	Five dimensions of global cultural flows: (a) ethnoscapes (b) mediascapes (c) technoscapes (d) finanscapes (e) ideoscapes Translocality Intercontextuality Post-national identity Diasporic public space Imagined worlds

Theorist	Definition	Primary Areas of Focus	Arguments	Constructs
Ulrich Beck (1992)	Globalization is the intensification of transnational spaces, events, problems, conflicts, and biographies The processes through which sovereign national states are crisscrossed and undermined by transnational actors with varying prospects of power, orientations, identities, and networks Should not be understood either as linear or all-encompassing; it is contingent and dialectical—global	Political, economic, and social globalization	There has been a change from the logic of wealth distribution in a society of scarcity to the logic of risk distribution in late modernity Society is confronted with socially created risks that endanger the survival of humankind; leading institutions (economic, political, legal, and administrative) not only produce those risks but also make the resulting risks "socially non-existent" (e.g., Mad Cow disease enabled by the government institutions allowing and not monitoring the feeding of cows with potentially dangerous foodstuffs)	*Risikogesellschaft*: Risk society Three Dimensions (a) extensions in space (b) stability in time (c) social density of the transnational networks, relationships, and image flows

(Continued)

Theorist	Definition	Primary Areas of Focus	Arguments	Constructs
Manuel Castells (1996, 1997)	The emergence of informationalism is the new material, technological basis of economic activity and social organization Three interdependent processes of the network society: (a) information technology revolution (b) economic crisis of capitalism and statism (c) blooming of new social movements Bipolar oppositions between the Net and the Self	Political, economic, social and cultural globalization	Shift emphasis from postindustrialism to informationalism Distinction between information society that emphasizes the role of information in society and has been part of all societies and the "informational society" in which information generation, processing, and transmission become the fundamental sources of productivity and power because of the new technological conditions emerging Networks constitute the new social morphology of our societies The processes of social transformation of The Network Society encompass social and technical relationships of production, culture, and power Power is no longer concentrated in institutions, organizations, or symbolic controllers; it is diffused in global networks of wealth, power, information, and images that circulate in a "dematerialized" geography Networks connect and disconnect	The Network Society Informational society The Power of Identity Real virtuality New system of communication, based in the digitized network Integration of multiple communication modes, which includes and comprehensively covers all cultural expressions Timeless time Instant time of computer networks/clock time Space of flows Cyberspace/place bound localities

Theorist	Definition	Primary Areas of Focus	Arguments	Constructs

Anthony Giddens (1990, 1996)	"The intensification of worldwide social relations which link distant localities in such a way that local happenings are shaped by events occurring many miles away and vice versa." A dialectical process	Political, social, and economic globalization	Modernization renders social processes—time-space distanciation, disembedding, and reflexivity—that make social relations more inclusive across the globe
			
			Globalization is a process of uneven development that fragments as it coordinates
				Time-space distanciation
				Disembedding
				Reflexivity
				Four Dimensions of modernity
				  (a) capitalism
				  (b) surveillance
				  (c) military order
				  (d) industrialism

David Harvey (1989)	The transition from Fordism to flexible accumulation via the mediations of time and space	Cultural and economic globalization Postmodernity	The experience of compressed time and space is the most important change in society Fragmentation, pluralism, and the authenticity of other voices and worlds pose acute problems of communication and the means of exercising power through command	Space-Time compression Time can be reorganized in such a way as to reduce the constraints of space and vice versa

(Continued)

Theorist	Definition	Primary Areas of Focus	Arguments	Constructs
David Held, Anthony McGrew, David Goldblatt, & Jonathan Perraton (1999)	The widening, deepening, and speeding up of worldwide interconnectedness in all aspects of contemporary social life	Political, economic, and social	The spatio-temporal and organizational attributes of global interconnectedness in discrete historical periods Four impacts of globalization (a) decisional (b) institutional (c) distributive (d) structural	Spatio-temporal dimensions of globalization The extensity of global networks The intensity of global interconnectedness The velocity of global flows The impact propensity of global interconnectedness
Samuel Huntington (1993)	The Clash of Civilizations	Political globalization	The dominating source of conflict in the new world will be cultural, not ideological or economic Cultural characteristics less mutable than political or economic	Civilization Identity Civilization: the highest cultural grouping of people and the broadest level of cultural identity people have, short of that which distinguishes humans from other species

Theorist	Definition	Primary Areas of Focus	Arguments	Constructs
Roland Robertson (1990, 1992, 1997)	The compression of the world and the intensification of consciousness of the world as a whole Universalization of particularism and the particularization of universalism	Cultural globalization	How people experience globalization The establishment of cultural, social, and phenomenological linkages between the self, the national society, the international system of societies, and humanity	Relativization: each unit in the emerging world takes shape relative to others that surround it; challenges the stability of perspectives Emulation: a single arena in which all actors pursue their goals in deliberate comparison with one another Globalization: the universal ideas and processes in globalization are interpreted and absorbed differently according to the vantage point and history of particular groups Interpenetrations: nexus of universalism becoming concrete and the particular becoming diffused

(Continued)

Theorist	Definition	Primary Areas of Focus	Arguments	Constructs
James Rosenau (2003)	The tensions between opposites that presently underlie the course of events and the development or decline of institutions	Political globalization	To understand the dynamics found within globalizing and local forces; explores how individuals orient themselves globally and locally and the relationship between these orientations and global issues such as human rights, global economy, and global governance	Distant Proximities Fragmegration: pervasive interaction between fragmenting and integrating dynamics unfolding at every level of the community Local worlds: insular, resistant, exclusionary, and affirmative Global worlds: affirmative, resistant, specialized, and territorial

Theorist	Definition	Primary Areas of Focus	Arguments	Constructs
Saskia Sassen (2001, 2002)	Economic globalization entails the importance of social connectivity and central functions, cross–border mergers and alliances, and denationalized elites and agendas	Economic and social globalization	Restructuring of global cities leads to growing economic and social polarization The growth of the producer services sector is the transforming feature of global cities Place is central to the ways in which economic globalization is constituted The role of gender in shaping migration, transnational production, and a new configuration of inequality	A new geography of centrality and marginality Global digital era

(Continued)

Table 10.1 (Continued)

Theorist	Definition	Primary Areas of Focus	Arguments	Constructs
Immanuel Wallerstein	Capitalist world systems spread across the globe World system: a unit with a single division of labor and multiple cultural systems	Economic globalization	Core, semiperipheral, and peripheral positions in the world economy are relatively stable because of military strength, ideological commitment to the system as a whole, and division of the majority into a larger lower stratum and a smaller middle stratum The semiperiphery prevents polarization and conflict	World System Core Semiperiphery Periphery
Malcolm Waters (1995)	A social process in which the constraints of geography on social and cultural arrangements recede and in which people become increasingly aware that they are receding	Political, economic, social, and cultural globalization	Traces globalization through three arenas of social life: the economy, the polity, and culture	Material exchanges localize Political exchanges internationalize Symbolic exchanges globalize

nation-state is being reinforced or even enhanced (Hirst & Thompson, 1997). In sociology and political economy, there are serious disputes regarding the social consequences of the political, economic, and environmental changes wrought through globalization processes and the development of new information technologies (Schaeffer, 1997). Geographers emphasize the spatio-temporal dimensions of social life, some suggesting that time and space are now compressed and spatial barriers have collapsed, whereas others posit that there is even greater sensitivity to the variations of space (Harvey, 1989). New types of strategic territories articulate the cross-border flows central to globalization (Sassen, 2002). For some economists, globalization is the triumph and glory of capitalism and a free market over other forms of economic structuring, whereas for others the global transformation of labor markets and immigration patterns portends dire consequences for very large segments of the world's population (Carnoy, Castells, Cohen, & Cardoso, 1993). The principal challenge of globalization is related to issues of inequality, including the "disparities in affluence and also gross asymmetries in political, social, and economic opportunities and power" (Sen, 2002, p. 4).

Communication scholars' theoretical predilections toward communication determine, in part, their views of the communication/organization/globalization relationship. For some, communication is a tool, a resource, and a rational selection mode that facilitates or inhibits organizational survival within the constraints and opportunities offered through globalization. Globalizing forces are a fact to which individuals and organizations must adjust. There is a recognition that communicative action influences and is influenced by the forces of globalization, but the institutional and environmental energies embedded within today's technologies, social exchanges, and competitive markets create a powerful structural fulcrum that strongly sways collective and individual action. These scholars are interested primarily in theories related to the globalization of organizations and, hence, utilize theories that help explain the creation, maintenance, and dissolution of specific types of organizational structures and networks (e.g., Cushman & King, 1993; Jang & Barnett, 1994; Monge & Fulk, 1999).

For others, communication is an interpretive symbolic process that plays a constitutive role in shaping individual identity and organizational reality. Globalization is intersubjectively constructed and meaningfully evolves as individuals, groups, and organizations struggle to survive and compete across the world stage. Globalization transforms our work and our social lives (Cheney, Lair, & Gill, 2001; Conrad & Poole, 1997; Holmer Nadesan, 2001). The language of the workplace represents processes of power and control (Banks & Banks, 1991). The shift to network structuring is theorized to result in the weakening of social bonds, the loss of shared experiences, and the loss of trust and commitment (Sennett, 1998). Globalization contributes to new formations of identities (ethnic, sexual, professional, political, religious) that challenge traditional definitions of who we are. Scholars in this tradition tend to focus primarily on the organization of globalization and are concerned with issues such as how marginalized groups manage/resist the tensions associated with the dynamic processes identified above (e.g., Deetz, 1992; Papa, Auwal, & Singhal, 1995; Trethewey, 1999). Feminist scholars view the institutions and processes of globalization as gendered, primarily created by and advantaging white Western male elites (Gottfried, 2000). Globalization, it is argued, is often detrimental to women on a global scale, although the adverse effects are often ignored. Townsley (2002), for example, empirically explores the ways in which the privileging of "flexibility" as a mode of production and service in neo-liberal economics and neo-Fordist regimes stymies women's full-fledged workplace participation and advancement.

In general, organizations are theorized variously to be at the root of the changes in contemporary experience, the cause of most of the problems associated with globalization, and the solution to the many challenges that we face. Organizations are largely responsible for the geographic dispersal and mobility that characterize globalization, while the construction of hyper-modern office buildings, smart buildings, and global business centers, all created by and for large-scale organizations, affects how we all live and conduct our daily lives (Ciccolella & Mignaqui, 2002). The joint collaborations of nongovernmental organizations (NGOs), intergovernmental organizations (IGOs), corporate entities, and e-movements have changed the nature of collective action. Moreover, the technological and structural innovations that have such widespread implications for our everyday experiences, our sense of self, our relationship to our communities, and so on are often the unintended consequences of the search to decrease transaction costs of global organizations.

In general, organizations recursively structure, respond to, and restructure the global system. Issues as diverse as individuals' rights to privacy, terrorism, the transmission of SARS, affordability of medications for AIDS victims, human rights, individual safety, the development and sale of chemical weapons, copyright infringement arising from downloading music from the Internet, air pollution, and global warming have several things in common, all of which implicate organizational communication practices: (a) They cannot be addressed successfully by individuals acting alone; (b) they will not be solved unilaterally, bilaterally, or even regionally; (c) they require cooperation from organizations across several sectors of society; and (d) information about these problem is no longer within the purview of any one individual, group, or organization. Digitized technology, the World Wide Web, and collaborative communication systems mean that there is no longer a monopoly of information held by any one elite group. Thus, there is an inevitable involvement of many different types of actors who had heretofore been denied access to or entry into the problem-solving arena.

Thus, it is not surprising that much organizational communication scholarship tends to reflect what social scientists call the transformationalist thesis of globalization (Held et al., 1999). Globalization is seen as a central driving force behind the rapid political, social, economic, and communicative changes taking place in contemporary society. Organizational activities are the primary means by which individuals, small clusters of people, and large groups influence the trajectory of globalization. Organizations may adhere to dominant cultural patterns, but simultaneously they adapt patterns and structures to accommodate differences in, and pressures of, the global system. Significantly, unlike hyperglobalists (those who see globalization ushering in a new economic era that is creating new patterns of beneficiaries) and skeptics (globalization is not considered as anything new, and the same inequalities will remain and perhaps increase), transformationalists do not hypothesize about the long-term positive or negative effects of globalization; within this perspective, either scenario is possible (Held et al., 1999).

The emergence of globalization as an important theoretical perspective in contemporary organizational communication research is evidenced in many ways. Peter Monge (the same scholar who asked me the question at the 1992 ASU conference) urged communication scholars in his 1998 ICA Presidential address, "Communication Structures and Processes in Globalization," to "reflect on our discipline from the perspective of globalization" (p. 143). He, too, set an agenda for organizational communication:

> Organizational communication needs to examine global organizations, their roots in local societies, their homogenizing influences, and their impacts on individuals, relationships and families. It needs to expand its horizons beyond large profit making corporations and examine not-for-profit organizations, non-governmental organizations, international labor unions, worker collectives, and even the worldwide influence of religious organizations. It needs to address practical issues of child labor exploitations, equal pay for equal work, language problems in the workplace, gender inequalities, full and fair disclosure of corporate information and many others. The global imperative requires no less than that we apply our communication theories to address practical human issues. (1998, p. 150)

In the last 5 years, the field of organizational communication certainly has taken up this call. *The New Handbook of Organizational Communication* included a chapter on "Globalizing Organizational Communication" (Stohl, 2001). Organizational communication journals recently have devoted special issues and forums to organizational ethics and corporate responsibility in the global system (Conrad, 2003; May & Zorn, 2003). Organizational communication dissertations on globalization have been completed at many universities (e.g., Galarneault, 2003; Gibbs, 2001; Shumate, 2003; Townsley, 2002). The number of graduate and undergraduate courses on globalization is proliferating (see Arquette, 2003). Most organizational textbooks now include references to globalization and organizational communication (e.g., Conrad & Poole, 1997, Eisenberg & Goodall, 2004). At the time of this writing, the most recent textbook to be published in the area is titled *Organizational Communication in an Age of Globalization* (Cheney, Christiansen, Zorn, & Ganesh, 2003).

Theorizing Globalization

Few terms have been stretched as far or proved to be as infinitely extendable as the word "globalization." Few terms have come into widespread use at such "global speed" . . . taken over from English by every other language on earth. And few terms have been so widely disseminated in a context of widespread social atopia, without any prior inventory of its possible significance or time for scrutiny by citizens, thus leaving an aura of doubt concerning the conditions and meaning of its source. (Mattelart, 2002, p. 591)

But what exactly do we mean by globalization, and how do we theorize about it? It is somewhat ironic that globalization has become such a widely popular term and is used so frequently that it has lost a great deal of its meaning and focus. Generally, unlike early conceptualizations of convergence and divergence, today's theories of globalization try to capture the oppositional and dialectic forces that simultaneously obliterate, maintain, and maximize homogeneity/heterogeneity within the global system. For example, Castells (1996) identifies the central issue of the "informational age"[2] as "the bipolar opposition between the Net and the self" (p. 3). Sassen (2001) suggests that "the geography of globalization contains dynamics of both dispersal and centralization" (p. 3). Appadurai (1997) writes, "The central problem of today's global interactions is the tension between cultural homogenization and cultural heterogenization" (p. 230). Mittleman's

(2000) book *The Globalization Syndrome* is subtitled *Transformation and Resistance*.

The metaphors associated with globalization have also evolved from simple, linear, complementary metaphors to richer and more complex and competing images. For example, like Ritzer's (1993) work described above, Barber (1992) utilized McDonald's as a global metaphor but did so in a way that more clearly articulates the dialectical tensions and oppositional forces rooted in globalization. Juxtaposing what he describes as the "two axial principles of our age—tribalism and globalism" Barber (1992, p. 53) explains his use of the metaphors Jihad versus McWorld:

> The tendencies of what I am here calling the forces of Jihad and the forces of McWorld operate with equal strength in opposite directions, the one driven by parochial hatreds, the other by universalizing markets, the one recreating ancient subnational and ethnic borders from within, the other making national borders porous from without. The one thing they have in common; neither offers much hope to citizens looking for practical ways to govern themselves democratically. (p. 54)

Mirroring earlier theories of convergence, Barber identifies four global imperatives—market, resource, information technology, and ecological—that result in McWorld, which demonstrates increasingly similar organizational structuring and activities, interdependence, and homogeneity of values. Simultaneously, however, the many divergent sects and factions search for ways to maintain their image of self and cultural ways of life in light of the imperatives of convergence. As a result, Jihads develop. "Narrowly conceived, identity driven and separatist, and fragmented, these value-driven Jihads work against any type of interconnectedness, interdependence, and mutuality. The planet is falling precipitously apart *AND* coming reluctantly together at the same time," Barber (1992, p. 53) notes. Most significantly, his theory suggests that "neither McWorld nor Jihad is remotely democratic in impulse. Neither needs democracy, neither promotes democracy" (p. 56).

The very same tensions of globalization are found in the metaphors of Thomas Friedman's (2000) national best-seller on globalization, *The Lexus and the Olive Tree*. The Lexus automobile represents humankind's drive for sustenance, improvement, prosperity, modernization, and financial security, often through the utilization of computer technologies. The olive tree represents our need for roots (linguistic, geographic, and historical) and community. The olive tree anchors us; it gives us identity and self esteem. Both of these strivings exist coterminously:

> This is why under the globalization system you will find both clashes of civilization and the homogenization of civilizations, both environmental disasters and amazing environmental rescues, both the triumph of liberal, free market capitalism and a backlash against it, both the durability of nation states and the rise of enormously powerful nonstate actors. (2000, p. xxxi)

These tensions, however, lead Friedman to a very different set of conclusions about globalization. Unlike Barber, he argues that the rapid and fundamental changes in how we communicate about, invest in, and learn about the world lead to greater democracy and individual freedom.

The oppositional forces that permeate these metaphors are also commonly seen in the definitions of globalization. Some of the more well-known and often-cited definitions include globalization as "the twofold processes of the universalization of particularism and the particularization of universalism" (Robertson, 1990, p. 23), "bringing people closer together and places further apart" (Short, 2001, p. 15), and "The intensification of worldwide social relations which link distant localities in such a way that local happenings are shaped by events occurring many miles away and vice versa"(Giddens, 1990, p. 86). Rosenau, in his recent book *Distant Proximities: Dynamics Beyond Globalization* (2003), captures the contradictory nature of globalization well. Distant proximities, he writes:

> encompass the tensions between core and periphery, between national and transnational systems, between communitarianism and cosmopolitanism, between cultures and subcultures, between states and markets, between urban and rural, between coherence and incoherence, between integration and disintegration, between universalism and particularism, between pace and space, between the global and the local—to note only the more conspicuous links between opposites that presently underlie the course of events and the development or decline of institutions. (p. 5)

Rosenau coined the term "fragmegration" to convey "the pervasive interaction between fragmenting and integrating dynamics unfolding at every level of community" (p. 11). Consistent with other theories of globalization, the shaping, sustaining, and ameliorating of oppositions are grounded in the everyday practices rooted in interpersonal, group, organizational, interorganizational, and mass communication.

Communicating and Globalizing

> [T]he fundamental form of industrialized culture and society dominant for the past four centuries is now in a stage of transition. What we are witnessing, in

fact, may be one of the turning points in human history: where one fundamental form of culture and society—that of industrialized nations and their modes of communication and information—is declining, and a different form is emerging. (Mowlana, 1996, p. 39)

So, 20 years after my first research trip to New Zealand, there is a multitude of globalization theories and perspectives to choose from. Rather than discussing each one separately, I will explicate common themes and unpack the communication implications of this body of work writ large. The choice of which particular theory to use must be rooted in the context of a particular research question and agenda. My search for a unitary, comprehensive theory was naive. Globalization is far too complex and far-ranging to be situated easily within one perspective. However, it is clear to me that research in organizational communication needs to be grounded in the dynamic theories and constructs of globalization. Thus, it is to this overarching global perspective that I will address the rest of this essay.

Across theories, there is a fundamental agreement that globalization represents (a) deep-rooted transformations in the texture and experience of everyday life, (b) changes in the relationship between time and space, and (c) modifications in the relationships between the self and others. Boundaries and physical distances are seen to matter less in determining the shapes of societies, organizations, and individuals than they did in the past (Holm, 2003). Globalization is not a state of affairs; it embodies dynamic communicative, economic, cultural, and political practices and produces new discourses of identity. "It is not just an out-there phenomenon. It is an in-here phenomenon" (Giddens, 1996, p. 367).

Six dynamic and interdependent processes of globalization are embedded in virtually all theories of globalization:

1. The dramatic increase in economic interdependence worldwide

2. The intensification and deepening of material, political, and cultural exchanges

3. The global and rapid diffusion of ideas and knowledge enabled through new information technologies

4. The compression of time and space

5. The disembedding of events and institutions, which permits new realignments and restructuring of social interaction across time and space

6. Increases in global consciousness through processes of reflexivity

Communication is central to all six dynamic processes, providing many pathways for communication scholars to contribute to the understanding of organizing and globalization. German sociologist Ulrich Beck (2000) points out that globalization is produced and maintained in communicative action:

> The globalization process lies in the empirically ascertainable scale, density and stability of regional-global relationship networks and their self definition through the mass media, as well as of social spaces and of image-flows . . . a world horizon characterized by multiplicity and non-integration which opens out when it is produced and preserved in communication and action. (p. 12)

The Dramatic Increase in Economic Interdependence Worldwide

This first dynamic generates and is generated by new forms of organizational arrangements and communication processes. Interdependence necessitates flexible forms of cooperation within and between traditional and emerging organizational structures at the local, state, regional, and global levels. New types of cooperative agreements are being forged across domains (see, for example, Taylor & Doerfel, 2002), demanding reconsideration of issues related to corporate responsibility and organizational communication practices with both internal and external stakeholders. For example, my work with colleagues analyzes foreign automobile manufacturers' efforts to link up with civic organizations to help local communities facilitate new forms of social capital (Perrucci & Stohl, 1998) and also addresses the communicative implications of cooperation between a private international temporary work agency and state-supported unemployment bureaucracies (Townsley & Stohl, 2003).

The turbulence, volatility, and uncertainty associated with economic globalization require organizational responsiveness, adaptation, and efficiency in communication systems that are not found in traditional hierarchical organizations (Monge, 1995). These changes have many wide-ranging implications for the types of workplace training designed to improve the effectiveness of workers and managers (Garlarneault, 2003). Most scholars agree that global forms will resemble temporary systems and ad hoc collaborations, and they will transcend spatial and/or jurisdictional boundaries (Stohl & Walker, 2002; Weick & Van Orden, 1990). Virtual organizing becomes commonplace (DeSanctis & Fulk, 1999; Poole, 1999), and face-to-face interactions are not necessarily the primary forum for relationship building, maintenance, or dissolution. Global network organizations, according to Monge and Fulk (1999), (a) are built on flexible emergent communication networks, rather than traditional hierarchies; (b) develop highly flexible linkages that connect them to a changing, dynamic network of other organizations, transcending their local country–bound networks; and (c) contain a highly sophisticated information technology structure that supports flexible emergent systems of communication. In their view, the global organization reflects communication relationships that transcend organizational levels and boundaries, and "flexibility implies that these relationships wax and wane" (p. 71). Changing patterns of communication as well as new rhetorics of organizing are central to the ways in which contemporary organizations of all types adapt to what some call post-Fordist conditions (Gottfried, 2000; Mattelart, 2002), the informational society (Castells, 1996), or the postmodern condition (Harvey, 1989).

The Intensification and Deepening of Material, Political, and Cultural Exchanges

The erosion of economic, political, social, organizational, territorial, and cultural boundaries suggests the radical erosion of what people talk about, how they talk about it, how frequently they communicate, which connections are mobilized, where people live and to where they emigrate, the ways in which they utilize both old and new media, and how they organize. For some theorists, this increasing intensity causes and is caused by an increase in the functions that central locations play in the growing global span of organizations. Communication technologies may mean the end of distance, but location still matters. The very diffuseness of the global system demands concentrated financial infrastructures, management systems, and labor forces. Sassen (2000), for example, describes a "new frontier zone," a political-economic space that "produce[s] new institutional forms and alter[s] some of the old ones" (p. 164). New types of global cities become the linking pins, "global circuits" for particular national economies that heretofore were marginalized. Moreover, global cities and the "new form of territorial centralization" become the site not only of a vast telecommunications infrastructure, highly specialized services, and industrialized industries but also the site of increased density, immigration, diverse work cultures, and multicultural exchange. For Sassen and others, these global conditions potentially enable disempowered actors to gain visibility and hence provide new opportunities for marginal groups and the development of a global civil society (Kaldor, 2003; Keane, 2003).

The intensification of linkages across social domains also is evidenced in the exponential growth in international governmental and nongovernmental organizations (Lechner & Boli, 2000), as well as the number of labor unions, small businesses, and social movement organizations that situate themselves globally rather than locally (Aram, 1999). The organizational dimension of global change and the building of a global civic culture are extraordinary. There are now more than 30,000 NGOs and IGOs just working on ecology and development (Keck & Sikkink, 1998). The numbers of partnerships, collaborations, and knowledge exchanges that take place on a daily basis are incalculable when we consider the coalitions that are developing among NGOs, IGOs, corporations, and governmental groups to address issues such as human rights (inside and outside the workplace), disease, public safety, and sustainable development (Cooperrider & Dutton, 1999; Kaldor, 2003; Keane, 2003). Even in interpersonal relations, the role of global organizing is taking on an increasingly powerful role. All one needs to do is look at Yahoo! groups to find global organizations designed to help people find mates, discuss the latest books they have read, generate grassroots movements, play games, engage in numerous other activities.

The Global and Rapid Diffusion of Ideas and Knowledge Enabled Through New Information Technologies

The third dynamic gives rise to the quintessential organizing structure characteristic of the age of globalization—the network. Corporate networks, advocacy networks, terrorist networks, criminal networks, sport networks, tourist networks, interest-based networks, and so forth are integral parts of the global system. Monge and Contractor (2003) note:

> These organizational and social forms, which are neither classical markets nor traditional hierarchies (Powell, 1990) nor both (Piore & Sabel, 1984) are built around material and symbolic flows that link people and objects both locally and globally without regard for traditional national, institutional, or organizational boundaries. . . . Built on the basis of flexible, dynamic, ephemeral relations, these network flows constitute the bulk of organizational activity (Monge & Fulk, 1999). Thus, global organizations are processes, not places. (p. 4)

Castells (1996) sees the technological and managerial transformation of production relationships and work processes in today's society to be at the core of the new social structure. The fundamental changes in how we organize work, and the ways in which we distribute, consume, and accumulate material goods, are the primary means by which the informational paradigm and the processes of globalization affect society at large.

The rapid diffusion of information on a global scale has many implications for organizational communication. Traditional models of knowledge creation, transmission, utilization, management, learning, and sensemaking are no longer sufficient (Contractor & Monge, 2002; Hollingshead & Contractor, 2002). Weick and Van Orden (1990), for example, argue that global social change organizations must develop new forms of organizing that utilize new technologies and engage in new kinds of sensemaking. Because knowledge is subjectively consumed and created, incomplete, and culturally tacit, knowledge management in global organizations requires contextual adaptation and reconfiguration.

Changes in information technology create many possibilities that can have large consequences for the identities, capacities, development, and strategies of organizations, groups, and the technologies themselves. Whereas medium-sized to mass audiences were until quite recently accessible exclusively to those who controlled the centralized media apparatus, new technologies are now closing this "media gap." With the rise of micromedia (e.g., e-mail, chat rooms, and cell phones) and "middle" media (e.g., Web sites, Web zines, and Internet-based communication campaigns), organizations now have the potential to reach and involve their members in ways that until quite recently were not feasible (see, for example, Bennett, 2003). Large-scale audiences as well as highly targeted, specialized audiences thus have been brought into range for meaningful group participation by a wide range of public organizations, both new and old. Traditional models of power, privacy, and surveillance are also challenged by the capacities embedded in the new information technologies.

The Compression of Time and Space

The fourth process changes the physical and psychological typologies and infrastructures of communication networks in both large and small-scale organizations. Time-space compression involves the shortening of time and a shrinking of space (Waters, 1995). The explosive growth of connectivity and the subsequent compression of time and space alter the transmission of information among networks, shrinking costs, maximizing speed, broadening reach, and eradicating distance. It involves radical changes in the ways we experience and interpret events (Norris, 2001, p. 20). It also enables increased intensity and robustness of relationships among family, colleagues, and people who have never met but have a similar goal or economic, political, or personal interest.

Space and distance disappear when people who are in different locations but are linked to a common communication technology (e.g., television, the Internet) simultaneously experience the same event, such as the assassination of John Kennedy, the bombing of the World Trade Center, or the World

Trade Organization riots in Seattle (e.g., Monge 1998; Waters, 1995). Globalization theory distinguishes the first event from the other two insofar as in the latter events, new communication technologies (e.g., cell phones, the Internet, text messaging) enabled people across the world to simultaneously and interactively experience and organize the events together, facilitating the growth of a global consciousness through processes of reflexivity. Thus, globalization changes notions of present and absence: "it has made the identification and communication of boundaries—and associated notions of 'here' and 'there,' 'far' and 'near,' 'outside' and 'inside,' 'home' and 'away,' 'them' and 'us,'—more problematic than ever" (Scholte, 2000, pp. 48–49).

But organizational relationships and identifications are not the only things that change. David Harvey, a geographer who is a key figure in linking globalization and postmodernism, writes that a major consequence of time-space compression

> has been to accentuate volatility and ephemerality of fashions, products, production techniques, labor processes, ideas and ideologies, values and established practices. . . . Deeper questions of meaning and interpretation also arise. The greater the ephemerality, the more pressing the need to discover or manufacture some kind of eternal truth . . . (1989, p. 83)

The Disembedding of Events and Institutions, Which Permits New Realignments and Restructuring of Social Interaction Across Time and Space

The disembedding of human interaction from local to distributed contexts is strongly associated with the compression of time and space and is facilitated by and reacted to by all sorts of collective entities. As Giddens (1990) states, "In conditions of modernity, larger and larger numbers of people live in circumstances in which disembedded institutions, linking local practices with globalized social relations, organize major aspects of day-to day life" (p. 26). Melucci (1996), for example, demonstrates how the lifting out of human interaction from the constraints of time and space, from local to global contexts, has radically changed social movements. Whereas most social movement organizations typically involved solidarity rooted in face-to-face interactions and "the ability of members to recognize others, and to be recognized as belonging to the same social unit," today the ability to lift interaction out of the here and now enables collective action to arise as an "aggregation of atomized behaviors" (p. 23) that are completely externally oriented, that is, focused outside the boundaries of the group.

Castells (1996) describes the new ways in which the intensification of linkages and disembedding of events across time and space change the way we organize and interact in terms of "space of flows" and "timeless time." Space and time are the "fundamental material dimensions of human life," and the informational network society is organized around "command and control centers able to coordinate, innovate, and manage the activities and resources of networks of organizations in shorter and shorter time periods. Space is the material support of time-sharing social practices" (p. 441). In contrast to the space of place, where form, function, and meaning are self-contained within the boundaries of a physical unit, the *space of flows is the material organization of time-sharing social practices that work through flows*. Timeless time occurs because the sequential order of phenomena performed collapses through instantaneous, discontinuous, or discontiguous action. In other words, stable forms of place and identity are replaced with flexible flows drawn across borders.

Significantly, the subsequent disembedding of social institutions and organizations as they have been lifted out of their local contexts and restructured is a critical component of many of the most frightening organizations today (terrorist groups, international drug cartels, transnational crime syndicates, etc.) (Arquilla, Ronfeldt, & Zanini, 1999) as well as multinational organizations. Today's terrorist networks, for example, are often seen as "small worlds" with few degrees of separation and composed of strong ties across personal, cultural, and ideological domains, with powerful hubs dispersed throughout the globe (see Arquilla et al., 1999; Stohl & Stohl, 2002).

Increases in Global Consciousness Through Processes of Reflexivity

The reflexive changes in identities of peoples and groups moving from local centering to universal concerns implicates changes in discourses of identity and the constant reexamination of social practices in light of new information and new relationships (Giddens, 1990). People self-consciously orient themselves to the world as a whole; psychological barriers to intergroup identifications and one's place in the world are reconsidered, potentially broken down, and reconfigured. Even when individuals and groups consider themselves separate from, or different from, the rest of the world, globalization theories suggest they establish their position in relation to the global system, what Robertson (1990) calls "relativization."

This process reinforces alterations in cooperative and collaborative strategies and organizational structures for addressing social, economic, and political issues that individuals now perceive as transcending national borders or local entities. Global social capital is created, maintained, and dissolved in new types of organizational affiliations; public spaces and loosely coupled networks are created to express multiple identities; and new forms of organization and models of leadership, communicative channels, and emerging technologies are constitutive parts of this network of relationship (Bennett, 2003; Melucci, 1996).

Paradoxically, the increasing levels of global consciousness derived through processes of reflexivity and communication are also associated with increasingly local politics, a heightened sense of the importance of community, social movement organizing designed to counter the new world order, and individuals' desperate struggles for identity. Most theories of globalization recognize that the search for identity has become a fundamental source of social meaning in these times of universal technological and economic decentering and destructuring. At one level, organizational identifications are superseding national, cultural, and ethnic identifications; people are "citizens of the world" and part of an evolving global civic culture. On the other hand, many people organize along communal identities that communicate inwardly, sharply distinguishing between in- and out-groups, and resist the economic, social, cultural, and political integration that is upon us. In the second volume of his globalization trilogy, *The Power of Identity*, Castells (1997) explores these mutually opposing forces:

> For those social actors excluded from or resisting the individualization of identity attached to life in the global networks of power and wealth, cultural communes of religious, national, or territorial foundation seem to provide the main alternative for the construction of meaning in our society. (p. 11)

In summary, the organizational communication implications for each of these dynamics are merely illustrative. My purpose here was to demonstrate that globalization theories help scholars identify what types of communication/organizational changes are happening within contemporary society, the tensions and paradoxes embedded within these communication practices, and the implications for our sense of self, our community, our nation, and our world. Globalization theories do not provide all the answers to all the questions I had about my New Zealand organizational experiences, but they provide a rich and complex framework for approaching the organization and the critical issues I was trying to address. They enable me to better understand my place in the world, my responsibilities, and my possibilities. No, I was not to blame for those events so very far away; they were indicative of changes taking place all over the world. But neither were my own behavior, reactions, interpretations, and sense of self at that time or subsequently independent of the phenomena.

The six dynamic processes of globalization have resulted in a remarkable transformation of the circumstances in which we live our lives. Personal, social, professional, and political organizing will play a central role in how we address the challenges and opportunities inherent in this social revolution. The world is in flux, as must be the questions we ask, the ways we go about finding the answers, and the theories we use as a guide. Organizational communication scholars can be at the forefront of these changes, utilizing these theories as well as producing new ones. We must continue to creatively connect globalization with the other vital theoretical traditions contained in this volume. As Hannerz (1996) states, "A theorist's work is never done . . . ; there is always more thinking, rethinking, and unthinking waiting around the bends" (p. 22).

Notes

1. See, for example, the introductions to special issues including those by Calas (1994), Earley and Singh (1995), and Tichy (1990).

2. Castells (1996) makes an important distinction between the term "information society," which " emphasizes the role of information in society" and has been part of all societies, and the "informational society in which information generation, processing, and transmission become the fundamental sources of productivity and power because of the new technological conditions emerging in this historical period" (p. 21).

References

Appadurai, A. (1997). *Modernity at large: Cultural dimensions of globalization.* Minneapolis: University of Minnesota Press.

Aram, J. (1999). Constructing and deconstructing global change organizations. In D. Cooperrider & J. Dutton (Eds.), *Organizational dimensions of global change* (pp. 235–251). Thousand Oaks, CA: Sage.

Arquette, T. (2003). *Globalization and technology.* Retrieved June 28, 2004, from http://www.sla.purdue.edu/people/comm/arquette/

Arquilla, J., Ronfeldt, D., & Zanini, M. (1999). Networks, netwar and information-age terrorism. In A. Lesser, B. Hoffman, J. Arquilla, D. Ronfeldt, & M. Zanini (Eds.), *Countering the new terrorism* (pp. 39–84). Santa Monica, CA: RAND.

Astley, G. (1985). The two ecologies: Population and community perspectives on organizational evolution. *Administrative Science Quarterly, 30,* 224–241.

Banks, S., & Banks, A. (1991). Translation as problematic discourse in organizations. *The Journal of Applied Communication Research, 3,* 223–241.

Bantz, C. (1993). Cultural diversity and group cross-cultural team research. *Journal of Applied Communication Research, 20,* 1–19.

Barber, B. (1992, March). Jihad vs. McWorld. *The Atlantic Monthly,* 53–63.

Bartlett, C., & Ghoshal, S. (1989). *Managing across borders: The transnational solution.* Boston: Harvard Business School Press.

Beck, U. (1992). *The risk society. Toward a new modernity.* London: Sage.

Beck, U. (2000). *What is globalization?* Cambridge, UK: Polity.

Bennett, W. L. (2003). Communicating global activism. In W. van de Donk, B. Loader, P. Nixon, & D. Rucht (Eds.), *Cyberprotest: New media, citizens, and social movements* (pp. 123–148). New York: Routledge.

Burger, R, (2002). Strategy as vector and the inertia of coevolutionary lock-in. *Administrative Science Quarterly, 47,* 325–357.

Calas, M. (1994). Minerva's Owl? *Organization, 1,* 243–248.

Carnoy, M., Castells, M., Cohen, S., & Cardoso, F. (1993). *The new global economy in the information age: Reflections of our changing world.* University Park: The Pennsylvania State University Press.

Castells, M. (1996). *The rise of the network society.* Oxford, UK: Blackwell.

Castells, M. (1997). *The power of identity.* Oxford, UK: Blackwell.

Cheney, G., Christiansen, L., Zorn, T., & Ganesh, S. (2003). *Organizational communication in an age of globalization: Issues, reflections, practices.* Prospect Heights, IL: Waveland.

Cheney, G., Lair, D., & Gill, R. (2001). Trends at work at the turn of the 21st century: Implications for organizational communication. *Management Communication Quarterly, 15,* 632–641.

Ciccolella, P., & Mignaqui, I. (2002). Buenos Aires: Sociological impacts of the development of global city functions. In S. Sassen (Ed.), *Global networks, linked cities* (pp. 309–326). New York: Routledge.

Conrad, C. (2003). Setting the stage: Introduction to the special issue on "Corporate Meltdown." *Management Communication Quarterly, 17*(1), 5–19.

Conrad, C., & Poole, S. (1997). Introduction: Communication and the disposable worker. *Communication Research, 24,* 581–592.

Contractor, N. (2002). Introduction. New media and organizing. In S. Livingstone & L. Lievrouw (Eds.), *Handbook of new media* (pp. 201–205). London: Sage.

Contractor, N., & Monge, P. (2002). Managing knowledge networks. *Management Communication Quarterly, 16,* 249–258.

Cooperrider, D., & Dutton, J. (1999). *Organizational dimensions of global change: No limits to cooperation.* Thousand Oaks, CA: Sage.

Cushman, D., & King, S. (1993). High-speed management: A revolution in organizational communication in the 1990s. In S. Deetz (Ed.), *Communication yearbook 16* (pp. 209–236). Newbury Park, CA: Sage.

Deetz, S. (1992). *Democracy in an age of corporate colonization.* Albany: SUNY Press.

DeSanctis, G., & Fulk, J. (Eds.). (1999). *Shaping organizational forms: Communication, connection, and community.* Thousand Oaks, CA: Sage.

DiMaggio, P. J., & Powell, W. (1991). *The new institutionalism in organizational analysis*. Chicago: University of Chicago Press.

Earley, C., & Singh, H. (1995). International and intercultural management research: What's next? *Academy of Management Journal, 38*, 327–341.

Eisenberg, E., & Goodall, H. (2004). *Organizational communication: Balancing creativity and constraint* (4th ed.). New York: St. Martin's.

Feld, W., & Jordan, R. (1988). *International organization: A comparative approach*. New York: Praeger.

Friedman, T. (2000). *The Lexus and the olive tree*. New York: Random House.

Fukuyama, F. (1992). *The end of history and the last man*. London: Hamish Hamilton.

Galarneault, S. (2003). *Communicating complex connectivity: Global training for managers*. Unpublished dissertation, Purdue University.

Gannon, M. (2001). *Understanding global cultures: Metaphorical journeys through 23 nations*. Thousand Oaks, CA: Sage.

Ghoshal, S., & Bartlett, C. (1990). The multinational corporation as an inter-organizational network. *Academy of Management Review, 15*, 603–625.

Gibbs, J. (2001). *Global teams*. Unpublished dissertation, University of Southern California.

Giddens, A. (1990). *The consequences of modernity*. Stanford, CA: Stanford University Press.

Giddens, A. (1996). Affluence, poverty and the idea of a post scarcity society. *Development and Change, 27*(3), 365–377.

Gottfried, H. (2000). Compromising positions: Emergent neo-Fordisms and embedded gender contracts. *British Journal of Sociology, 51*, 235–259.

Habermas, J. (1984). *Theory of communicative action*. Boston: Beacon.

Hall, E. T. (1981). *Beyond culture*. Garden City, NY: Anchor.

Hannerz, U. (1996). *Transnational connections: Culture, people, places*. London: Routledge.

Harris, P., & Moran, R. (1999). *Managing cultural differences* (5th ed.). Woburn, MA: Butterworth-Heinemann.

Harvey, D. (1989). *The condition of postmodernity: An enquiry into the conditions of cultural change*. Oxford, UK: Blackwell.

Held, D., McGrew, A., Goldblatt, D., & Perraton, J. (1999). *Global transformations: Politics, economics, and culture*. Stanford, CA: Stanford University Press.

Hickson, D., Hinings, C., MacMillan, C., & Schwitter, J. (1974). The culture-free context of organisation structure: A tri-national comparison. *Sociology, 8*, 59–80.

Hirst, P., & Thompson, G. (1997). *Globalization in question*. Cambridge: Polity.

Hofstede, G. (1984). *Culture's consequences: International differences in work-related values*. Beverly Hills, CA: Sage.

Hollingshead, A., & Contractor, N. (2002). New media and organizing at the group level. In L. Lievrouw & S. Livingston (Eds.), *Handbook of new media* (pp. 221–235). London: Sage.

Holm, H. (2003). *Globalization and what governments make of it.* Unpublished manuscript, Danish School of Journalism, Aarhus, Denmark.

Holmer Nadesan, M. (2001). Post-Fordism, political economy, and critical organizational studies. *Management Communication Quarterly, 15,* 259–267.

Huntington, S. (1993). The clash of civilizations? *Foreign Affairs, 72*(3), 22–50.

Jang, H., & Barnett, G. (1994). Cultural differences in organizational communication: A semantic network analysis. *Bulletin de Methodologie Sociologique, 4,* 31–59.

Kaldor, M. (2003). *Global civil society: An answer to war.* Cambridge, UK: Polity.

Keane, J. (2003). *Global civil society?* Cambridge, UK: Cambridge University Press.

Keck, M., & Sikkink, K. (1998). *Activists beyond borders.* Ithaca, NY: Cornell University Press.

Krieger, J. (1999). *British politics in the global age: Can social democracy survive?* Cambridge, UK: Polity.

Krone, K., Garrett, M., & Chen, L. (1992). Managerial practices in Chinese factories: A preliminary investigation. *The Journal of Business Communication, 29,* 229–252.

Lechner, F., & Boli, J. (2000). *The globalization reader.* Oxford, UK: Blackwell.

Lipnack, J., & Stamps, J. (1986). *The networking book: People connecting with people.* London: Routledge & Kegan Paul.

Mattelart, A. (2002). An archeology of the global era: Constructing a belief. *Media, Culture, and Society, 24,* 591–612.

May, S., & Zorn, T. (2003). Forum introduction. *Management Communication Quarterly, 16*(4), 595–598.

Melucci, A. (1996). *Challenging codes: Collective action in the information age.* Cambridge, UK: Cambridge University Press.

Miles, R., & Snow, C. (1995). The new network firm: A spherical structure built on a human investment philosophy. *Organizational Dynamics, 23,* 5–18.

Mitroff, I. (1987). *Business NOT as usual: Rethinking our individual, corporate, and industrial strategies for global competition.* San Francisco: Jossey-Bass.

Mittleman, J. (2000). *The globalization syndrome: Transformation and resistance.* Princeton, NJ: Princeton University Press.

Monge, P. (1995). Global network organizations. In R. Cesaria & P. Shockley-Zalabak (Eds.), *Organization means communication: Making the organizational communication concept relevant to practice* (pp. 135–151). Rome: Servizio Italiano Pubblicazioni Internationali Srl.

Monge, P. (1998). 1998 ICA presidential address: Communication structures and processes in globalization. *Journal of Communication, 48,* 142–153.

Monge, P., & Contractor, N. (2003). *Theories of communication networks.* Oxford, UK: Oxford University Press.

Monge, P., & Fulk, J. (1999). Communication technologies for global network organizations. In G. DeSanctis & J. Fulk (Eds.), *Communication technologies and organizational forms* (pp. 71–100). Thousand Oaks, CA: Sage.

Mowlana, H. (1996). *Global communication in transition: The end of diversity?* Thousand Oaks, CA: Sage.

Nohria, N., & Berkley, J. D. (1994). The virtual organization: Bureaucracy, technology, and the implosion of control. In C. Heckscher & A. Donnellon (Eds.), *The post-bureaucratic organization: New perspectives on organizational change* (pp. 108–128). Thousand Oaks, CA: Sage.

Norris, P. (2001). *Digital divide: Civic engagement, information poverty, and the Internet worldwide.* Cambridge, UK: Cambridge University Press.

Ohmae, K. (1995). *The end of the nation state.* New York: Free Press.

Papa, M., Auwal, M., & Singhal, A. (1995). Dialectic of control and emancipation in organizing for social change: A multitheoretic study of the Grameem Bank in Bangladesh. *Communication Theory, 5,* 189–223.

Perrucci, R., & Stohl, C. (1998). Economic restructuring and changing corporate-worker community relations. In R. Hodson (Ed.), *Research in the sociology of work: The globalization of work* (pp. 177–195). Greenwich, CT: JAI.

Poole, M. S. (1999). Organizational challenges for the new forms. In G. DeSanctis & J. Fulk (Eds.), *Shaping organizational forms: Communication, connection, and community* (pp. 453–471). Thousand Oaks, CA: Sage.

Powell, W. (1990). Neither market nor hierarchy: Network forms of organization. *Research in Organizational Behavior, 12,* 295–336.

Rice, R., & Associates. (1984). *The new media: Communication, research and technology.* Beverly Hills, CA: Sage.

Ritzer, G. (1993). *The McDonaldization of society.* Boston: Pine Forge Press.

Robertson, R. (1990). Mapping the global condition: Globalization as the central concept. *Theory, Culture & Society, 7,* 15–30.

Robertson, R. (1992). *Globalization: Social theory and global culture.* London: Sage.

Robertson, R. (1997). Globalization: Time-space and homogeneity-heterogeneity. In M. Featherstone, S. Lash, & R. Robertson (Eds.), *Global modernities* (pp. 25–44). Thousand Oaks, CA: Sage.

Rosenau, J. (2003). *Distant proximities: Dynamics beyond globalization.* Princeton, NJ: Princeton University Press.

Sassen, S. (2000). Excavating power: In search of frontier zones and new actors. *Theory, Culture & Society, 17,* 163–170.

Sassen, S. (2001). *The global city* (2nd ed.). Princeton, NJ: Princeton University Press.

Sassen, S. (Ed.). (2002). *Global networks, linked cities.* New York: Routledge.

Schaeffer, R. (1997). *Understanding globalization.* Lanham, MD: Rowman and Littlefield.

Scholte, J. (2000). *Globalization: A critical introduction.* New York: St. Martin's.

Sen, A. (2002). *Development as freedom.* Oxford, UK: Oxford University Press.

Sennett, R. (1998). *Spaces of democracy.* Ann Arbor: University of Michigan Press.

Short, R. (2001). *Global dimensions: Space, place, and the contemporary world.* London: Reaktion Books.

Shumate, M. D. (2003). *The coevolution of a population with a community, organizations, and the environment: The emergence, evolution, and impact of HIV/AIDS NGOs.* Unpublished dissertation, University of Southern California.

Simmons, P., & Oudraat, C. (2001). *Managing global issues: Lessons learned.* Washington, DC: Carnegie Endowment for Peace.

Stage, C. (1999). Negotiating organizational communication cultures in American subsidiaries doing business in Thailand. *Management Communication Quarterly, 13,* 245–280.

Stohl, C. (1992). *Exploring the new organizational horizon: IGOS, INGOs, and BINGOs.* Paper presented at a conference on New Directions for Organizational Communication, Tempe, AZ.

Stohl, C. (1993a). European managers' interpretations of participation: A semantic network analysis. *Human Communication Research, 20,* 97–117.

Stohl, C. (1993b). International organizing and organizational communication. *Journal of Applied Communication Research, 21,* 377–384.

Stohl, C. (2001). Globalizing organizational communication. In F. Jablin & L. Putnam (Eds.), *The new handbook of organizational communication* (pp. 323–375). Thousand Oaks, CA: Sage.

Stohl, C., & Stohl, M. (2002, November). *The nexus and the organization: The communicative foundations of terrorist organizing.* Paper presented at the NCA Organizational Communication Preconference, New Orleans.

Stohl, C., & Walker, K. (2002). A bona fide perspective for the future of groups: Understanding collaborating groups. In L. Frey (Ed.), *New directions for group communication* (pp. 237–252). Thousand Oaks, CA: Sage.

Taylor, M., & Doerfel, M. (2002). Building interorganizational relationships that build nations. *Human Communication Research, 29,* 153–181.

Tichy, N. (1990). The global challenge for business schools. *Human Resource Management, 29,* 1–4.

Tomlinson, J. (1999). *Globalization and culture.* Chicago: University of Chicago Press.

Townsley, N. (2002). *A discursive approach to embedded gender relations in (Swedish) global restructuring.* Unpublished dissertation, Purdue University.

Townsley. N., & Stohl, C. (2003). Contracting corporate social responsibility: Swedish expansions in global temporary agency work. *Management Communication Quarterly, 4,* 599–605.

Trethewey, A. (1999). "Isn't it ironic?" Using irony to explore the contradictions of organizational life. *Western Journal of Communication, 63,* 140–167.

Triandis, H. (1983). Dimensions of cultural variation as parameters of organizational theories. *International Studies of Management and Organization, 12,* 139–169.

Triandis, H., & Albert, R. (1987). Cross-cultural perspectives. In F. Jablin, L. Putnam, K. Roberts, & L. Porter (Eds.), *Handbook of organizational communication: An interdisciplinary perspective* (pp. 264–296). Newbury Park, CA: Sage.

Waters, M. (1995). *Globalization*. London: Routledge.

Weick, K. (1999). Sense-making as an organizational dimension of global change. In D. Cooperrider & J. Dutton (Eds.), *Organizational dimensions of global change* (pp. 39–55). Thousand Oaks, CA: Sage.

Weick, K., & Van Orden, P. (1990). Organizing on a global scale: A research and teaching agenda. *Human Resource Management, 29*, 49–61.

Wiseman, R., & Shuter, R. (Eds.). (1994). *Communicating in multinational organizations*. Thousand Oaks, CA: Sage.

11

Conclusion

Engaging the Future of Organizational Communication Theory and Research

Steve May

Dennis K. Mumby

This book is rooted in the premise that organizational communication theory has, over the last 20 years, become wide-ranging and diverse in its epistemological, ontological, and methodological assumptions. This diversity reflects the growth and maturation of the field but also signals its increasing complexity. Today, students are faced with a dizzying array of theoretical perspectives and research agendas that require an intellectual familiarity that is difficult to attain and sustain, given recent developments in organizational communication. Our purpose has been to introduce students to the major theoretical developments, while neither claiming to be exhaustive nor providing simple overviews. Instead, the goal has been to present theory emergence and development as an engaged process that occurs through the work of real scholars who are grappling with particular organizational problems and issues. We invited prominent scholars—who have spent much of their career "engaging" one of the featured theoretical perspectives—to provide thorough, yet readable, chapters that explore the history, assumptions, development, propositions, research, and application of the theoretical perspectives that have significantly influenced (or are likely to influence) research, teaching, and practice in organizational communication.

More specifically, we wanted to give students in organizational communication a sense of the multiple scholarly traditions that characterize the field. We believe that students should be familiar with—and conversant in—at least each of these perspectives in order to be fully engaged in organizational communication. Second, we wanted to avoid producing another "handbook." Other authors have covered that terrain quite effectively (Clegg, Hardy, & Nord, 1996; Jablin & Putnam, 2001). Instead, we wanted to produce a book that provided students with a more personal glimpse at the ways scholars engage theory and research. Our assumption is that, once students realize that our prominent scholars' understanding has developed over time (replete with mistakes, wrong turns, and unexpected revelations), they will be motivated to pursue their own questions without intimidation from the received wisdom of the day. Every scholarly community that fosters creativity and innovation needs the courage, curiosity, and rebellious spirit that produce innovation and creativity. Our hope is that viewing "scholarship in progress" will energize students to extol, expand, and extend our current assumptions of organizational communication. Third, then, an additional goal of the book was to convey to readers the sense of excitement that comes from "taking on" a set of questions about organizational communication. As we noted in Chapter 1, although the remnants of the subdiscipline called organizational communication that emerged in the 1950s and 1960s are still the foundation for our current work, a variety of emerging perspectives have radically altered not only organizational communication theories but also organizational communication practices. Finally, the book also was designed to explore the mutual, reciprocal engagement of theory and practice in organizational communication. The volume has sought to explore how organizational communication theory and research, then, may be the catalyst, process, and outcome for/of various contextual factors in our culture. As is evident in each of the chapters, theory and research are simultaneously bound by, and create, cultural contexts.

Learning as Engagement: The Basis for Theory and Research Development

When we first began to discuss this project, in general, and explore its focus and direction, more specifically, recurring questions we asked ourselves were: What most engaged us as students of organizational communication?

and When and how did we develop an interest in, and enthusiasm for, better understanding communicating and organizing? Similarly, we asked: Under what circumstances are our own students engaged and active in learning about organizational communication? Finally, we also considered: What will motivate students of the future to not only embrace the lively, contested history of organizational communication, as a field of theory and practice, but also to participate in its ongoing emergence and evolution?

In response to each question—regardless of whether its focus was on the past, present, or future of organizational communication—our answer was similar. In each case, engagement with organizational communication was invariably associated with a teacher who had both the expertise and the patience to explore the various trajectories of theory and research, bringing them to life in ways that often contradicted the detached, objective writing of so many textbooks. For such teachers, organizational communication was not represented in a "canon" per se but, rather, was described as a struggle for competing ideas, as an ebb and flow of various scholarly perspectives, and as a situated dialogue with other scholars. Much like practices of organizing themselves, the field was discussed and debated as an emergent activity, one constantly shaped by the influence of new theories and innovative research agendas—sometimes located within an exemplary book or article, a strong academic program, a dialogic conference, an innovative set of research questions, a creative methodology, or, certainly, a group of collaborative scholars. Regardless of the "location" of the field's emergence, though, it has been, is, and will be best engaged in a reflexive and evocative manner that disrupts our taken-for-granted assumptions and commonsense notions of the "natural."

In this book, then, we have sought, in some ways, to simulate the excitement that is produced when organizational communication scholarship is taught not as a static entity but as an engaged set of practices that are challenging, transformational, and, occasionally, contradictory. Such practices, as you have seen, may not only affect the development of theory and research but also affect scholars' own identities.

Yet, the "author function" (Foucault, 1984) in scholarship often seeks to produce a monumental history of a field that purports to be impartial and neutral, with little emphasis on change, rupture, or discontinuity. By contrast, we have tried to open up the coherent narrative of authors and their theoretical perspectives in order to show how they have actively engaged in a body—or, in some cases, intersecting bodies—of scholarship that is still evolving. As we noted in Chapter 1, a "discourse of vulnerability" (Mumby, 1997) questions the author's role as a disinterested observer who adopts an omniscient view of organizational phenomena and, as a result, asserts authoritative knowledge claims. We appreciate each author's willingness to engage in his or her own vulnerability and to respond to our request to describe both his or her own development as a scholar and the role of theory and research in that development. As a result of their vulnerability, we hope that you have learned not only about organizational communication but also about how successful, prominent scholars develop questions, pursue ideas, engage theory, and create practice. In that sense, we hope that each of the chapters—and the book, as a whole—has provoked both an understanding of our past(s) and the possibility(ies) for our future.

In the remainder of the chapter, we will briefly revisit some of the key ideas presented by each author and offer a few questions that are prompted by his or her engagement of organizational communication theory and research. We hope these questions will provide readers with potential directions for future research as they engage in their own scholarly projects. Finally, we will conclude with a discussion of the role of engaged teaching that draws on many of the perspectives presented by the authors.

Postpositivism

In Chapter 2, Steve Corman provided a useful historical review of the different types of positivism, outlined several principles of postpositivism, and explored the relationship between postpositivist and antipositivist positions. Perhaps most important, he described the assumptions of postpositivism, articulating various points of convergence with other theories in the book. Postpositivism, for example, assumes that interpretations emerge from a person's position in a specific context. However, to reach a status of knowledge, the interpretations should be tested and criticized. Therefore, post positivists do not reject the notion of interpretation, but they do suggest that interpretations must eventually be validated in order to be evaluated.

Although these commonalities with other perspectives may appear unexpected to some readers, Corman argued that positivism—as a precursor to postpositivism—has a long and overlooked history that includes multiple variations including classical positivism (scientism, empiricism, and naturalism), logical positivism (rational progress, verifiability, and antirealism), and instrumental positivism (inductivism, reductionism). These different, yet related, strands of positivism, he noted, are often conflated with postpositivism, causing confusion regarding the principles and assumptions used by postpositivist scholars.

Postpositivism, he explained, should be understood as "a fundamental reform of positivist principles." Corman noted, for example, that postpositivists still value a scientific orientation to understanding social phenomena, but they also accept many of the criticisms of the different positivisms, seeking opportunities to transcend them. Postpositivism, according to Corman, is best defined as "a philosophy of science that respects the spirit of science in the context of fundamental reforms of positivistic principles" (p. 21). These reforms produce a series of principles that are central to postpositivism, including falsificationism, naturalism, realism, transformational models, and emergent objectivity.

Scholarship, from this perspective, proceeds by a process of conjectures and refutations. It does not necessarily achieve definitive conclusions, yet it does generate reliable knowledge. In order to progress, research should focus on disconfirming or falsifying instances, through methods such as statistical testing. In addition, postpositivists believe that there is an essential unity between the social sciences and natural sciences. As Corman explained, "features of human communication and its context are influenced by obdurate characteristics of the physical world. In addition to being subjects, communicators are physical objects" (p. 24). By extension, social phenomena have a reality that is independent of a person's perception. As he argued, it is plausible, for example, to believe that phenomena exist even when we do not directly perceive them.

Yet, "there can be *generative mechanisms* or systems that, while not observable themselves, are responsible for things we can observe" (p. 27). When we do observe phenomena, such as communication, we must have a good system of evaluation, keeping in mind that "objectivity, for the postpositivist, inheres in the standards developed and enforced by a community of practice" (p. 29). That is, objectivity is not characterized by any single observation, but rather by an emergent property of organized skepticism and questioning. The ongoing development of theory and research, then, is balanced by a "context of discovery" that features curiosity and innovation and a "context of justification" that features testing and evaluation.

Given Corman's discussion of postpositivism, students interested in further exploring this perspective might consider the following questions: To what extent is postpositivism convergent with, or divergent from, other theoretical perspectives of organizational communication? What are the ways in which the principles of positivism and postpositivism are reconcilable or irreconcilable? In what ways and to what extent does postpositivism capture the processes of communication? What models might integrate the physical act of communicating, the content of that communication, and organizational activities? Is postpositivism best suited for developing theory, building theory, or testing theory? How might scholars best address the tension between discovery and justification in their theory and research?

Social Constructionism

In Chapter 3, Brenda Allen explored the basic assumptions of social constructionism for organizational communication, with a primary emphasis on the centrality of language and the significance of social interaction processes. According to Allen, social constructionism foregrounds sociocultural forces and also encourages us to challenge taken-for-granted knowledge. Perhaps most important, she also noted the theory's potential to encourage us to imagine and enact alternative realities, in general, and alternative identities and organizations, specifically. She reminded us, for example, that discursive micro-practices are intertwined with broader cultural discourses to produce relations of power that have wide-ranging implications for all of us. In particular, Allen acknowledged that organizations are important sites for learning about our identities—and those of others.

Allen also suggested that social constructionism is not limited to one narrow methodology. She explained that a range of qualitative methods—including ethnography, ethnomethodology, narrative analysis, participant observation, and autoethnography—may be most appropriate to pursue the questions raised by social constructionism. Regardless of the method used, however, Allen cautioned us that we must focus our attention simultaneously on multiple levels of analysis, considering both the general and local contexts that are crucial for the production and reproduction of social realities.

In addition, her chapter explored a range of implications and offered a variety of possible questions for students of organizational communication to consider: What organization-based identities are made available to us, given our specific location within various positions of race, sex, class, age, ethnicity, sexual orientation, geographic location, and so on? What, if any, identities are resisted and, when they are, how is that process accomplished? How has communication within and across organizations evolved over time and space to either enable or constrain alternative modes of organizing and identity construction? More specifically, Allen suggested that we further study socialization processes that enact "outsider-within" identities that may emerge in work settings or in anticipatory socialization settings such as educational institutions. Whether that identity is being formed in the family, the school, the church, the community, or the workplace, though, Allen urged us to study the ways in which social actors continue to negotiate their identities on an ongoing basis. What, then, are the various mechanisms for identity formation in the multiple organizations that are a part of our lives? Are they consistent? Contradictory? What role do we play in our identity re-formation? Finally, reconsidering the effect of theory development on identity itself, how have theories of organizational communication located or dislocated particular understandings of our organizational lives? The latter question requires us to seriously reflect upon our own representational practices in organizational communication theory and research (May, 1993). As Clegg and Hardy (1996) have noted, how we represent (i.e., socially construct) organizations—and the people within them—is "always an effect of theoretical privilege afforded by certain ways of seeing, certain terms of discourse, and their conversational enactment" (p. 4).

Rhetorical Theory

In Chapter 4, George Cheney, assisted by Dan Lair, explored the long history of rhetorical studies, identifying key moments, concepts, and persons in the development of organizational rhetoric. Rhetoric's contribution to organizational communication, according to Cheney, is its heuristic value and its sensitivity to "the uses and adaptations of language and other symbols, particularly as they relate to various audiences" (p. 56). For Cheney, engagement with rhetorical theory and criticism, as a set of connected practices, both defines and illuminates the central phenomena of organizational communication. In his chapter, Cheney defines rhetorical criticism as "the description, interpretation, analysis, and critique of organized persuasion—and, by extension, identification. Similar to other authors in the book, Cheney focuses on the "organized" nature of persuasion that focuses our attention beyond literal, discrete notions of a bounded organization to wider institutional activities.

Based on this broad view of organization, scholars of organizational rhetoric have produced a range of research on public relations and issues management, corporate apologia and crisis management, social movements, public policy, organizational identity, and knowledge management, among other topics. Each of these diverse, yet related, areas of research is bound by a common interest in the practice of persuasion in and about organizations, yet not necessarily limited by the time and space of a single organization. This broader perspective allows us to study multiple domains of analysis, from a single message; to organizational missions, visions, and values; to broader discourses about organizational quality, empowerment, and change.

Looking to the future, Cheney noted that one of the most important contributions the study of organizational rhetoric can offer is to examine the nexus of persuasive communication where politics, economics, and culture converge. Given the myriad configurations of organizations today—and their relationship to other realms—we can take from Cheney's chapter a series of questions to consider: What are the specific rhetorical strategies used by organizations—and their members—to maintain legitimacy; gain credibility; discredit competitors; select, train, manage, and evaluate employees; rationalize misconduct; and strategize for the future? What is the relationship between "internal" and "external" forms of organizational communication, as organizations serve multiple constituencies? How are organizations' communication strategies tied to such broader cultural discourses as "freedom," "equality," and "justice"? What social, political, economic, and ideological discourses are taken for granted, with regard to organizational practices? What communication logics are used in various "rhetorical situations" relevant to organizations, such as advertising, public relations, marketing, employee relations, labor-management negotiations, and organizational consulting? What is the speaker/message/audience relationship in such situations? At the very least, Cheney has argued that we should also consider "issues of globalization, citizen participation, consumerism, civil rights, military hegemony, environmental stewardship, and corporate responsibility" (p. 77) in our organizational communication scholarship. In such cases, we must consider how power and authority are mobilized, rhetorically, to bring about one outcome rather than another, particularly in today's increasingly mediated environment.

Critical Theory

In Chapter 5, Stan Deetz explained that critical theory has been used to study the structures, social relations, and practices in organizations, with particular attention to systems of inappropriate control and distorted decision making. Focusing on both micro and macro relations, critical theory has sought to better understand the relationships between power, language, and conflict as they are embedded in a wide range of cultural practices, including the production of knowledge, identity, and decision making. Deetz construed a broad meaning of critical theory of organizations to include scholarship that has an orientation toward "investigating exploitation, repression, social injustice, asymmetrical power relations (generated from class, gender, or position), distorted communication, and misrecognition of interests" (p. 86).

Deetz explained that the various strands of critical theory may include Frankfurt School critical theorists, conflict theorists, feminists, labor process theorists, poststructuralists, race and postcolonial theorists, and, finally, the occasional Burkean and structurationist. Although these perspectives differ in significant ways, Deetz argued that many share similar historical roots and, as a result, they have mutually transformed one another in their ongoing intellectual and practical development. In addition, each fosters the development of wider and more democratic participation in organizational and/or cultural decision making in order to better represent the different interests of workers/citizens necessary for responsive and responsible communities. At its core, critical theory should engage us to explore dominant, resistant, and alternative practices that either enable or constrain cooperative, transparent, and, ultimately, ethical governance. For Deetz, transforming communication to be more democratic "must look to the formation of knowledge, experience, and identity, rather than merely to their expression" (p. 86).

As a form of engaged scholarship, then, critical theory offers a variety of opportunities for the future development of theory and research. As Deetz noted, "critical theory is far less interested in predicting the future than in making it" (p. 104). As such, critical scholarship will most certainly make its future by influencing and being influenced by the various theoretical strands noted above. It will focus on a range of questions, including some of the following: What is the relationship between power, knowledge, and identity, and how is that relationship articulated in general trends and specific practices? How do discourses of work circulate within, between, and among other realms of life? What are the means by which communicative processes of dissensus and consensus are produced? Who participates in such practices, to what end, and with what interests? What are the mechanisms by which organizations and their stakeholders produce discursive closure and/or suppress conflict? What are the histories of cultural inequities, and how are they reproduced in and through today's organizations? How, if at all, might business organizations balance the drive for profitability with the need for social "goods" that extend beyond mere consumption? Finally, how might organizational communication scholars be useful agents of organizational and cultural change?

Postmodern Theory

In Chapter 6, Bryan Taylor noted that postmodernism, as a term, defies easy explanation and has served several functions: as a theory, as a political tool; and as a cultural cliché. Although its use is increasingly common, popular use makes its meaning more difficult to discern. Taylor suggested that most scholars who claim postmodernism are committed to studying the relationship among power, knowledge, and discourse as they are negotiated through social struggles. In addition, Taylor described the different, but related, features of postmodernity, as a historical moment, and of postmodernism, as a theoretical perspective. The former describes a break between modern and postmodern (or contemporary) conditions, whereas the latter describes a set of assumptions that create heightened reflexivity regarding the role of scholars in the production/reproduction and presentation/re-presentation of organizations.

Postmodernity, Taylor explained, is characterized by several conditions, including: the disintegration of colonial systems; the decline of industrial capitalism and the subsequent rise of a global information economy; the emergence of integrated global media systems; the creation of aesthetic practices that reject linear logic, coherence, and realism; the questioning of grand narratives that have supported dominant institutions; and the erosion of traditional identities that have been based on a sense of stability. Based on these historical conditions, Taylor explained how and why postmodern theory developed in concert with this transitional cultural context.

Postmodern organizational communication theory, as a result, is characterized by a set of assumptions about organizations and their time/place under postmodern conditions. For example, postmodern theorists view organizations as intertextual (or discourse-based) and organizational cultures and the identities they create as fragmented and decentered. Taylor also argued that postmodern theory assumes that organizational power, knowledge, and discourse are inseparable and that their relationships—including resistance to them—should be explored more fully. Finally, he acknowledged that scholars should consider how they represent organizations and, as a result, should be increasingly reflexive about their own practices.

Both postmodernity and postmodern theory pose a variety of challenging questions for persons interested in engaging them on a more concrete level: What is the nature and scope of organizations in a postcolonial world? In what ways have global media and information systems affected our cultural understanding of work? What narratives are being told about today's organizations, and how do they affect our identities? What are the consequences of employees gaining new flexibility and responsibility to become entrepreneurial change agents? In what ways has decentralized authority and local autonomy in decision making affected communication in and across organizations? How have multi-skilling, multitasking, and flexible work processes affected employees' experience of work? How do the permeable and unstable boundaries among traditionally distinct groups (e.g., customers, suppliers, competitors) alter production and consumption processes? How are power, knowledge, and discourse deployed in specific organizational contexts? How and why are some organizational members able to resist and others not? How are organizations represented (e.g., in research, in media, on the Internet) and with what consequences? These questions, and many others like them, are a mere starting point for persons interested in engaging postmodernism more thoroughly.

Feminist Theory

In Chapter 7, Karen Ashcraft explained that feminist scholarship is truly plural. She noted that although the term "feminist" is broadly applied to persons interested in gender inequality, multiple perspectives may be included under the heading, including liberal, radical, cultural-revisionist, psychoanalytic, Marxist, socialist, poststructuralist, postcolonial, existentialist, and standpoint. As she noted in her introductory comments, similar to many of the other theoretical perspectives, "the history of feminist studies is rich with internal struggle—between epistemological and political imperatives, between symbolic and material realities, between deconstructive and reconstructive impulses, between conceptions of power as imposed and self-policed, between stable and fragmented accounts of 'woman,' and so forth" (p. 152). Focusing less on reproducing past typologies, Ashcraft sought to identify what distinguishes feminist communication perspectives on organization, noting how feminist theories have understood the relationships between gender, organization, and discourse and how feminist scholars have located themselves on the modernist-postmodernist continuum.

Ashcraft noted that feminist theory is characterized by several features. First, it assumes that gender is fundamental to the ways in which social identities and relations of power are formed, maintained, and altered. Second, feminist scholars suggest that work is a central site that structures those gender identities and power relations and, additionally, gender is a key mechanism and outcome of work. That is, organization is simultaneously gendered both as a process and as a product. Third, feminist scholarship notes that, regardless of context, dominant forms of organizing systematically de-privilege women/femininity in comparison to men/masculinity. Fourth, feminism also recognizes that gender and power are not static, unified, or determined. Rather, they are fluid, contingent, and in process. They are reproduced in both formal and informal, public and private contexts and, in fact, feminist scholars challenge such dichotomies. Fifth, communication—as the process by which gender, power, and organization are accomplished—is a means not only for control but also for resistance. Finally, feminist scholars apply many of the preceding assumptions to their own research practices as well. From a feminist perspective, scholars are held accountable "for practicing reflexivity regarding the relation between knower and known, or exploring relevant connections among one's personal experience, political location, and intellectual activity" (p. 155). Extending the common adage that "the personal is political," Ashcraft noted that scholarly decisions about the conduct of research are both personal and political.

What does Ashcraft's chapter suggest for persons interested in a more engaged understanding of feminist theory and its multiple forms? Although a set of questions here certainly could not exhaust the range of possibilities, we might consider the following: In what sense does Ashcraft suggest that organizational communication scholars are better positioned to examine the gendered character of organization than, say, scholars in sociology and management? How is gender related to race, class, ethnicity, and sexual orientation, and how should these relationships be studied? What are the organizational sites and practices whereby gender is made visible or obscured? What is the relationship between masculinity and femininity, and how is it constructed in and through organizing? What are the specific micro and macro practices that produce gendered work? What are the effects of "feminine styles" of managing and organizing? How have "public" and "private" spheres of life been organized, particularly in terms of labor practices? How might organizational communication research further complicate the tensions of power and resistance, work and pleasure, rationality and emotionality? In what ways have binary and essentializing logics, in general, structured our assumptions about gender? How have organizational communication theorists preserved, promoted, and/or concealed gendered organization through the form and content of their representational discourse? How might we conduct research in ways that are consistent with feminist principles, including an emphasis on praxis?

Structuration Theory

In Chapter 8, Scott Poole and Bob McPhee discussed the influence of Anthony Giddens's structuration theory on organization studies, with specific attention to its impact on organizational communication. They explored the ways in which structuration theory accounts for the constitutive relationship between agency and structure, and, as a result, how it is also able to encompass both stability and change. Poole and McPhee described structuration as a process-based theory of communication and organization that explains how social systems—including organizations—are produced and reproduced through the "duality of structure." Structuration theory, they suggested, defines systems as "the product of human actions operating through a duality in which structures are both the medium and the outcome of actions" (p. 175). Focusing on the role of interaction as the means by which structuring occurs, then, the theory addresses both human action and social structure in a common framework.

In order to understand the full scope of structuration theory, however, Poole and McPhee noted that organizational communication scholars must account for a variety of features, including system/practice/structure, production and reproduction, agency (via discursive, practical, and unconscious levels of consciousness), and modalities of action such as meaning, power, and norms. In addition, they noted that structuration theory also emphasizes the role of time and space in the agency/structure relationship. Finally, they also argued that structuration theory offers an explanation for various units of analysis, including individuals, groups, organizations, and society. As Poole and McPhee suggested, structuration theory may offer practical knowledge because, as we better understand structuring processes, we can then learn how to maintain or alter social systems such as organizations.

For students of organizational communication, structuration theory poses a variety of interesting questions: What are the typical and atypical rules and resources that are drawn on in organizing activities? What is the dialectical tension between action and structure, and how does it vary within and across social systems? What is the role of social interaction in the production and reproduction of organizational stability or change? How can we best understand constraints on action that may be affected by location in a social system, by context, and by history? In what ways are technologies sedimented structural elements that may either enable or constrain action? How, if at all, is the duality of structure enacted in a different manner in various units of analysis, such as the individual, the group, the organization, and society? Each of these question and many others raised at the conclusion of their chapter provide additional possibilities to engage structuration theory at a deeper level.

Worldview

In Chapter 9, Jim Taylor moved to a different level of abstraction and analysis in his discussion of organization and worldview. In that chapter, Taylor explored a fundamental question central to organization studies: What is an organization? On the surface, the question seems fairly straightforward. Under closer examination, though, Taylor argued that fully understanding "organization" is more complex than it first appears. In his effort to answer the question, he challenged once common conceptions of organizations as static, stable, and reified. Conventional definitions of organization presumed a coherently structured system that affords an opportunity for objective analysis and intervention. By contrast, a definition based on worldview, he argued, reveals that organizations are characterized by chaos and complexity and are created through co-orientational practices. From this perspective, organization is "a congeries of communities of practice, each characterized by its particular cognitive domain . . . and simultaneously linked to, and alienated from, other communities . . . with which they share a common fate" (p. 216).

According to Taylor, the synthesis of coordinated actions that give reality to an organization necessitates communication. Communication, in such communities of practice, begins with two "never quite" convergent viewpoints, each with its own unique means-ends rationality. It results in organization as a never-ending search for meaning and closure, for "the resolution of irresolvable contradictions, for a solution to the dilemma of means that fit badly with ends, and for identities that in the act of self-affirmation may be denials of others" (p. 216). Such an endless search is best explained by chaos and complexity theory, which Taylor prefers as an alternative image of organization for the future. Instead of stable, coherent structures, complexity theory offers attractors that are focal points for the emergence of organization. Waxing and waning, these attractors pull resources, personnel, and interaction into their orbit, thereby creating patterns and cycles of activity that show a semblance—at least for a time—of stability and order. The centripetal forces of attractors, then, provide the basis for the creation, maintenance, and transformation of organization—sometimes gradually and sometimes abruptly.

As with the preceding chapters, Taylor's discussion of worldview and organization prompts several questions that compel us to reconsider our basic definitions of organization and communication: What is the relationship between the history of our rationales, myths, definitions, and images of organization and our communicative practices? What is the relationship between emergence and order, stability and change, in a co-orientational model of organization and communication? What are the contradictions that embody organizing practices, and how are they related to expressed intentions? What are the mechanisms by which language creates cognitive domains that link humans in action? What narratives have created productive and/or unproductive co-orientation? How, if at all, might organizational scholars and practitioners predict and/or manage the emergence of organization? What effect will globalization have on communities of practice and coordinated action in geographically dispersed organizations?

Globalization Theory

In Chapter 10, Cynthia Stohl noted the profound impact of globalization on our development of organizational communication theory and research. Her goal was to explain how an active engagement with globalization theories will help us better understand what "communication/organizational changes are happening within contemporary society, the tensions and paradoxes embedded within these communication practices, and the implications for our sense of self, our community, our nation, and our world" (p. 255).

No single perspective offers more challenges or more opportunities, given the fluid, rapid changes in our global environment. Globalization, Stohl argued, has produced a radical transformation of everyday life, as it has changed the relationship between time and space and modified the relationship between self and others. Organizational communication, as a field of study, must take into account a wide array of global conditions, including economic interdependence that stretches the limits of the economic/political tension and the widespread and rapid exchanges of products, services, and knowledge via information technologies. In addition, globalization has produced both a profound compression of time and space that has subsequently reconfigured labor and social relations, as well as a heightened sense of reflexivity. Paradoxically, though, a rising global consciousness derived through processes of reflexive communication is "also associated with increasingly local politics, a heightened sense of the importance of community, social movement organizing designed to counter the new world order, and individuals' desperate struggles for identity" (p. 254).

As Stohl explained, globalization has changed the dynamic between the cooperative and competitive conditions of business, to the extent that individuals perceive that organizations now transcend national boundaries or local confines. Global organizing, then, creates new social capital; creates, maintains, and transforms new organizational forms; and produces loose affiliative networks created through communication technologies. The result, according to Stohl, is that globalization requires more flexible, adaptable forms of organizing between local, state, regional, and global entities. Not surprisingly, then, "the turbulence, volatility, and uncertainty associated with economic globalization require organizational responsiveness, adaptation, and efficiency in communication systems that are not found in traditional hierarchical organizations" (p. 249).

Such temporary systems of organizing will no doubt require more thoughtful theorizing and raise a series of questions for scholars of organizational communication who want to engage globalization in a meaningful manner: What are the effects of new communication technologies on global political, economic, and social structures? What kinds of infrastructure, organizational structures, management approaches, and labor forces are most suitable to globalization? How, if at all, should cultural differences be negotiated within and across organizational boundaries? What forms of knowledge production, utilization, transmission, and storage will be sufficient in a global network? How might global business exchange either facilitate or negate the possibilities for a global civic culture? How might new information technologies transform identities, power relations, and the rights and responsibilities of workers/citizens? Finally, how might the "disembedding" of human interaction from local to distributed contexts affect our interpretations of events and our understanding of communication, in general?

Teaching as Engagement: Re-Creating Critical Learning Contexts

As we explained in Chapter 1, all theories are partial, perspectival, political, and contested. As a result, our research, teaching, and service in organizational communication are never neutral. As Paulo Freire (1985) reminds us, we need to know the type of assumptions we ascribe to and for whose interests we work. We hope that the chapters in this volume have assisted you in better understanding other scholars' assumptions and have guided you as you develop your own. Although the chapters represent a rich, diverse array of perspectives, we must remember that our current understanding is highly situated and relatively perishable. However, what remain fairly constant, albeit never neutral, are the theoretical and ethical orientations that converge in our philosophies of scholarship.

Given our own critical orientations, we assume that scholarly decisions may be forms of "symbolic violence" (Bourdieu & Passeron, 1990) because they serve some interests at the expense of others. Our use of the term "violence" here does not suggest that all research (and discourse generally, as Foucault suggests) is necessarily destructive, but rather that everything is potentially dangerous. From a critical perspective, scholarly decisions should be viewed as a contested terrain over "whose form of knowledge, history, visions, language, culture, and authority will prevail as a legitimate object of learning and analysis" (Giroux, quoted in Freire & Macedo, 1987, p. 20). For us, accepting the danger within the contested terrain of scholarship requires that we acknowledge how our decisions affect ourselves, our students, our institutions, our communities, and our cultures. We believe that such an acknowledgment not only affects the nature and scope of our theory and research but also affects the pedagogical decisions we make in the classroom.

As organizational communication educators, these decisions are particularly important because corporate values, discourses, and practices have increasingly "colonized" the content and process of education (Deetz, 1992). For instance, educational institutions, including universities, often use corporate models of efficiency (e.g., instructor as authority figure; regulation of time, discipline, and turn-taking; performance appraisal through grades; taking attendance) and the discourse and metaphors of the workplace (e.g., learning by objectives, mastery of skills, criteria for evaluation, meeting deadlines). As a result of this sedimented and naturalized corporate bias, education has often been assimilated into training. Knowledge is treated like a commodity to be produced for, and consumed by, passive students primarily interested in the exchange value of their learning in the economic marketplace. More and more frequently, the value of education is determined by its economic utility rather than by its social and political uses. Not surprisingly, then, students tend to dichotomize theory and practice, the academic world and the "real world."

An engaged, reflexive response to this dilemma requires, simultaneously, a discourse of critique and a discourse of possibility. This dialectic between deconstruction and reconstruction is important in order to challenge taken-for-granted assumptions and to offer alternative means for participation in not only economic, but also political and social, realms of life. There are several means to pursue this dialectic. First, it is important to engage in teaching with the belief that knowledge is a process that is mutually accomplished in the day-to-day performance of dialogue within and beyond the classroom. As teachers, our role is not so much to transmit knowledge as to facilitate creating a context for the construction of knowledge. In our teaching, then, we attempt to create a dialogic education, whereby teacher and students alike have a mutual interest in, and responsibility for, learning. If facilitated effectively, a classroom should be a site for lively discussion, debate, and critical inquiry that more closely approximates an active civic life than a passive corporate life. We hope that this volume helps facilitate that engaged learning process.

Second, we enter teaching environments with the belief that learning is created in the interplay between theory and practice, reflection and experience. As in praxis, theory and practice are inextricably interwoven in a dialectical tension between centripetal and centrifugal forces. Theory (and reflection), for instance, is often depicted as unified and coherent, whereas practice (and experience) is frequently reflected in diversity and ambiguity. It is the intersection and interaction of these tensions that often provide the most valuable learning. For example, in this volume, we have seen how the historical development of various theoretical perspectives has guided organizational practice, as well as the ways that organizational experiences have been used to revise and alter those theories. By historicizing the theory/practice relationship, we come to realize that organizations have been constituted in multiple ways in relation to the social, political, economic, and technological conditions of the time. We hope that, as readers, you have also learned that those theories are embedded in your own organizational experiences, affording you the opportunity to critique the appropriateness of the theories for practice. Finally, we expect that you will use your own critiques to explore alternative forms of organizing that you consider appropriate for your own vision of work in our culture.

Our goal was not only to produce a book that, as a pedagogical tool, builds students' knowledge and skills in order to meet corporate demands; it was also to foster a dialogue that stimulates students' critical thinking in order to engage in ethical, civic action. This is particularly salient, we believe, as we enter a new era for reconsidering and reconstructing organizations based on innovative scholarship. In the end, then, our purpose was not necessarily to provide a set of clear-cut answers regarding how to engage theory and research. Rather, our intent has been to raise a series of questions about the past, present, and future of organizational communication, based in our belief that a discussion of scholars' active engagement provides an opportunity for new developments.

At this time, such developments are especially important, given our assumption that the business organization, in particular, has become the central institution in our society, often eclipsing the state, family, church, and community in its power (Deetz, 1992). Organizations pervade our lives not only through their economic impact but also through their social, political, technological, and ideological influence. Often, the effects are observable and immediate, through corporate downsizing, corporate welfare, corporate discrimination and harassment, and corporate degradation of the environment. In other cases, the effects are more subtle and long-lasting, through the naturalization and reification of the time, space, and structure of work. Such effects should remind us that our scholarship provides us with new possibilities for rethinking and restructuring our organizations so that they are simultaneously productive and humane, responsive and responsible. To do so, however, requires a dialectical attention to, and understanding of, what is visible and invisible, spoken and unspoken, and present and absent with regard to organizational communication theory and research.

References

Bourdieu, P., & Passeron, J. C. (1990). *Reproduction in education, society, and culture* (R. Nice, Trans.). Newbury Park, CA: Sage.

Clegg, S., & Hardy, C. (1996). Organizations, organization, and organizing. In S. Clegg, C. Hardy, & N. Nord (Eds.), *Handbook of organization studies* (pp. 1–28). Thousand Oaks, CA: Sage.

Clegg, S., Hardy, C., & Nord, W. (1996). *Handbook of organization studies.* Thousand Oaks, CA: Sage.

Deetz, S. (1992). *Democracy in an age of corporate colonization: Developments in communication and the politics of everyday life.* Albany: State University of New York Press.

Foucault, M. (1984). What is an author? In P. Rabinow (Ed.), *The Foucault reader* (pp. 101–120). New York: Pantheon.

Freire, P. (1985). *The politics of education, cultural power, and liberation* (D. Macedo, Trans.). South Hadley, MA: Bergin and Garvey.

Freire, P., & Macedo, D. (1987). *Literacy: Reading the word and the world.* South Hadley, MA: Bergin and Garvey.

Jablin, F. M., & Putnam, L. L. (Eds.). (2001). *The new handbook of organizational communication: Advances in theory, research, and methods.* Thousand Oaks, CA: Sage.

May, S. K. (1993). The modernist monologue in organizational communication research: The text, the subject, and the audience. In G. Barnett & L. Thayer (Eds.), *Communication and organizations: Emerging perspectives* (pp. 1–19). Norwood, NJ: Ablex.

Mumby, D. K. (1997). Modernism, postmodernism, and communication studies: A rereading of an ongoing debate. *Communication Theory, 7,* 1–28.

Author Index

Subject Index

About the Editors

Steve May (PhD, University of Utah, 1993) is Associate Professor in the Department of Communication Studies at the University of North Carolina at Chapel Hill. His research focuses on the relationship between work and identity, as it relates to the boundaries of public/private, work/family, and labor/leisure. His research has explored the role of corporate counseling programs during organizational change and crisis, including downsizing, labor strikes, and accidents. Most recently, he has studied the challenges and opportunities for organizational ethics and corporate social responsibility. His current book projects include *Case Studies in Organizational Communication: Ethical Perspectives and Practices* (in press) and *Communication and Corporate Social Responsibility*, with George Cheney and Juliet Roper. He has served as the Forum Editor of *Management Communication Quarterly* and is currently a Leadership Fellow and an Ethics Fellow at The Institute for the Arts and Humanities.

Dennis K. Mumby (PhD, Southern Illinois University, 1985) is Professor in the Department of Communication Studies at the University of North Carolina at Chapel Hill. His research focuses on the relationships among discourse, power, gender, and organization. He has published in journals such as *Academy of Management Review*, *Communication Monographs*, *Communication Theory*, and *Management Communication Quarterly*. His most recent book, coauthored with Karen Lee Ashcraft, is *Reworking Gender: A Feminist Communicology of Organization* (2004).

About the Contributors

Brenda J. Allen (PhD, Howard University, 1989) is Chair of the Department of Communication at the University of Colorado at Denver, where she teaches courses on organizational communication, diversity, small group communication, and qualitative research methods. Her scholarship focuses on social identity and organizational communication. She is the author of *Difference Matters: Communicating Social Identity* (2004), as well as several articles and book chapters on gender, race, and feminism. She recently began an ethnographic study of a transgender identity center in Denver, Colorado.

Karen Lee Ashcraft (PhD, University of Colorado at Boulder) is an Associate Professor in the Department of Communication at the University of Utah. Her research examines gender, power, professional identity, and alternative organizational forms and has appeared in such forums as *Administrative Science Quarterly*, *Academy of Management Journal*, *Communication Monographs*, and *Communication Theory*. Her coauthored book with Dennis Mumby, *Reworking Gender* (2004), examines the role of feminist communication scholarship in contemporary critical organization studies. Her current research examines the cultural organization of professional identity. Focused on the case of U.S. commercial airline pilots, this project explores the discursive and material development of occupational selves and relations across multiple sites of organizing. The study investigates how gender, race, and class become relevant players in the organization of labor identity, as well as the role of communication in that process.

George Cheney (PhD, Purdue, 1985) is a Professor in Communication at the University of Utah. He is also an Adjunct Professor in Management Communication at The University of Waikato, Hamilton, New Zealand. Recognized for both teaching and research, he has published widely in the area of organizational communication, including a number of studies of organizational rhetoric. His other interests are identity and power in organizations, employee participation and workplace democracy, quality of worklife, business ethics (especially corporate social responsibility), globalization and marketization, and the rhetoric of war and peace. A past chair of the National Communication Association's Organizational Communication Division, he has lectured in Western Europe and Latin America.

Steven R. Corman is a Professor in the Hugh Downs School of Human Communication at Arizona State University. He received his PhD in Communication Theory from the University of Illinois at Urbana–Champaign in 1988. He is Chair of the Organizational Communication Division of the International Communication Association as well as being an Associate Editor of *Human Communication Research*. He also serves on the editorial boards of *Communication Monographs*, *Management Communication Quarterly*, and *Progress in Communication Sciences*. His publications on communication networks, interaction processes and content analysis, and computer models of communication have appeared in these outlets and in others such as *Communication Theory*, *Communication Research*, *Social Networks*, and *Technology Studies*. He recently edited (with Marshall Scott Poole) a volume titled *Perspectives on Organizational Communication: Finding Common Ground* (2000).

Stanley Deetz is Professor of Communication at the University of Colorado at Boulder. Prior to joining the CU faculty in 1997, he taught for several years at Rutgers University, chairing the department there during the 1980s. He is the author of *Leading Organizations Through Transitions* (2000), *Doing Critical Management Research* (2000), *Transforming Communication, Transforming Business* (1995), and *Democracy in an Age of Corporate Colonization* (1992) as well as editor or author of eight other books. He has published approximately 100 essays in scholarly journals and books regarding stakeholder representation, decision making, culture, and communication in corporate organizations and has lectured widely in the United States and Europe. He was a Senior Fulbright Scholar at Goteborgs Universitet (Sweden, 1994). He is a Fellow of the International Communication Association, having served as its president, 1996–1997, and has held many other elected professional positions. He is also an active consultant for companies in the United States and Europe.

Robert D. McPhee (PhD, Michigan State University, 1978) is a Professor in the Hugh Downs School of Human Communication at Arizona State University. Specializing in communication theory and methods and in organizational communication, he has served as Chair of the Organizational

Communication Division of the National Communication Association, as Associate Editor of *Human Communication Research*, and as Book Review Editor of *Communication Theory*. Among his specific research interests are organizational hierarchies, organizational knowledge, the communicative constitution of organizations, and structuration theory.

Marshall Scott Poole (PhD, University of Wisconsin, 1980) is Professor of Communication and Information and Operations Management at Texas A&M University. He has conducted research and published extensively on the topics of group and organizational communication, computer-mediated communication systems, conflict management, and organizational innovation. He has coauthored or edited 10 books, including *Communication and Group Decision-Making, Organizational Change and Innovation Processes: Theory and Methods for Research, Theories of Small Groups: Interdisciplinary Perspectives*, and *Handbook of Organizational Change and Innovation*.

Cynthia Stohl (PhD, Purdue University, 1982) is Professor of Communication at the University of California, Santa Barbara. She teaches a variety of courses at both the graduate and undergraduate levels in organizational, global, and group communication and has published widely in these areas. Her empirical research centers on organizational networks, collective action, and workplace participation in the United States, New Zealand, and several Western European countries. She is currently a co–principal investigator on a National Science Foundation Grant, "Technological Change and Collective Association: Changing Relationships Among Technology, Organizations, Society, and the Citizenry." She is the author of more than 60 articles in management, communication, and sociology journals and handbooks. Her book *Organizational Communication: Connectedness in Action* (1995) received the National Communication Association Award (1995) for the "best book" in organizational communication, and her article (co-authored with George Cheney et al.) "Democracy, Participation, and Communication at Work" received the 1998 National Communication Association Organizational Communication Division Award for best article.

Bryan C. Taylor is an Associate Professor in the Department of Communication, University of Colorado, Boulder. His research and teaching interests include Cold War and nuclear rhetoric, high-technology organizational culture, qualitative research methods, and cultural studies of technology and media. He is the recent coauthor, with Thomas R. Lindlof, of *Qualitative Communication Research Methods* (2nd ed., 2002).

James Taylor, author or coauthor of six books and some 70 published articles, is emeritus professor and interim chair of the Communication

Department at the University of Montreal. He has pioneered approaches to the study of the role of language in the constitution of human organizations, emphasizing in his work the contrasting roles of conversation and text in the construction of social reality. A member of the Board of Directors of the International Communication Association, he has lectured extensively in Finland, Denmark, France, Spain, Germany, the Netherlands, England, Argentina, New Zealand, and Australia. He is currently working on two new books, one in collaboration with colleagues at the University of Montreal and one that is the culmination of a 4-year research project conducted under the auspices of the University of Waikato, in New Zealand. Recent work includes two books, *The Emergent Organization* (2000) and *The Computerization of Work* (2001), and some 25 articles in peer-reviewed journals and books. He has received Best Article and Best Book awards from the International Communication Association and the National Communication Association.

CPSIA information can be obtained
at www.ICGtesting.com
Printed in the USA
LVHW04s2334140918
590112LV00005B/72/P